D1474242

Societal Impact on Aging Series

Series Editor

K. Warner Schaie, PhD
Director, Gerontology Center
College of Health and Human Development
The Pennsylvania State University
University Park, PA

Steven H. Zarit, PhD, is a research educator and clinician whose work has focused on the mental health problems of older people and their families. He is Professor of Human Development and Assistant Director of the Gerontology Center at the Pennsylvania State University and Adjunct Professor, Institute of Gerontology, College of Health Sciences, Jönköping University, Jönköping, Sweden. Dr. Zarit has conducted pioneering work on the problems faced by families of people with Alzheimer's disease and related memory disorders, and on interventions to relieve the stresses of family caregiving. He has also investigated adaptation in very late life, and the role of mastery and control in supporting independent functioning. He is the author or co-author of several books, including *Mental Disorders in Older Adults: Fundamentals of Assessment and Treatment* with Judy M. Zarit. He is a member of the Board of Directors of the Alzheimer's Association, the Medical and Scientific Advisory Council of the Alzheimer's Association, and the Research Advisory Board of the Lighthouse, Inc. of New York. He is associate editor of the journal, *Aging and Mental Health,* and has served on editorial boards of several journals.

Leonard I. Pearlin, PhD, is Emeritus Professor at the University of California, San Francisco and is now Graduate Professor of Sociology at the University of Maryland, College Park. His research has focused on the social origins of stress and its health consequences across the life course, and on the personal resources that protect people from the harmful effects of difficult life circumstances. Pearlin has been a major contributor to the theoretical development of the stress process model widely used in research.

K. Warner Schaie, PhD, is an Evan Pugh Professor of Human Development and Psychology and director of the Gerontology Center at Pennsylvania State University. He also holds an appointment as affiliate professor of psychiatry and behavioral science at the University of Washington. He has previously held professorial appointments at the University of Nebraska, West Virginia University, and the University of Southern California. Dr. Schaie received his BA degree from the University of California at Berkeley and MS and PhD from the University of Washington, all in psychology. He also holds an honorary PhD from the Friedrich Schiller University of Jena, Germany. He is author or editor of 35 books, including the textbook *Adult Development and Aging* (with S. L. Willis) and *Handbook of the Psychology of Aging* (with J. E. Birren), both of which are now in their fifth edition. He has directed the Seattle Longitudinal Study of Cognitive Aging since 1956 and is the author of more than 250 journal articles and chapters on the psychology of aging. Dr. Schaie is the recipient of the Robert W. Kleemeier Award for Distinguished Research Contributions from the Gerontological Society of America, the Distinguished Scientific Contributions Award from the American Psychological Association, and the Lifetime Research Career Award from the Mensa Research Foundation.

Personal Control in Social and Life Course Contexts

Steven H. Zarit
Leonard I. Pearlin
K. Warner Schaie

Editors

Springer Publishing Company

Springer Publishing Company, Inc.
536 Broadway
New York, NY 10012-3955

Acquisitions Editor: Helvi Gold
Production Editor: Sara Yoo
Cover design by Joanne Honigman

01 02 03 04 05 / 5 4 3 2 1

Library of Congress Cataloging-in-Publication Data

Personal control in social and life course contexts / Steven H. Zarit, Leonard I. Pearlin, K. Warner Schaie, editors.
    p. cm. — (Societal impact on aging)
    Proceedings of a conference held Oct. 9-10, 2000 at Pennsylvania State University, sponsored by the University's Gerontology Center.
    Includes bibliographical references and index.
    ISBN 0-8261-2402-X
    1. Gerontology—Congresses.   2. Aging—Congresses.   3. Control (Psychology) in old age—Congresses.   4. Aged—Social conditions—Congresses.   5. Aged—Psychology—Congresses.
I. Zarit, Steven H.   II. Pearlin, Leonard I. (Leonard Irving), 1924-
III. Schaie, K. Warner (Klaus Warner), 1928-   IV. Series.
HQ 1061 .P345 2003
305.26—dc21   2002035277
                                                                      CIP

Printed in the United States of America by Maple-Vail.

Contents

Contributors

Ronald P. Abeles, PhD
Office of the Director, NIH
Office of Behavioral and Social
  Sciences Research
Bethesda, MD

William R. Avison, PhD
University of Western Ontario
Department of Sociology
London, Ontario
Canada

Fredda Blanchard-Fields, PhD
Georgia Institute of Technology
School of Psychology
Atlanta, GA

John Cairney, PhD
McMaster University
Department of Psychiatry and
  Behavioral Neuroscience
Hamilton, Ontario
Canada

Laura L. Carstensen, PhD
Stanford University
Department of Psychology
Stanford, CA

Margaret E. Ensminger, PhD
Johns Hopkins University
School of Hygiene and Public
  Health
Department of Health Policy and
  Management
Baltimore, MD

Phillip Gardiner, PhD
Office of Health Affairs
300 Lakeside Drive, 12th Floor
Oakland, CA

Linda K. George, PhD
Duke University
Department of Sociology
Durham, NC

Jutta Heckhausen, PhD
University of California, Irvine
Department of Psychology
Irvine, CA

Scott M. Hofer, PhD
Pennsylvania State University
Department of Human
  Development and
  Family Studies
University Park, PA

Pamela Braboy Jackson, PhD
Indiana University
Department of Sociology
Bloomington, IN

Neal Krause, PhD
University of Michigan
School of Public Health and
    Institute of Gerontology
Ann Arbor, MI

Sara A. Leitsch, PhD
University of Michigan
School of Social Work
Ann Arbor, MI

Corinna E. Löckenhoff
Stanford University
Department of Psychology
Stanford, CA

Kyriakos S. Markides, PhD
University of Texas Medical
    Branch
Division of Sociomedical
    Sciences
Preventive Medicine/Community
    Health
Galveston, TX

Jane D. McLeod, PhD
University of Indiana
Department of Sociology
Bloomington, IN

Richard A. Miech, PhD
John Hopkins University
Department of Mental Hygiene
Baltimore, MD

Mark F. Pioli, PhD
University of Maryland
Department of Sociology
College Park, MD

Richard H. Price, PhD
University of Michigan
Psychology Department
Ann Arbor, MI

Scott Schieman, PhD
University of Maryland
Department of Sociology
College Park, MD

Richard Schulz, PhD
University of Pittsburgh
Department of Psychiatry and
    University Center for Social
    and Urban Research
Pittsburgh, PA

Michael J. Shanahan, PhD
University of North Carolina
Department of Sociology
Chapel Hill, NC

Marilyn McKean Skaff, PhD
University of California–
    San Francisco
Department of Family
    Community Medicine
San Francisco, CA

John J. Wilkins III
North Carolina Agricultural and
    Technical State University
Department of Animal Sciences
Greenboro, NC

Carsten Wrosch, MA
Carnegie Mellon University
Department of Psychology
Pittsburgh, PA

Preface

This is the 14th volume in a series on the broad topic "Societal Impact on Aging." The first five volumes of this series were published by Lawrence Erlbaum Associates under the series title "Social Structure and Aging." The present volume is the ninth published under the Springer Publishing Company imprint. It is the edited proceedings of a conference held at Pennsylvania State University, October 9–10, 2000.

The series of Penn State Gerontology Center conferences originated from the deliberations of a subcommittee of the Committee on Life Course Perspectives of the Social Science Research Council, chaired by Matilda White Riley, in the early 1980s. That subcommittee was charged with developing an agenda and mechanisms that would serve to encourage communication between scientists who study societal structures that might affect the aging of individuals and those scientists who are concerned with the possible effects of contextual influences on individual aging. The committee proposed a series of conferences that would systematically explore the interfaces between social structures and behavior, and in particular to identify mechanisms through which society influences adult development. When the second editor was named director of the Penn State Gerontology Center, he was able to implement this conference program as one of the center's major activities.

The previous 13 volumes in this series have dealt with the societal impact on aging in psychological processes (Schaie & Schooler, 1989); age structuring in comparative perspective (Kertzer & Schaie, 1989); self-directedness and efficacy over the life span (Rodin, Schooler, & Schaie, 1990); aging, health behaviors, and health outcomes (Schaie, Blazer, & House, 1992); caregiving in families (Zarit, Pearlin, & Schaie, 1993); aging in historical perspective (Schaie & Achenbaum, 1993); adult intergenerational relations (Bengtson, Schaie, & Burton, 1995);

older adults' decision making and the law (Smyer, Schaie, & Kapp, 1996); the impact of social structures on decision making in the elderly (Willis, Schaie, & Hayward, 1997); the impact of the workplace on aging (Schaie & Schooler, 1998); mobility and transportation (Schaie & Pietrucha, 2000); the evolution of the aging self (Schaie & Hendricks, 2000); and societal impact on health behavior (Schaie, Leventhal, & Willis, 2002).

The strategy for each of these volumes has been to commission six reviews on three major topics by established subject-matter specialists who have credibility in aging research. We then invited two formal discussants for each chapter—usually one drawn from the writer's discipline and one from a neighboring discipline. This format seems to provide a suitable antidote against the perpetuation of parochial orthodoxies as well as to make certain that questions are raised with respect to the validity of iconoclastic departures in new directions.

To focus the conference, the editors chose three aspects of the conference topic that are of broad interest to gerontologists. Social and behavioral scientists with a demonstrated track record were then selected and asked to interact with those interested in theory building within a multidisciplinary context.

Considerable evidence has accrued that the sense of personal control, or mastery, has beneficial effects on people's well-being. Not all of the reasons for this association are understood, although it may be supposed that when people see the circumstances of their lives as being amenable to their direction and control, the circumstances will appear less ominous and threatening. It is equally reasonable to assume that a high level of mastery would function as a self-fulfilling prophecy: beliefs about personal control enable individuals to take actions on their own behalf. Whatever the bases of its contributions to well-being, it is clear that the sense of personal control enhances and that its lack is inimical to well-being.

Mastery is of special critical importance to older populations; although the sense of mastery is as instrumental to the well-being of older people as to younger people, the conditions supporting the sense of mastery probably undergo accelerated change in the later years. Mastery in general warrants the attention of scholars, but it is thought to have particular relevance to the study of aging.

The volume begins with an examination of the theoretical framework of mastery and control as it applies to the study of aging. Mastery and control are potential resources that can contain or mediate the effects of stressful life events. Little attention, however, has been paid on how mastery changes with aging or whether mastery and control have similar or different functions in later life compared to earlier phases of the life span. Mastery may be a resource that older people can draw on to compensate for decrements in other domains. Conversely, there may be situations in which mastery and control lead to poorer adaptation because of life circumstances or institutional forces that do not lend themselves to the exertion of personal control. The volume begins with an overview of the concept of personal control, including a discussion of the evolution of this concept and its implications for functional consequences as individuals age. Chapter 2 elaborates on these issues by focusing specifically on the social foundations of personal control in late life.

The second topic in this volume deals with the cultural and social sources of mastery and control and how these variations may lead to differences in functions and outcomes of mastery. Factors such as social class, education, race and ethnicity, affective feelings of mastery and control, and, in turn, a sense of mastery may be more or less typical and adaptive in different social settings. Examination of how mastery functions in different cultures can further illuminate its role in supporting well-being in later life. Chapter 3 focuses on cultural variations in the meaning of control, and chapter 4 examines the relationship between social structures, stress, and the exercise of personal control.

The third topic is concerned with the functions of mastery. After all, our interest in mastery is based on indications that it can contribute to the well-being of older people. However, the ways that mastery exercises this effect and the range of the effects are not sufficiently understood at this time. For example, we may ask whether mastery is effective because it enriches the coping repertoire of individuals. Likewise, the range of effects of mastery has not yet been fully evaluated. It is known that mastery influences mental health, but it is not clear whether mastery also influences such diverse actions and disposition as alienation, social activities, and religious sentiments. Chapter 5 examines these issues and focuses on the relation between planful competence, the life course, and aging. Chapter 6 considers the issues and evidence of a life span theory of control. Finally, the afterword brings these matters back to practical implications of the concept of personal control.

We are grateful for the financial support of the conference that led to this volume, which was provided by conference grant AG 09787-10 from the National Institute on Aging, and by additional support from the vice president for research and dean of Graduate School of the Pennsylvania State University. We are also grateful to Judy Hall and Lindsey Estright for handling the conference logistics, to Anna Shuey for coordinating the manuscript preparation, and to Pamela Davis for preparing the indexes.

K. Warner Schaie
September 2001

REFERENCES

Bengtson, V. L., Schaie, K. W., & Burton, L. (1995). *Adult intergenerational relations: Effects of societal changes.* New York: Springer.

Kertzer, D., & Schaie, K. W. (1989). *Age structuring in comparative perspective.* Hillsdale, NJ: Erlbaum.

Rodin, J., Schooler, C., & Schaie, K. W. (1990). *Self-directedness and efficacy: Causes and effects throughout the life course.* Hillsdale, NJ: Erlbaum.

Schaie, K. W., & Achenbaum, W. A. (1993). *Societal impact on aging: Historical perspectives.* New York: Springer.

Schaie, K. W., & Hendricks, J. (Eds.). (2000). *Evolution of the aging self: Societal impacts.* New York: Springer.

Schaie, K. W., Blazer, D., & House, J. (1992). *Aging, health behaviors, and health outcomes.* Hillsdale, NJ: Erlbaum.

Schaie, K. W., Leventhal, H., & Willis, S. L. (2000). *Societal impacts on health behaviors in the elderly.* New York: Springer.

Schaie, K. W., & Pietrucha, M. (Eds.). (2000). *Mobility and transportation in the elderly.* New York: Springer.

Schaie, K. W., & Schooler, C. E. (1989). *Social structure and aging: Psychological processes.* Hillsdale, NJ: Erlbaum.

Schaie, K. W., & Schooler, C. E. (1998). *Impact of the workplace on older persons.* New York: Springer.

Smyer, M., Schaie, K. W., & Kapp, M. B. (1996). *Older adults' decision-making and the law.* New York: Springer.

Willis, S. L., Schaie, K. W., & Hayward, M. (1997). *Impact of social structures on decision making in the elderly.* New York: Springer.

Zarit, S. H., Pearlin, L., & Schaie, K. W. (1993). *Social structure and caregiving: Family and cross-national perspectives.* Hillsdale, NJ: Erlbaum.

CHAPTER 1

Personal Control: Some Conceptual Turf and Future Directions

Leonard I. Pearlin and Mark F. Pioli

It is accurate to state that personal control is generally acknowledged to be a fundamental psychological disposition and a powerful analytic tool in research into well-being. A substantial body of research has accumulated indicating that there is something about this disposition that helps to explain the differences among individuals and groups in their aspirations and achievements and in the ways they deal with adversities. Yet, although considerable writing has been directed to specifying what that something is, we remain uncertain what manner of beast we have by the tail or how we might tame it to serve our interests. What is amply certain is that it is worth hanging on to and waiting to see where we are led.

Behind our uncertainties about how and why personal control should make a difference in our lives is a lack of agreement about the very construct of personal control, how it should be assessed, and what it should be called. Thus, subsumed by the general notion of personal control are multiple concepts that probably share some core of meaning but that are evaluated and measured by quite different means and bear different labels. In these respects, the notion of personal control is not unlike a number of other constructs that are part of the discourse of the social and behavioral sciences. It is not unusual in these fields to find either that different concepts have overlapping, if not identical, meanings or that the same concept may be used in ways that convey quite different meanings. This kind of slippage can lead people who believe they are addressing the same issue to discover that they are actually talking about quite different matters or, conversely, to learn that they are speaking about the same thing though using different language. Indeed, we shall probably have the occasion to observe these ambiguities even within the narrow confines of this volume.

However, these ambiguities should be judged neither as the product of indifferent scholarship tolerated by the imprecise social and behavioral sciences nor as cause for despair. Although clarity is most assuredly favored over confusion, the obscure and overlapping boundaries of personal control and its subsumed concepts may be more reflective of their usefulness and vitality than of their impoverishment. Concepts that attract the attentions of large numbers of researchers over a protracted length of time are likely to acquire an accumulation of nuance, with their original meaning either becoming lost or having to compete with accrued meanings. This accrual, moreover, may be particularly pronounced when the concept is adopted by researchers representing different disciplines, pursuing different agendas, and guided by different theoretical orientations. It is further accelerated when researchers of the different disciplines are not disposed to read each others' work, as is often the case. By contrast, we submit, concepts that are of marginal utility and infrequently used more easily maintain clearly delineated boundaries and meanings.

We do not intend to argue for complacency. Given the prominence of the construct in the social and behavioral sciences, it is periodically necessary to take stock of our progress and the work that remains to be done. This is a major mission of this and the other chapters included in this volume. Indeed, a conference held at Pennsylvania State University over a decade ago had a similar mission, with papers dedicated to the examination of concepts related to personal control and self-directedness. At that conference, Rodin (1990) critically reviewed some of the definitions and processes of personal control. We attempt here to pick up where she left off, but less with the intention of further specifying the construct of personal control or elaborating a taxonomic guide (see Skinner, 1996) than exploring some of its potential analytic applications and uses.

THE MULTIPLE LABELS AND MEANINGS OF CONTROL

Like others, we regard personal control as a generic construct under whose wings are several related but distinguishable concepts. Among these related concepts are self-efficacy, locus of control, mastery, fatalism, learned helplessness, and empowerment. It seems to us that what distinguishes these concepts is not only their definitions, even when clear and comprehensive definitions can be found, but also differences in how they are assessed and the scholarly uses to which they are put. A quick and highly selective excursion through these concepts is intended to highlight some of these differences as well as areas of overlap.

Self-Efficacy

Although the label *self-efficacy* is relatively recent, the theory probably has had greater influence on the current thinking of social psychologists than other concepts subsumed by the overarching construct of personal control. It is our opinion that its prominence in the literature stems less from the magnitude or power of the research it has stimulated than from the thoughtful and persuasive theoretical specification and elaboration given it by Bandura (1977, 1997). It is a case where theoretical development has outpaced empirical underpinnings. Essentially, the theory begins with the assumption, certainly not shared by all critics (e.g., Burger, 1992; Burger & Cooper, 1979; Schooler, 1990), that it is a universal desire of individuals to control their environments. According to Bandura (1977), actual control efforts rest on two expectancies, one, that the sought-after outcome is achievable, the other that individuals see themselves as being capable of engaging in the behavior that will produce the desired outcome. There are multiple sources of self-efficacy, perhaps most important among them being learning from prior successful experiences. It is assumed that because success breeds success, self-efficacy and its expectations tend to become generalized from one situation to another.

Bandura regarded the learning and acquisition of self-efficacy as a tool for behavior modification, such as helping individuals overcome phobias and other aversions they might harbor or to enhance health behaviors. Because of this use of the construct, self-efficacy came to be seen as asocial and acontextual. In later writing, Bandura (1997) and others (e.g., Gecas, 1989) took issue with these views, arguing for the importance of culture in shaping expectancies and for the importance of individual expectancies as a force underlying collective actions and social change. We can note in this connection that the foundations for such arguments are difficult to establish empirically, because there is no single measure of the construct that permits such relationships to be observed and validated. Instead, the assessments of self-efficacy are typically tailored to specific tasks and contexts. The specificity of its measures, though in some respects useful, tends to stand as a barrier to making empirically based comparisons across social or cultural groups or to observing systematically the developmental changes of individuals across time. From a social-psychological perspective, self-efficacy embodies a theoretically interesting and important set of ideas, but currently it is more easily adapted to inquiries into highly specific situations than to the tracing of its social sources and consequences.

Locus of Control

The concept of locus of control was developed by Rotter (1966), and, like the construct of self-efficacy that came a decade later, it seemed to capture immediately the attention of many scholars. It is not an exaggeration to state that his contributions have been instrumental in bringing to awareness the importance of the sense of control. This awareness was greatly aided by the scale constructed by Rotter that was designed to assess the extent to which people feel they possess the power and/or obligation to control a broad and varied range of events and conditions. Those who believed that events and circumstances are amenable to influence through the actions of individuals are considered to be guided by internality; in contrast, people who regard the same events and circumstances to be the result of uncontrollable forces are guided by externality.

The presence of a standardized measure, though flawed in some respects, and the thinking that led to it were powerful stimuli to the work of other scholars and resulted in an outpouring of studies and literature, including an annual series reporting advances in research into locus of control (Lefcourt, 1981, 1983, 1984). Indeed, this outpouring prompts the speculation that concepts that are accompanied by reliable measures easily adapted to the methodology and varied subject matter of surveys are likely to be adopted more quickly and widely by researchers than concepts whose measurements are elusive. Rotter's locus of control measure, made up of a large number of items whose manifest content seems to extend in multiple directions, suggests that weak (albeit reliable) measures of strong constructs may yield richer results than exquisite measures of weak constructs.

The work subsequent to Rotter's seminal paper in 1966 led to an enrichment of the concept (e.g., Gurin, Gurin, & Morrison, 1978) and to a number of useful modifications of the original measure. One modification stemmed from the recognition that the Rotter measure subsumed three distinct loci of control: internal, chance, and powerful others (Levenson, 1974). Next, this multidimensional treatment was adapted to the measurement of locus of control in specific domains, such as in health (Wallston & Wallston, 1978). Still another application has been to issues concerned with aging and the life course. One effort along these lines has questioned whether there is a loss of internality that occurs with late life, a question to which there is as yet no clear answer (e.g., see Lachman & Jelalian, 1984). Krause, finally, has applied a modified measure of locus of control to older samples, observing its functions as a buffer to chronic economic strains (1987a) and its associations with different dimensions of social support (1987b). Although the construct of locus of control seems to have fallen out of vogue in recent years, the movement toward domain-specific measures and their application to the life course are very much in evidence (e.g., Lachman, 1986).

Mastery

The third concept, mastery, is like both self-efficacy and locus of control in that it too essentially concerns personal control. However, it is somewhat distinguished from locus of control by its more limited focus on the control of conditions that individuals regard as importantly affecting their own personal lives, not on all environmental conditions. It also differs somewhat in the way it is measured, which is with a relatively short but robust scale developed by Pearlin in the early 1970s (Pearlin, 1975; Pearlin & Schooler, 1978). It is perhaps most distinctive with regard to the research uses to which it has been put. As is reflected in Chapter 4 (this volume), mastery has tended to be incorporated into models of the stress process, where it is analytically treated as a condition that not only can directly affect health outcomes but also can stand as a resource that functions to moderate or cushion the impact of stressful experience on those outcomes.

Another kindred concept deserving recognition because of the attention given it in recent years (Mirowsky & Ross, 1990; Ross, Mirowsky, &

Cockerham, 1983; Wheaton, 1985) is the notion of *fatalism*. There are, we submit, at least two forms of fatalism that can be distinguished. One involves the belief that the conditions and experiences of one's life, whatever they are, are pre-scripted by some unseen force, perhaps astrological or divine. Because one is powerless to establish a course of action that deviates from the preordained scenario, any effort to avoid or otherwise exercise personal control is obviated. A second type of fatalism arises out of people's experiences in attempting to manage situations that eventually prove to be highly resistant to personal control. For example, we have been able to observe an erosion of mastery in situations where people confront a formidable pile-up of stressors following involuntary job loss (Broman, Hamilton, & Hoffman, 1990; Pearlin, Lieberman, Menaghan, & Mullan, 1981) and where caregivers must deal with the inexorable course of Alzheimer's disease (Aneshensel, Pearlin, Mullan, Zarit, & Whitlach, 1995). These kinds of situations can lead people to become resigned to their inability to alter the exigencies they face in such situations and to cede some measure of mastery or self-efficacy. Fatalism of both types may be linked to the level of personal control, but the nature of these linkages differs according to types of fatalism we are considering. In the first instance, personal control is made moot by the conviction that the circumstances of life have been laid out for the individual by an omnipotent force and, therefore, are beyond the control of the individual. The second form of fatalism, very different from a passive resignation to what is "meant to be," is explained not by the nature of one's belief system but by the nature of the particular life circumstances one confronts. Specifically, where individuals experience these circumstances as intractable and rigidly resistant to efforts to change them, they may come to acknowledge defeat by what they are unable to control, like it or not.

Two additional concepts involving personal control may be briefly discussed. One concerns the notion of *empowerment*. Bandura (1997) regards empowerment more as political hyperbole than as a viable concept, largely because the term suggests that those with power can bestow it on others who are without it (p. 77). We are sympathetic to Bandura's reservations about the naivete or manipulativeness that may underlie the use of the term, especially when it implies that it can be transferred from one individual to another. However, we do believe that empowerment as a concept has some utility when it is viewed as a disposition that institutions are able to foster in their constituents. For example, it is reasonable to suppose that political systems have it within their grasp to shape the distribution of power and mastery among social and economic groups in societies. Looked at this way, the notion of empowerment can expand our thinking about the social origins of personal control. Although by its nature personal control is a disposition possessed by individuals, it does not necessarily originate within individuals but, instead, may be acquired from the institutions and collectivities of which individuals are a part. We return later in the chapter to consider further the relationship between individuals and collectivities with regard to mastery and control.

Learned Helplessness

Finally, a word about the interesting concept of learned helplessness specified by Seligman (1975). It entails the conviction, learned from repeated experience, that there is little or no connection between the intended and the actual consequences of one's actions. To some extent, it is the converse of self-efficacy. However, the notion of learned helplessness has not been adopted to an appreciable extent by scholars concerned with personal control. This seems to be less a result of the potential relevance of learned helplessness to matters of personal control than to the fact the inquiries into the construct have largely been confined to exploring its relationship to depression (e.g., Abramson, Metalsky, & Alloy, 1989).

Looking back over the rather rich array of concepts relevant to personal control, it can be seen that each contributes its own perspectives to an understanding of the concept, each has both strengths and weaknesses, each has helped to illuminate the relationships of personal control to personality, behavior, and/or distress, and each has its methodological challenges. Much of the remainder of this chapter suggests ways in which the conceptualization of personal control can be further extended and applied. However, we can assert here that if we were to present a wish list for future work, we would want a theory that moves the sense of control from its historic concern with individual differences toward a firmer link to the larger society and its systems of stratification. In this regard, we are also in full agreement with Skaff's call (this volume) for theories that attend to cultural influences.

There is one more salient item on our wish list to which we now turn our attention: It concerns the development of theories and measures of personal control that are more attuned to and congenial with the study of life course changes. In the following discussions, we occasionally employ mastery as interchangeable with the more generally used sense of control.

CONTROL AND THE LIFE COURSE

Most scholars agree that personal control is a learned view of self, not a fixed attribute of personality. Because it is learned, it is presumably also amenable to relearning and change. Despite the general understanding that it is a learned disposition, there has been remarkably little inquiry into how and under what conditions the sense of personal control might change, especially as people traverse the life course. Of particular interest are changes that emerge in an orderly or predictable manner as people pass through the multiple life course transitions entailing the entrance into and exits from various roles and statuses. An example of such change that accompanies an important role transition can be drawn from research into caregiving to relatives with Alzheimer's disease, a role that is all too commonly and unexpectedly acquired by older people. In a study that followed a sample of caregivers over a period of several years, it was observed that the global level of mastery among the caregivers was likely to rise with the termination of the role resulting from the death of the relative (Aneshensel et al., 1995; Skaff, Pearlin, & Mullan, 1996). Such a finding provisionally suggests that people's sense of control is likely to be elevated when they no longer need to confront on a daily basis important circumstances that are beyond their control.

Conventional wisdom would suggest that, in general, the sense of control would begin to diminish as people enter late life and are increasingly and repeatedly reminded of their lessened ability to manage as they once did the conditions and demands of their various activities and relationships. The available evidence, however, provides a less conclusive picture of the sense of control in late life (Lachman, 1986). On one hand, deaths of friends and loved ones, loss of valued social roles, and shifts in the balance of power in key relationships, such as with children, have the potential to reduce an individual's sense of control (Rodin, 1986; Rodin & Timko, 1992). Similarly, the declines in physical and mental capacity associated with age may dilute the sense of control (Mirowsky, 1995; Schieman & Turner, 1998). On the other hand, Johnson and Barer (1997), for example, report a surprisingly high level of mastery in a sample of oldest-old living independently in the community.

Pearlin (1994), in his analysis of qualitative interviews conducted with this sample, sought some explanation for this somewhat unexpected finding. One explanation lies with reported shifts in the priorities that people in late life attach to different areas of their lives and on which they base their estimates of mastery. What earlier might have been of salient importance, such as active involvement in voluntary associations or even in the lives of children and grandchildren, now attaches to different arenas of activity, particularly the satisfaction of the logistical needs of daily life, such as meal preparation and meeting other quotidian demands. The qualitative data, then, indicate that the oldest-old are able to maintain a sense of control by adopting as their standards of judgment the more narrowed areas of life over which they can, in fact, exert control. Indeed, there was some suggestion in these interviews that being the sole survivor or among the last survivors of one's age peers was itself used by the survivors as evidence of their mastery. However painful the loss of friends and relatives is, being able to "tough it out" seemed to be a source of pride and strength among some of the oldest-old.

Perceived Control and Life Trajectories

It seems to us that in certain respects our thinking about the sense of control does not match up well with our thinking about aging and life course transitions over the long run. We particularly have in mind the linkage of the sense of control to distal outcomes and the eventual achievement of these outcomes. It seems to us that such achievement depends on a host of intermediate control–outcome linkages. To illustrate, consider a freshman student who feels fully confident that she or he possesses all of the qualifications to achieve sought-after financial riches. But standing between the present moment and the distant outcome is tomorrow's midterm examination, followed 3 years later by the finals the person must take before graduation, then finding a job having an opportunity structure that can accommodate the person's aspirations, moving up through a series of job advancements over the next 20 or 30 years, then, finally, producing the outcome over which the individual had perceived control some decades earlier.

Whereas it is relatively simple to assess the relationship between the sense of control and the management of a situation that is contemporaneous or temporally proximate, it is incomparably more complicated to follow the process through which an earlier sense of control leads to temporally distal outcomes. However, it is likely that embedded in the life course trajectories of many people are deferred or delayed outcomes whose primordial foundations entail an earlier sense of control over the contingencies that are expected to arise in the distant future. Of course, there is no certainty that a strong sense of mastery will ultimately be linked to valued and expected outcomes. This kind of linkage, we suppose, depends on situations in which mastery contributes to an outcome, where, in turn, this success then reinforces the sense of mastery, which then heightens the chances of successfully affecting a related outcome, and so on, until through a series of incremental steps one finally arrives at the long-cherished place in life. Alternately, initial disadvantages (e.g., being born poor in an inner-city neighborhood) may inhibit the development of a strong sense of mastery and the benefits it may confer. In the context of the life course, control and outcome should not be viewed as freestanding episodes, but instead as forming contingency chains reaching into the future.

Perhaps the forging of an integrated succession of mastery–outcome experiences over the life course can be regarded as a component of successful aging. But successful aging depends on much more than desire alone. As Riley and her colleagues (Riley, Foner, & Riley, 1998; Riley, Kahn, & Foner, 1994) have emphasized, it also requires that individuals live under environmental conditions whose realities encourage and reward the sense of control. We know that the sense of control is least likely to be enjoyed by people with the fewest social and economic advantages, and we can confidently surmise that these are the same people who are least able to successfully negotiate the intermediate steps leading to desired long-term outcomes. Any research into the life course should track and compare the life course trajectories of people whose social and economic resources differ. However, the observation of the linkages of control and outcome across time requires both considerable methodological and conceptual sophistication, neither of which we possess at this time.

In a form and from a perspective much more modest than suggested above, we have attempted to bring together the notion of mastery and the life course. One aspect of this approach entails people's reconstruction of their sense of control over their past life course trajectories, leading up to the present time. Concretely, a sample of Alzheimer's caregivers was asked to provide a global retrospective review of their mastery. Thus, past mastery was assessed through a battery of seven items, prefaced by this query: "[T]hese statements are about the control you think you had over the earlier years of your adult life. Looking backward to the past, how much do you agree or disagree with these statements?" Respondents were then presented with statements such as these: "Things have pretty much worked out according to my plans," "My life has turned out to be different from what I tried to make it," "I was the master of my life," and "Sometimes I felt that I was being pushed around in life." In another study of people 65 years and older that is just getting under way, we will extend the application of mastery to the life course by asking people about their anticipated control over their futures. The assessment of anticipatory mastery is also made on the basis of answers to multiple items, including "What happens to me in the future mostly depends on me," "I am the master of my future," "I can create the kind of future life I want for myself," and "My future is beyond my control." Both past and anticipated mastery can be examined in conjunction with our measure of current global mastery.

Obviously, these global assessments of the past and future cannot take the place of repeated assessments of mastery at regular intervals and across a substantial span of time. Subsumed within these global measures are undoubtedly countless swings and variations in the sense of control across the life course that are associated with changes in the conditions and outcomes over which control is directed. However, people apparently do make such assessments, and early analysis of the measure of mastery over the past indicates that this dimension of control contributes to well-being independently of the contributions made by current mastery. It remains to be seen whether similar statements can be made with regard to anticipatory mastery. Regardless of where the analyses of these measures may eventually take us, they can be seen as but one way to more closely link the sense of control to life course trajectories.

It is evident that there are large gaps in our current knowledge concerning the connections between mastery and the life course. However, these gaps should not obscure what is most significant and what repeatedly shows up in the research literature, namely, that it is better for individuals to be armed with a sense of control than to be without it. This statement, of course, is supported by a considerable body of evidence showing mastery and control to be associated with well-being and that it can function to blunt what would otherwise be the more inimical impact of stressors (see Avison, this volume). This evidence alone should spur our inquiries into control and the life course. At this time, nonetheless, we are largely in the dark regarding the interplay of mastery with the assumption and enactment of new roles and the yielding of old roles, the structure of experience, and the quality of life across an expanse of time. We revisit some of these issues below.

THE MULTIPLE DIMENSIONS AND APPLICATIONS OF PERSONAL CONTROL

The conceptual flexibility of personal control and the many analytic uses to which it can be put contribute to its attractiveness as well as to its ambiguities. In addition to its utility in looking at connec. ns to life course changes, it has a number of other potential applications. Whereas the application of the sense of control to life course issues may involve its temporal dimensions—past, present, and future—its application to other issues reveals additional aspects that deserve further attention and development.

Global versus Domain-Specific Control

Probably the most commonly recognized specification of personal control is that distinguishing its global and domain-specific manifestations. The distinction between them is not for the purpose of questioning whether one is better than the other and therefore should be employed in preference to the other. Indeed, it is doubtful whether either global or specific measures alone are sufficient to yield all the detailed information we seek in many of our studies. The salient goal is to understand how and when each can be used, either separately or in conjunction with one another, to gain maximum analytic yield in our research. To elaborate this matter, it is useful to differentiate two types of specific domains for which measures have been developed: *role-specific* and what may be described as *function-specific.*

Role-specific mastery, of course, refers to the control that people sense they are able to exercise over conditions they encounter within the context of their institutionalized roles. The sense of control in these domains is potentially of great importance, for the enactment of the roles typically extends over broad arcs of the life course. Moreover, the very fact that these roles are located within institutions that are important to society at large—family, occupation, and economy among them—gives mastery over the conditions they embody a corresponding importance to their individual incumbents. Indeed, these roles are likely to be among the central elements in the organization of people's lives and of their identities. Finally, mastery of these roles cannot be taken for granted, for they entail complex interlocking relationships, expectations, and obligations among all of those who are part of what Merton (1957) has termed the role set.

The connections between global and role-specific mastery are not yet well understood. Although we can be quite confident that such connections exist, their strength and the mechanisms through which they are established probably vary with different roles and at different periods of the life course. It is reasonable to suppose that the global ways that people are disposed to view themselves can tell us something of how they view themselves in the context of the more specific tasks and social relationships of their roles. Thus, we can speculate that a global sense of control functions as a self-fulfilling prophecy in the enactment of specific roles. That is, a belief that in general we are able to control the conditions of our lives may encourage the belief that the conditions of specific roles are also within our control. These beliefs, in turn, are expressed in actions consistent with the beliefs, such as actively coping with unwanted circumstances. At the same time, it is also reasonable to suppose that the influence between global and role-specific mastery is reciprocal, such that its presence in a particular role influences its global level. The channels through which role-specific mastery may influence the global await illumination. One likelihood is that the influence of role-specific mastery on global mastery varies as a function of the saliency of that role. At this time, we are willing to venture the opinion that global mastery cannot be calculated by simply averaging its role-specific manifestations.

Moreover, whatever may be the reciprocal influence between the two, they do not have identical origins nor do they produce identical consequences. Neither the global nor the role-specific can be treated as a proxy for the other. These assertions are supported by data drawn from our study of caregivers to spouses with Alzheimer's disease in which measures of both global and role-specific mastery were used. These data reveal that only global mastery is closely correlated with people's socioeconomic characteristics, education and income in particular. Additionally, global mastery alone is related to long-term health outcomes, such as symptoms of chronic illness and self-rated health. By contrast, there are certain role-related outcomes, namely, feelings of role captivity and role overload, with which only role-specific mastery are associated. The two dimensions are equally related to depression and anxiety, but role-specific mastery is more closely associated with anger. We present these differences not for the purpose of undertaking an explanation here, but to underscore that each can potentially underlie the different outcomes that are under observation. Analytically, they may be placed usefully in the service of quite different questions, or, conversely, they may provide different answers to the same questions.

As noted, we think it is also useful to distinguish function-specific from role-specific mastery. By function, we essentially refer to the patterns of activities that are associated with the satisfaction of daily needs and proclivities. Although some of these functions may involve the enactment of roles, they tend either to cut across the boundaries of multiple roles or to be entirely outside the boundaries of any role. Perhaps the best known example of functional mastery is control over the protection and enhancement of health, for which specific measures have been developed (e.g., Wallston & Wallston, 1978). The notion of functional control is also implicated in everyday discourse, found in such expressions as "controlling myself" or "controlling my emotions." There are other functional areas that can also be considered to fall under this heading: activities associated with the logistical requirements of daily life (e.g., shopping and homemaking), the maintenance of lifestyle proclivities (e.g., social and leisure activities), and the organization and use of time.

Much of what we said above concerning the connections between global and role-specific mastery would apply as well to function-specific domains. That is, we can speculate that there is some reciprocal influence between the global and the function-specific domains. Indeed, reciprocal influence may exist between role- and function-specific mastery as well as between each of these and global mastery. However, the patterns and directions of influence between any of these dimensions of mastery have yet to be fully examined.

Independent versus Negotiated Control

We typically think of mastery or personal control as dispositions and behaviors of individuals, separate and apart from relationships and interactions with other individuals. There are conceivably many activities and situations that are entirely consistent with this thinking. For example, there are occupations marked by a high degree of self-directedness, where people enjoy considerable latitude in setting job goals, establishing priorities, and selecting task methods (Kohn et al., 1997; Kohn,

Naoi, Schoenbach, Schooler, & Slomczynski, 1990; Kohn & Schooler, 1982). Thus, the artist may with confidence in his or her own unique creative judgments and skills succeed in producing a work that is precisely what he or she hoped for and expected. However, it is much easier to think of instances where the sense of mastery and the actions stemming from it operate not in social separateness, but within social relationships having clear interpersonal obligations and expectations. This is typically the case with role-specific mastery, because by definition one's role is always part of a larger role set. The self-directed artist who works in splendid isolation, for example, may not have independent control of his or her activities outside the studio. Despite the control he or she might be able to exercise at the easel, the artist may have to negotiate with a spouse or roommate over which of them is responsible for the shopping, how to reconcile incompatible food tastes, how much money to spend, and whose turn it is to wash the dishes.

The point to be drawn from this discussion is that mastery in many situations may be the product of successful negotiation with others, not something that springs up within or is sustained by the individual alone. Agency, the ability to act on one's own behalf, is not necessarily exercised in a vacuum; more typically, especially within role sets, it is the joint product of all who also have a stake in and are affected by the actions of individuals. One's sense of personal control, therefore, may be supported by a willingness to yield or share control with others who are judged to have a legitimate stake in the outcomes one seeks to bring about. This line of inquiry, it seems to us, can help to bring some additional light both to the exercise of individual mastery and to the stability of the social systems in which the actions of the individual are located.

Collective versus Individual Control

There is a somewhat different aspect of the social dimensions of personal control that may also be usefully taken into account. The above discussion considered how the level of one's mastery may be the product of give-and-take interactions among individuals whose interests are interdependent. By contrast are outcome expectations that are shared by individuals constituting a larger collectivity whose members may be largely anonymous and engage in few if any interpersonal exchanges. Most important, the outcome expectations, though shared by others, are seen as beyond the reach of individual attainment. Under these conditions, we submit, agency lies with the collectivity, not its individual constituents.

This is a matter to which Bandura (1997, 477–525) has astutely devoted considerable attention. He seems to emphasize the sense of control that individuals bring with them in shaping the activities and goals of collectivities, such as political parties. When we think of people like Martin Luther King Jr., who through his own efficacy helped to activate and inspire the civil rights movement, we can agree with this emphasis. We would argue that influence on mastery and the sense of control more often operates in the opposite direction, from the collectivity to its individual members. It is not difficult to find examples of how personal control might be shaped by collective efficacy and action. Thus, it may be only after they join a union that individuals feel that they personally have the capability of contributing to the improvement of noxious work conditions, not through their individual efforts alone but through participation in collective action. Or parents who find their sense of control depleted by their unsuccessful attempts to improve public education experience a turnabout when they join a militant school association. Anyone, certainly, who has ever participated in a protest movement or gathered for a cause on the Mall in Washington, DC, has probably experienced an uplift in mastery, but it is a mastery largely acquired through participation in and identification with the collectivity.

The Direct versus Indirect Exercise of Control

Implicitly underlying the distinction between individual and collective efficacy is the difference between agency that is *directly* exercised by an individual in achieving his or her desired outcomes and agency that is *indirectly* exercised through appeals to more efficacious forces for intercession on behalf of that individual. As proposed above, participation in larger collectivities for the purpose of attaining shared goals is but one instance of indirect control. In addition, aspects of social support are relevant to matters of mastery and control. We know from our research and that of others (Smith et al., 2000) that there is a fairly robust correlation between global mastery and social support. This relationship suggests a pair of possibilities: first, that people with a high level of mastery are better able to enlist support systems; and, second, that one's success in attaining sought-after ends is enhanced by activating the appropriate social support. This is perhaps most evident in cases where instrumental support is mobilized. Take as an illustration a person with a high level of mastery who because of an injury needs some assistance. More than an injured counterpart with limited mastery, this person is likely to have created a viable network of supporting friends and acquaintances who will bring in casseroles, provide transportation, and cater to other necessities of life. In whatever way mastery may help to build such supports, once in place it is through the actions of the support system that the individuals are able to realize this desired outcomes.

In the above illustration, then, the significant actions prompted by the individual's sense of mastery is directed to the marshaling of appropriate supports, who then become the agents for producing desired and expected outcomes. This process may also provide a framework for looking at people's mastery in relation to their use of religion and its belief systems. We refer here to appeals to a deity or other higher power to intervene in one's behalf. Although some religious beliefs can reasonably be regarded as an expression of passive resignation or an acceptance of an unshakable fate, appeals to a deity do not necessarily involve the yielding of control by individuals. It is more akin to exercising personal control in tandem with that possessed by another and more powerful entity. To the extent that religious beliefs encourage the active and purposive supplication for intervention, the use of religion is similar to the use of social support. That is, the individual senses that through the use of specified practices he or she will succeed in activating the favorable attention of the higher power and that power will then act in behalf of the supplicant. We can think of a double agency working in tandem. The individual first acts as his or her own agent through his or her control of the channels leading to another powerful entity. That power, in turn, will presumably exercise its power and control in a manner consistent with the attainment of the individual's desired outcomes. In exploring the application of mastery to social and spiritual life, then, it may be reasonable to think of mastery not as starting and stopping with the individual but as operating in chains of control in which one's mastery is linked to that possessed by other bodies.

CONCLUSION

It seems hardly necessary at this time to espouse the importance of the sense of control. Its importance has been repeatedly demonstrated, particularly as an explanatory construct in accounting for observed differences in the ways people are able to manage the demands of life and to take actions on their own behalf. The salient issue is not whether the construct deserves continued attention; by all indications it does. More at issue is the recognition of the many matters of social and psychological life to which it can be applied.

A central feature of personal control, which we sought to underscore in this chapter, concerns its flexible multidimensionality. Its multidimensional character immediately surfaces when we begin to think of the domains over which control potentially extends. Thus, it can refer to global control over the important circumstances across the entirety of one's life course, past, present, and future. It is equally applicable to the more specific domains over which one exercises control. As we suggested, these domains are of two types: role-specific and function-specific. Indeed, it may be useful to think of a third specific domain, this one involving the self. Thus, the notion of self-control, which includes control over one's emotions and impulses and the social presentation of self, is part of everyday discourse.

In addition to its various dimensions, we also examined how personal control is exercised, the mechanisms through which the sense of control may be converted to actual control. In this connection, we noted the operation of self-fulfilling prophecies, where individuals' control beliefs can both perceptually diminish the magnitude of threat in a situation and, at the same time, reduce barriers to actions capable of overcoming the threat. Other possible mechanisms that were identified were more social in their nature. Specifically, control may be exercised through alliances with other entities, including groups and collectivities seeking the same or similar outcomes, the mobilization of social support and assistance, or through appeals to a higher power identified by one's belief system. Moreover, the outcomes that are sought and the actions that are taken may be the product of negotiation with others whose interests are also at stake. Personal control and its relevant mechanisms may be personal and direct or social and indirect. Which dimensions and mechanisms of control are selected for study depend, of course, on what is being sought to learn.

From a sociological perspective, the salient and challenging future tasks of research into personal control are to explore more extensively the interconnections between personal control, its cultural, social, and situational contexts, and its patterned changes across the life course. These contexts, though frequently ignored, essentially envelope personal control. Thus, we know that they can influence the levels at which people enjoy a sense control and, as we suggest above, such contexts may also represent the arenas in which control is negotiated and through which it is implemented. How these kinds of interconnections are relevant to the study of life course trajectories largely awaits further inquiry. At this time, however, we feel on safe ground to speculate that its sources, its salient dimensions, and the mechanisms through which it is realized are all likely to shift as people traverse the life course. What does not change with the life course, we can confidently assert, is the critical importance of personal control to well-being.

REFERENCES

Abramson, L. Y., Metalsky, G. I., & Alloy, L. B. (1989). Hopelessness depression: A theory-based subtype of depression. *Psychological Review, 96,* 358–372.

Aneshensel, C. A., Pearlin, L. I., Mullan, J. T., Zarit, S. H., & Whitlach, C. (1995). *Profiles in caregiving: The unexpected career.* San Diego: Academic Press.

Bandura, A. (1977). Self-efficacy: Toward a unifying theory of behavioral change. *Psychological Review, 84,* 191–215.

Bandura, A. (1997). *Self-efficacy: The exercise of control.* New York: Freeman.

Broman, C. L., Hamilton, V. L., & Hoffman, W. S. (1990). Unemployment and its effect on families: Evidence from a plant closing study. *American Journal of Community Psychology, 18,* 643–659.

Burger, J. M. (1992). *Desire for control: Personality, social, and clinical perspectives.* New York: Plenum Press.

Burger, J. M., & Cooper, H. M. (1979). The desirability of control. *Motivation and Emotion, 3,* 381–393.

Gecas, V. (1989). The social psychology of self-efficacy. *Annual Review of Sociology, 15,* 291–316.

Gurin, P., Gurin, G., & Morrison, B. M. (1978). Personal and ideological aspects of internal and external control. *Social Psychology, 41,* 275–296.

Johnson, C. L., & Barer, B. M. (1997). *Life beyond 85 years: The aura of survivorship.* New York: Springer.

Kohn, M. L., Naoi, A., Schoenbach, C., Schooler, C., & Slomczynski, K. M. (1990). Position in the class structure and psychological functioning: A comparative analysis of the United States, Japan, and Poland. *American Journal of Sociology, 95,* 964–1008.

Kohn, M. L., & Schooler, C. (1982). Job conditions and personality: A longitudinal assessment of their reciprocal effects. *American Journal of Sociology, 87,* 1257–1286.

Kohn, M. L., Slomczynski, K. M., Janicka, K., Khmelko, V., Mach, B. W., Paniotto, V., Zaborowski, W., Gutierrez, R., & Heyman, C. (1997). Social structure and personality under conditions of radical social change: A comparative analysis of Poland and Ukraine. *American Sociological Review, 62,* 614–638.

Krause, N. (1987a). Chronic strain, locus of control, and distress in older adults. *Psychology and Aging, 2,* 375–382.

Krause, N. (1987b). Understanding the stress process: Linking social support with locus of control beliefs. *Journals of Gerontology: Social Sciences, 42,* 589–593.

Lachman, M. E. (1986). Locus of control in aging research: A case for multidimensional and domain-specific assessment. *Journal of Psychology and Aging, 1,* 34–40.

Lachman, M. E., & Jelalian, E. (1984). Self-efficacy and attributions for intellectual performance in young and elderly adults. *Journal of Gerontology, 39,* 577–582.

Lefcourt, H. M. (Ed.). (1981). *Research with the locus of control construct: 1. Assessment methods.* New York: Academic Press.

Lefcourt, H. M. (Ed.). (1983). *Research with the locus of control construct: 2. Developments and social problems.* New York: Academic Press.

Lefcourt, H. M. (Ed.). (1984). *Research with the locus of control construct: 3. Extensions and limitations.* New York: Academic Press.

Levenson, H. (1974). Activism and powerful others: Distinctions within the concept of internal-external control. *Journal of Personality Assessment, 38,* 377–383.

Merton, R. K. (1957). The role set: Problems in sociological theory. *British Journal of Sociology, 8,* 106–120.

Mirowsky, J. (1995). Age and the sense of control. *Social Psychology Quarterly, 58,* 31–43.

Mirowsky, J., & Ross, C. E. (1990). Control or defense? Depression and the sense of control over good and bad outcomes. *Journal of Health and Social Behavior, 31,* 71–86.

Moghaddam, F. M., & Studer, C. (1998). *Illusions of control: Striving for control in our personal and professional lives.* Westport, CT: Praeger.

Pearlin, L. I. (1975). Status inequality and stress in marriage. *American Sociological Review, 40,* 344–357.

Pearlin, L. I. (1994). The study of the oldest-old: Some promises and puzzles. *International Journal of Aging and Human Development, 38,* 91–98.

Pearlin, L. I., Lieberman, M., Menaghan, E., & Mullan, J. T. (1981). The stress process. *Journal of Health and Social Behavior, 22,* 337–356.

Pearlin, L. I., & Schooler, C. (1978). The structure of coping. *Journal of Health and Social Behavior, 19,* 2–21.

Riley, M. W., Foner, A., & Riley, J. W., Jr. (1998). The aging and society paradigm. In V. L. Bengston & K. W. Schaie (Eds.), *Handbook of theories of aging* (pp. 327–344). New York: Springer.

Riley, M. W., Kahn, R. L., & Foner, A. (Eds.). (1994). *Age and structural lag: Society's failure to provide meaningful opportunities in work, family, and leisure.* New York: Wiley.

Rodin, J. (1986). Aging and health: Effects of the sense of control. *Science, 233,* 1271–1276.

Rodin, J. (1990). Control by any other name: Definitions, concepts, and processes. In J. Rodin, C. Schooler, & K. W. Schaie (Eds.), *Self-directedness: Cause and effects throughout the life course* (pp. 1–17). Hillsdale, NJ: Erlbaum.

Rodin, J., & Timko, C. (1992). Sense of control, aging, and health. In M. G. Ory, R. P. Abeles, & P. D. Lipman (Eds.), *Aging, health, and behavior* (pp. 207–236). Newbury Park, CA: Sage.

Ross, C. E., Mirowsky, J., & Cockerham, W. C. (1983). Social class, Mexican culture, and fatalism: Their effects on psychological distress. *American Journal of Community Psychology, 11,* 383–399.

Rotter, J. B. (1966). Generalized expectancies for internal versus external control of reinforcement. *Psychological Monographs, 80*(1, Whole No. 609).

Schieman, S., & Turner, H. A. (1998). Age, disability, and the sense of mastery. *Journal of Health and Social Behavior, 39,* 169–186.

Schooler, C. (1990). Individualism and the historical and social-structural determinants of people's concerns over self-directedness and efficacy. In J. Rodin, C. Schooler, & K. W. Schaie (Eds.), *Self-directedness: Cause and effects throughout the life course* (pp. 19–49). Hillsdale, NJ: Erlbaum.

Seligman, M. E. P. (1975). *Helplessness: On depression, development, and death.* San Francisco: Freeman.

Skaff, M. M., Pearlin, L. I., & Mullan, J. T. (1996). Transitions in the caregiving career: Effects on the sense of mastery. *Psychology and Aging, 11,* 247–257.

Skinner, E. A. (1996). A guide to constructs of control. *Journal of Personality and Social Psychology, 71,* 549–570.

Smith, G. C., Kohn, S. J., Savage-Stevens, S. E., Finch, J. J., Ingate, R., & Lim Y.-O. (2000). The effects of interpersonal and personal agency on perceived control and psychological well-being in adulthood. *Gerontologist, 40,* 458–468.

Wallston, B. S., & Wallston, K. A (1978). Locus of control and health: A review of the literature. *Health Education Monographs, 6,* 107–117.

Wheaton, B. (1985). Personal resources and mental health: Can there be too much of a good thing? *Research in Community and Mental Health, 5,* 139–184.

Commentary

Some Thoughts on Aging, Social Structures, and Sense of Control[1]

Ronald P. Abeles

Leonard Perlin and Mark Pioli (this volume) provide a thorough overview of many, if not most, of the significant recent and continuing conceptual issues in research involving personal control. They review quite adeptly the multiple labels and meanings of personal control and explore various implications flowing from the multiple conceptualizations of personal control. In keeping with their explorations, I would like to comment briefly on two broad areas deserving of more research. I consider first the relationship between social structures and personal control and, second, change and stability during old age in personal control.

A MODEL OF SENSE OF CONTROL

Before proceeding with these brief discussions, it may be helpful to review the components of sense of control.[2] Figure 1.1 synthesizes the major strains in the current literature and provides a model that represents the components of sense of control and schematizes their interrela-

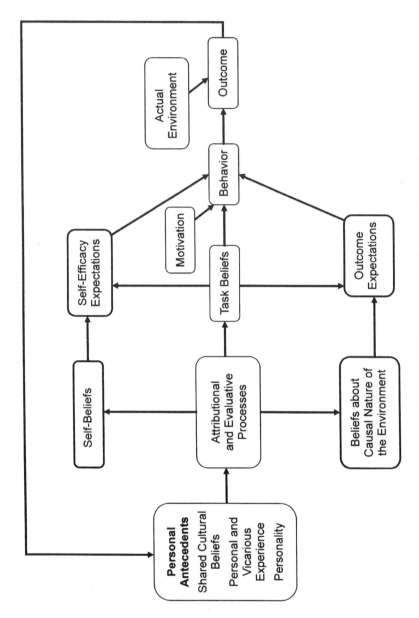

FIGURE 1.1 A model of sense of control.

tions (Abeles, 1991; Fung, Abeles, & Carstensen, 1999). In viewing this model, five points are noteworthy. First, it refers primarily to internal, cognitive structures and processes. That is, it conceptualizes control in terms of subjective experiences within a person's mind. It is not a model of actual or objective control. (See Schulz, Wrosch, and Heckhausen, this volume, for a discussion of objective control.) Although most elements are internal, a few presumed antecedents and consequences are external to the individual. Second, sense of control is not a unitary concept, but is composed of multiple component beliefs and expectations regarding oneself and the environment. Third, the model postulates processes that are dynamic and also dialectical; these processes include a feedback loop from outcomes back to the hypothesized antecedents of sense of control. This loop implies that accumulating experiences result in both short- and long-term changes in sense of control as a person undergoes development and aging. Fourth, the least elaborated or specified part of the diagram refers to the hypothesized antecedents of sense of control, which reflects the relative lack of research on antecedents. Fifth, the question of global versus domain-specific sense of control may be handled by presuming that multiple senses of control (each with the components detailed in Figure 1.1) as well as a generalized sense of control may exist. The model does not, however, specify how the domain-specific and the global sense of control are interrelated.

As schematized in Figure 1.1, the model portrays the components of sense of control and their role in influencing whether someone will perform a particular behavior and how the results of that behavior feed back to affect the person's sense of control. Sense of control consists of beliefs and expectations about the self and about the environment. According to this model, people's *self-beliefs* about their own ability (e.g., skills) and capability (e.g., to exert effort) combine with *task beliefs* about the nature of the task (e.g., how difficult it is, whether it requires skill or luck) to produce their *self-efficacy expectations*: a sense of whether they could successfully perform the behaviors needed to achieve the particular desired outcome.

People's *beliefs about the causal nature of the environment* focus on whether they perceive the environment to be governed by lawful or orderly processes such that outcomes (e.g., success or failure) are contingent upon people's behaviors as opposed to random forces (i.e., noncontingent). Environmental contingency may stem from physical (e.g., the laws of nature) or social rules (e.g., norms). Believing that an environment is contingent does not necessarily mean that people believe that they have control, because their own outcomes may be perceived as more contingent upon the behaviors of others than upon their own efforts. Beliefs about the causal nature of the environment also combine with task beliefs to produce *outcome expectations* (i.e., whether performing action A is generally likely to result in outcome B). Thus, people's sense of control consists of the complex interrelationships among their self-beliefs, self-efficacy expectations, beliefs about the causal nature of the environment, and outcome expectations.

SOCIAL STRUCTURES AND SENSE OF CONTROL

Now, let us turn briefly to the question of how social structures may affect people's sense of control. To accomplish this, we need to amend the model of sense of control by adding a new box representing social structural antecedents, which presumably precede personal antecedents of shared cultural beliefs, experiences, and personality. What should this box contain? How do its contents impact upon sense of control? The answer to the first question depends on how detailed and how distal in a hypothesized causal chain we want to be. Perhaps it should include such concepts as the following:

- Social stratification systems (based on education, income, gender, race/ethnicity, or age) that allocate people to different roles, life chances, and experiences
- Role sets (see Pearlin & Pioli, this volume)
- Immediate social environments, in which social stratification systems and roles express themselves. These are the socially structured situations in which we live out our daily lives, such as schools, offices, and homes.

Perhaps the most psychologically relevant or causally proximal social structure in this short list is the immediate social environment. Social stratification systems and role sets operate, to a major degree, by placing us in particular immediate social environments in which we live out our daily lives. This sequence of macro and distal social structural processes operating through micro and proximal social environments is depicted in Figure 1.2.

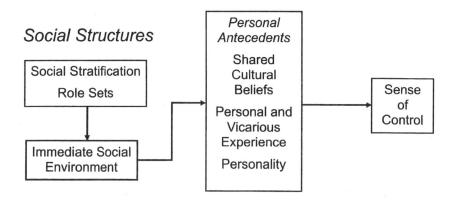

FIGURE 1.2 Antecedents of sense of control.

IMMEDIATE SOCIAL ENVIRONMENTS

To which aspects of immediate social environments should we be paying attention in order to study potential links between social structures and sense of control? How are "social facts" translated into "psychological facts"? Among possible processes are cultural belief systems, information environments, contingency and sensitivity, and affordance of control.

Cultural Beliefs

By virtue of belonging to particular social groups and enacting particular roles, we are exposed to and learn, if we are properly socialized, cultural belief systems. These include elaborate systems (e.g., religion and science) for explaining how both the social and physical worlds operate and the appropriate means for achieving desired ends, including whether particular outcomes are contingent or noncontingent upon people's behaviors. (See Skaff and Gardiner, this volume.) At the level of the immediate social environment, cultural beliefs operate through shared social schemas about the rules of the situation (i.e., how people with particular characteristics are expected to behave). One component to cultural belief systems is beliefs about people's capabilities at different ages, such as ageism. Presumably, cultural beliefs could affect both global and domain-specific senses of control, with perhaps greater influence on global sense of control.

Biased Information Environments

Being in an immediate social environments may result in selective exposure to information from mass media as well as other people (e.g., opinion leaders and reference groups) that reinforce beliefs and expectations about oneself and the environment. The social psychological and political science literature demonstrates that we tend to converse with others who hold similar opinions and who rely upon and are exposed to similar sources of information (Sears, 1967, 1969). Such biased information environments may contribute to socialization to roles and belief systems, including global and domain-specific senses of control. This possible avenue of influence has not been studied very much, if at all, from a life course or aging perspective, and surely not in terms of impact upon sense of control.

Contingency and Sensitivity

Immediate environments differ in their actual responsiveness to people's behaviors (Skinner, 1995). That is, environments can be characterized in terms of how contingent they are: Is there an actual link between what you do and how the social and physical environments respond to your behaviors? Are responses systematic or random (chaotic)? As we age, our social environments tend to become less responsive to our behaviors, and our outcomes are more dependent or contingent upon the behaviors of others, such as friends, family, and health care providers. At the same time, the environment may become more responsive to the behaviors and demands of interaction partners, such as caretakers, who are better positioned to organize the physical, temporal, and social environment according to their own needs (e.g., scheduling of meals; Baltes, 1996).

In addition, the social environment may become less likely to provide appropriate or what others have called "sensitive" responses to our behaviors as we age (Skinner, 1995). For example, social partners may reliably and consistently respond to verbal requests for assistance (i.e., the environment is contingent), but their replies may always be in the form of unhelpful information, such as about the weather (i.e., the environment's responses are inappropriate or insensitive). This may result from diminished social contacts or from interaction partners, such as caretakers, who reinforce behaviors that make their lives easier rather than taking into account our desires and goals. Perhaps the most dramatic demonstration of this tendency is research by Margaret Baltes (1996) on interaction patterns between nursing home residents and staff. Baltes and her colleagues found that staff were more reinforcing (i.e., responsive) to dependent behaviors than to independent behaviors. (Although there is probably no one-to-one correspondence between dependency and sense of control, they are probably highly correlated.)

Affordance of Actual Control

Immediate environments may be highly contingent, even sensitive, but permit little actual control. For example, total institutions, such as military organizations and prisons, create highly contingent environments but limit the degree of choice and ability to exert actual control. Of course, even in such extreme environments, one's position in the institution conditions one's degrees of freedom for action. Moreover, there are domains in which the institution is indifferent to how its inmates or citizens behave. We do not have to restrict our view to total institutions to recognize that social institutions create environments differing in how much actual control its role incumbents may exercise. In their now classic studies of occupational effects on personality, Kohn and Schooler (1982) characterized everyday occupations in terms of span of control, time pressure, and complexity. For our purposes, it is interesting to note that these dimensions of jobs predicted workers' sense of control some 10 years after initial measurement. Note also that social stratification systems (e.g., social class) operate to place people into jobs differing along these dimensions. The less education people have, the more likely they are to be in jobs with low span of control, high time pressure, and low complexity (e.g., working on an assembly line).

STABILITY AND CHANGE IN SENSE OF CONTROL

I would like to turn to the question of change in sense of control as people age. As we all know, aging is often characterized in dismal terms of declines in biological, cognitive, and social reserve capacity. Although some areas of functioning (e.g., pragmatic knowledge and emotional regulation) may improve with aging, many theorists have speculated that age-related impairments increasingly prevent older people from exercising control. Increasing disability may lead to fewer choices in activities and in the capability of successfully engaging in activities. At the same time, the social environment may become less responsive (i.e., contingent) and may provide beliefs and expectations (i.e., age-based stereotypes) about increasingly poor performance by older people in most domains of daily life. In sum, old age seems to be associated with physical, psychological, and social conditions hostile to a strong sense of control. With aging, forces within and outside of the person are likely to lead to a diminishing sense of control. (For one recent discussion of this literature, see Fung et al., 1999.)

So say our theories. However, as Pearlin and Pioli noted (this volume), research does not uniformly support this hypothesis of decline in sense of control in old age. Indeed, most of the studies show no age trends. This leads me to wonder whether we are studying the wrong question. Perhaps we should be addressing the question of why people continue to maintain a sense of control in old age. Why do they continue to hold an illusion of control (Langer, 1975; Taylor, 1989; Taylor et al., 2000)? We need more research on why and how sense of control is maintained in face of the "slings and arrows of outrageous fortune."

Along with other researchers, Pearlin and Pioli suggested that the illusion may be maintained by a kind of selective perception or reevaluation of priorities. That is, people may devalue domains in which they are no longer able to exercise control and focus their psychic and physical energy on those over which they still can exercise control. This explanation is compatible with Paul and Margaret Baltes' theory of selective optimization with compensation (Baltes & Baltes, 1990) and with Laura Carstensen's theory of socioemotional selectivity (Carstensen, 1993). In addition to selection of domains, the model of sense of control suggests that we should also look toward attributional (e.g., positivity bias) and evaluative processes (e.g., social comparisons) that may work to maintain beliefs into old age about causality, one's own competence, and outcome expectancies. In effect, people are constantly adapting and recalibrating in a highly successful effort to maintain their sense of control. My suspicion is that such processes may well work for many people as they age. However, it does seem that at some point—in advanced old age, perhaps—reality must break through. When one's sphere of action becomes extremely limited, for example, after a broken hip, then perhaps one can no longer recalibrate and reevaluate self-beliefs and expectation; thus, the illusions about control are abandoned (Abeles, 1991).

CONCLUSION

Rather than concluding with this somber dose of reality, let me say that we should continue exploring the conditions that develop and sustain a sense of control. Pearlin and Pioli have identified many interesting and important issues deserving of additional research. In my brief comments, I have focused on possible antecedents of sense of control, with an emphasis on pathways by which social structures may affect sense of control. I also touched on a few possible psychological and social psychological processes. In addition, I highlighted the question of why there is so little evidence for declines in sense of control with aging. How do people maintain their sense of control? Perhaps the operative concept should be illusions of control. In any event, certainly more empirical research is needed to explore these questions. But that should not come as a surprise. Did a researcher or financial supporter of research ever conclude that "more research is *not* needed"?

NOTES

1.   The opinions expressed in this chapter are those of the author's and do not necessarily reflect or represent those of the National Institutes of Health. This chapter was prepared as part of the author's official duties as an employee of the United States Government and is therefore in the public domain.
2.   *Sense of control* is used as an umbrella to cover several related concepts, such as locus of control over reinforcements, self efficacy, personal efficacy, and perceived control.

REFERENCES

Abeles, R. P. (1991). Sense of control, quality of life, and frail older people. In J. E. Birren, J. Lubben, J. Rowe, & D. Deutschman (Eds.), *The concept and measure of quality of life in frail elderly* (pp. 297–314). San Diego: Academic Press.

Baltes, M. M. (1996). *The many faces of dependency in old age.* New York: Cambridge University Press.

Baltes, P. B., & Baltes, M. M. (Eds.). (1990). *Successful aging: Perspectives from the behavioral sciences.* New York: Cambridge University Press.

Carstensen, L. L. (1993). Motivation for social contact across the life-span: A theory of socioemotional selectivity. In J. E. Jacobs (Ed.), *Nebraska symposium on motivation* (Vol. 40, pp. 209–254). Lincoln: University of Nebraska Press.

Fung, H. H., Abeles, R. P., & Carstensen, L. L. (1999). Psychological control in later life: Implications for life-span development. In J. Brandtstädter & R. M. Lerner (Eds.), *Action and self-development: Theory and research through the life course* (pp. 345–372). Thousand Oaks, CA: Sage.

Kohn, M. L., & Schooler, C. (1982). Job conditions and personality: A longitudinal assessment of their reciprocal effects. *American Journal of Sociology, 87,* 1257–1286.

Langer, E. (1975). The illusion of control. *Journal of Personality and Social Psychology, 32,* 311–328.

Sears, D. O. (1967). Selective exposure to information: A critical review. *Public Opinion Quarterly, 31,* 194–213.

Sears, D. O. (1969). Political behavior. In G. Lindzey & E. Aronson (Eds.), *The handbook of social psychology* (pp. 315–458). Reading, MA: Addison-Wesley.

Skinner, E. A. (1995). *Perceived control, motivation, and coping.* Thousand Oaks, CA: Sage.

Taylor, S. E. (1989). *Positive illusions: Creative self-deception and the healthy mind.* New York: Basic Books.

Taylor, S. E., Kemeny, M. E., Reed, G. M., Bower, J. E., & Gruenewald, T. L. (2000). Psychological resources, positive illusions, and health. *American Psychologist, 55,* 99–109.

Commentary

Embedding Control Beliefs in Social and Cultural Context

Linda K. George

I t is an honor to have the opportunity to comment upon the superb chapter by Leonard Pearlin and Mark Pioli. I have admired Len Pearlin—the scholar and the man—for more than two decades. I've never read anything that he's written without coming away seduced by his elegant thinking and writing, learning from his theoretical sophistication, and stimulated by his insights. This chapter is no exception.

I will begin with a review of what I consider the major contributions of Chapter 1. Subsequently, I will speculate a bit about how this chapter contributes to some larger questions concerning the sources and benefits of control beliefs. Note my use of the term *control beliefs* rather than *locus of control* or *sense of control*. My choice of terms has two advantages. First, it is intended as a generic term to encompass not only locus/ sense of control but also mastery, self-efficacy, and so forth. Although the distinctions between types of control beliefs are often important in the context of specific research questions, my discussion will focus on the broad range of control beliefs. Second, we should continually remind ourselves that sense of control, self-efficacy, and similar constructs are beliefs about control, rather than control itself. Such recognition also reminds us that the large knowledge base on beliefs is a relevant source for developing hypotheses about the specific nature and functions of control beliefs.

HIGHLIGHTS OF THE CHAPTER

Three major themes of this chapter make important contributions to our conceptual thinking about control beliefs. Moreover, these themes are either unique or have received limited attention in scholarship to date.

A first and critically important issue is the link between control beliefs and location in the social structure, especially stratification systems. As the authors note, this has been a badly neglected aspect of research on control beliefs and has left us with an overly individualistic bias, limiting our understanding of both the sources of control beliefs and the ways they affect behavior. In addition, intraindividual change in control beliefs, over time may, to a significant degree, reflect socially structured opportunities and constraints. That is, higher levels of social and economic resources may foster increasingly internal control beliefs, whereas social and economic impoverishment have the opposite effect. Moreover, even in the absence of resources, opportunities may be sufficient to cultivate beliefs in one's ability to ensure pleasurable achievements and outcomes. This is strongly suggested by the classic observations by Barker (1968) on undermanned and overmanned environments. Barker observed that it is a surplus of opportunities (an undermanned environment) that lead to active pursuit of goals—and possibly increased feelings of control, whereas opportunity deficits (an overmanned environment) lead to passivity and fatalism.

A second important theme of Pearlin and Pioli's chapter is the need to look temporally at control beliefs. As they point out, one possibility is that there are predictable life course trajectories of control beliefs. Such trajectories are likely if control beliefs are linked to life course patterns of resources (ranging from income to relationships to health) or the age stratification system itself (e.g., the respect and esteem allocated to age strata). But, as the authors point out, a variety of other temporal issues also merit exploration. Their examples include the possible independent effects of perceptions of past and future control on health and well-being. Another important area of investigation concerns the role of time in predicting stability or change in control beliefs.

For example, are a series of failures experienced in a short period of time more likely to erode control beliefs than an equal number of failures experienced over a longer period of time?

The third compelling theme of this superb chapter is the distinctions Pearlin and Pioli develop among types of control: global versus domain-specific, independent versus negotiated, collective versus individual, and direct versus indirect. The distinction between global and domain-specific control beliefs is well-known conceptually, although the specific outcomes associated with these types of control and the relationships between them remains poorly understood. The other three distinctions, however, are unique and important contributions, each of which brings to mind a plethora of research questions. I will limit myself to a single issue that cross-cuts these three distinctions. The common denominator of these distinctions is that control can be exercised in a variety of ways beyond the obvious route of personal effort. Negotiated, collective, and indirect controls are all characterized by the mobilization of others for the purpose of enhancing one's personal goals. These are important conceptual distinctions, but it is not clear whether or not individuals perceive these routes to goal attainment as methods of control. It is possible that people perceive these as appropriate strategies for pursuing one's goals but do not interpret them as demonstrating a sense of personal control. More likely, there is individual variation in the extent to which these are recognized by actors as control behaviors, with some individuals seeing their roles in bringing about goal-directed outcomes, whereas other do not. Consequently, it is not clear how and under what conditions such strategies affect control beliefs. This is clearly an important issue for future research.

BROADER ISSUES

As important as this chapter is in advancing our thinking about the nature, types, and consequences of control, I found that it triggered two larger issues in my mind. At a general level, both questions concern the role of culture in control beliefs. It is interesting to note that, although Pearlin and Pioli pay substantial attention to the role of social structure in control beliefs, they do not discuss the possible role of culture. In addition, these questions seem to me to probe at the heart of why we study control and ponder its implications for personal biography.

Developing Control Beliefs

My first question is, how do we develop control beliefs, or, alternatively, where do control beliefs come from? A corollary issue is whether global and domain-specific control beliefs are developed by the same processes. Although developing control beliefs is not a primary focus of this chapter, the authors comment on it in a variety of places. Pearlin and Pioli seem to subscribe to the view that development of control beliefs is experience-based. Specifically, the authors state that "it is because success breeds success that self-efficacy tends to become generalized." This suggests that they view global control as a result of generalizing from our experience of success—or, presumably, failure. Although the authors also state that "global mastery cannot be calculated by averaging its role-specific levels," the notion that success breeds success suggests that global control beliefs will be based largely on experience.

To my knowledge, there is no firm research evidence demonstrating the processes by which individuals develop global and domain-specific control beliefs. Thus, the propositions posed by Pearlin and Pioli may be accurate. But I see another scenario as equally or perhaps even more compelling. According to this scenario, global and domain-specific control beliefs emerge from quite different processes.

I view a global internal sense of control—the joint expectancies that most outcomes are controllable by nature and within our personal ability to control—as a core value of American society and perhaps other western societies as well. Because it is a core value, it is instilled in individuals in the same way as other core values: via a variety of socialization experiences that transmit cultural worldviews to societal members. That is, I suspect that we acquire global control beliefs in much the same way we come to understand that individualism, hard work, and democracy are core societal values. If this scenario is accurate, global control beliefs are learned via widespread socialization experiences rather than by direct personal experience.

In contrast, I agree with Pearlin and Pioli that domain-specific control beliefs are likely to be based on direct experience. As a consequence, domain-specific control beliefs should vary more across individuals than global control beliefs—a testable proposition. Other testable propositions emerge from this proposed contrast in processes of developing control beliefs as well, for example:

H1:   The relationships between global and domain-specific control beliefs will be quite modest.

H2:   Domain-specific control beliefs will be more changeable than global control beliefs.

H3:   Changes in experience-based domain-specific control beliefs are unlikely to affect global control beliefs.

If my hypotheses are accurate, many individuals live significant proportions of their lives—perhaps their entire lives—with substantial discrepancies between global beliefs of predominantly internal control and multiple specific domains in some of which their experiences suggest a relative lack of control. This raises additional questions: Isn't this a source of dissonance and discomfort? How do individuals handle this discrepancy so that it is not uncomfortable? Answers to these questions seem to be available if we turn to the broader research base on belief discrepancies in general and self-esteem in particular.

Research on the self-esteem motive (e.g., Dodgson & Wood, 1998; Gecas & Burke, 1995) and self-discrepancy theory (Higgins, 1987, 1989) suggest that (1) the preservation and enhancement of self-esteem are nearly universal human motivations and (2) individuals use a variety of strategies to protect and enhance self-esteem. (An important exception to these propositions is depressed individuals, who typically have very low levels of self-esteem and make few, if any, cognitive or behavioral efforts to raise their sense of self-worth.) Control beliefs, I would argue, are, in part, integral components of the self-concept and serve as one of numerous psychological "yardsticks" against which we assess our level of global self-esteem. The distinction common in the self-efficacy literature between beliefs that outcomes are potentially controllable and beliefs that we have the personal capacities to control those outcomes is especially relevant to self-concept and self-esteem. In general, we would expect people who view outcomes that are important to them as potentially controllable but do not believe that they have the capacities required to control those outcomes to experience (or feel psychological pressures to experience) low levels of self-esteem. Undoubtedly, this scenario frequently occurs. Feelings that one cannot cope with or manage issues that others apparently find easy to manage successfully can threaten or erode self-esteem.

But threats to self-esteem do not invariably lead to its erosion. Many individuals use a variety of strategies to deflect threats to self-worth and self-efficacy. Those same strategies would seem to be effective in preventing dissonance or distress when global control beliefs are at odds with domain-specific control beliefs. A few examples will illustrate this point. One strategy for preserving self-esteem in the face of threat is to value those domains in which we are successful as self-relevant and to view domains where we are less accomplished as irrelevant to self-esteem (Rosenberg, 1979). Similarly, individuals may come to value those areas in which they experience a sense of control and to ignore or devalue areas of life in which they experience a lack of control. Thus, by focusing attention on the experience of control, lack of control in other domains can be discounted, and its challenge to global beliefs of internal control can be defused.

A second strategy for protecting self-esteem has been demonstrated in research on the distinctive features of self-attribution. The self-serving bias (Brown & Rogers, 1991; Miller & Ross, 1975), which is very common, is a cognitive scheme in which we take credit for bringing about positive outcomes (an internal attribution) but deny that anyone could control negative outcomes (an external attribution). Recall that only perceptions that outcomes are controllable but that one lacks the capacity to control them are likely to threaten self-esteem. By defining negative outcomes as uncontrollable, self-esteem is protected. In addition, one is left with the belief that all positive outcomes are a result of personal control and effort—a belief that can be used to buttress global feelings of internal control. Indeed, it is interesting to speculate whether there would be a self-serving attribution in societies where internal control is not a fundamental cultural value.

Both of the above strategies are primarily cognitive in nature. Behavioral strategies also can be used to protect self-esteem and, I would argue, permit global beliefs of internal control to be relatively unchallenged by personal experience. One mechanism for protecting or enhancing self-esteem is to place oneself in social environments where, using self-comparisons, we look good compared to others in those environments— what has occasionally been termed the "big fish in a small pond" strategy (Bachman & O'Malley, 1986; Rosenberg, 1979). Similarly, one strategy for sustaining feelings of internal control is to restrict one's major environments to those where one can achieve positive outcomes that reinforce feelings of control. Indeed, Pearlin and Pioli make this point when describing an earlier study in which the oldest-old reported surprisingly high levels of mastery. "It appears," the authors write, "that the oldest-old are able to maintain a sense of control by using as standards of judgment the more narrowed areas of life over which they can, in fact, exert control."

Thus, there are multiple ways to leave one's general sense of internal control intact despite evidence to the contrary in domain-specific areas.

Indeed, the fascinating concept of illusion of control recognizes the strong motives and social pressures to believe in personal control, even if that conclusion is at odds with reality. The term *illusion of control* refers specifically to the fact that mentally healthy individuals routinely overestimate the extent to which they control outcomes in situations where the actual odds of success as a result of personal effort are known (Langer, 1975). In a larger sense, however, there are a myriad of strategies that individuals use to sustain a sense of internal control. Clearly, not everyone avails themselves of these control-enhancing strategies. But research on the illusion of control suggests that we pay a high price for committing ourselves to reality rather than illusion. The most accurate predictions of the likelihood of success at tasks where the odds of success were known were provided by patients diagnosed with major depressive disorder (Alloy & Abramson, 1979; Langer, 1975).

Why Is a Sense of Control Beneficial?

The second major question that arose as I pondered Chapter 1 is an obvious one, but one that I would argue we have yet to answer completely. Why is a sense of control good for us? A broad body of research indicates that, with the exception of extremely high levels of internal control beliefs, both global and domain-specific beliefs in internal control are related to a range of positive outcomes, including academic and occupational success (Sanna & Pusecker, 1994; Schwalbe, 1985; Tuckman & Sexton, 1990), success in interpersonal relationships (Fan & Mak, 1998), and better physical and mental health (Pearlin, Lieberman, Menaghan, & Mullan, 1981; Sutton & Kahn, 1984). The same research supports the opposite conclusion: Belief in external control (especially lack of control due to fate or powerful others) is associated with stressful conditions and psychological distress, especially depression.

Despite literally thousands of investigations of sense of control and related constructs, the reasons why internal control beliefs are beneficial remains unanswered. Admittedly, much of the research on the benefits of internal control beliefs suggests possible pathways by which a sense of control exerts its salubrious effects, and a few studies document the ways in which a sense of control mediate the effects of causally prior factors on outcomes of interest (e.g., Heidrich, 1996; Pearlin et al., 1981). But we lack empirical evidence that documents the processes that mediate the effects of control beliefs on outcomes.

The most frequently proposed explanations that I have seen focus on the role of internal control beliefs (1) in encouraging active coping,

(2) in fostering more positive (or at least less negative) appraisals of stressful situations, and (3) in promoting better quality social support networks and more effective use of those networks in times of need. All of these are reasonable hypotheses; I would offer an additional one. If I am correct in hypothesizing that internal control beliefs are a core value in our society, then believing and behaving in accordance with those values should promote social solidarity and be rewarded in a variety of socially sanctioned ways. In essence, endorsing internal control beliefs is one avenue by which we participate in a sustaining cultural identity.

The proper test for hypotheses about cultural values is examination of cross-cultural differences. More specifically, we would expect that internal control beliefs would be transmitted and positively sanctioned in societies with an individualistic orientation. Conversely, internal control beliefs may be less common, less rewarded, and, perhaps, exhibit weaker (or even negative) relationships with indicators of personal success and well-being in societies with a collectivistic orientation. Indeed, evidence supporting these hypotheses is observed in cross-cultural research (Bond, 1988; Cousins, 1989; Heine & Lehman, 1997; Yik, Bond, & Paulhus, 1998). Most of these studies examined control beliefs among Chinese and Japanese people.

RELIGIOUS BELIEFS AND INDIRECT CONTROL

A final issue concerns the authors' proposition that religious beliefs may serve as a form of indirect control. The authors' proposition strikes me as generally accurate, and some research evidence supports a somewhat more elaborate thesis. Two streams of research offer evidence relevant to this proposition. First, several studies report that people who regularly participate in religious services have higher levels of internal control beliefs than people who attend religious services infrequently or not at all (e.g., Gartner, Larson, & Allen, 1991; McIntosh & Spilka, 1990).

The second body of research focuses on individuals' views on the nature of God or a higher power and the implications of those views for personal well-being. To simplify, albeit in a reasonable way, there are two primary images of God endorsed by large proportions of Americans. In one image, God is viewed as an authority figure, sitting in judgment of our behavior and expecting obedience to religious precepts. In the other, which most Americans endorse, God is viewed as a loving figure, desiring only the best for us, willing to work with us and for us to secure our needs and desires. It is belief in this second image that would provide the opportunity for exercising indirect control through God. Indeed, there is increasing evidence that images of being in partnership with a kind, loving God are associated with higher levels of life satisfaction (Pollner, 1989), better mental health in general (Koenig et al., 1992; Pargament, Smith, Koenig, & Perez, 1998), more active coping during times of stress (Pargament, 1997; Pargament et al., 1992), and less negative effects of stressful experiences on mental health, especially depression (Bickel et al., 1998; Koenig, Pargament, & Nielson, 1998). In contrast, images of God as a harsh authority figure are associated with lower levels of life satisfaction (Pollner, 1989) and mental health (Bickel et al., 1998; Pargament, 1997).

Thus, there is evidence that religious beliefs can be associated with beneficial outcomes, probably as a result of the experience of indirect control. But the whole story is more complex: It is only beliefs in a kind and loving God or higher power that exhibit the beneficial outcomes observed more broadly for internal control beliefs.

CONCLUSION

In conclusion, I commend Pearlin and Pioli for their chapter, which is an excellent orientation to thinking about issues of control and their importance both for social and behavioral research and for people's lives. The chapter intrigued me, taught me, inspired me to think about new issues, and whetted my appetite for the remainder of the volume.

REFERENCES

Alloy, L. B., & Abramson, L. Y. (1979). Judgement of contingency in depressed and nondepressed students: Sadder but wiser? *Journal of Experimental Psychology, 108,* 441–485.

Bachman, J. G., & O'Malley, P. M. (1986). Self-concepts, self-esteem, and educational experiences: The frog pond revisited. *Journal of Personality and Social Psychology, 50,* 35–46.

Barker, R. (1968). *Ecological psychology.* Stanford, CA: Stanford University Press.

Bickel, C. O., Ciarrocchi, J. W., Sheers, N. J., Estadt, B. K., Powell, D. A., & Pargament, K. I. (1998). Perceived stress, religious coping, and depressive affect. *Journal of Psychology and Christianity, 17,* 33–42.

Bond, M. H. (Ed.). (1988). *The cross-cultural challenge to social psychology.* Beverly Hills, CA: Sage.

Brown, J. D., & Rogers, R. J. (1991). Self-serving attributions: The role of physiological arousal. *Personality and Social Psychology Bulletin, 17,* 501–506.

Cousins, S. D. (1989). Culture and self-perception in Japan and the United States. *Journal of Personality and Social Psychology, 56,* 124–131.

Dodgson, P. G., & Wood, J. V. (1998). Self-esteem and the cognitive accessibility of strengths and weaknesses after failure. *Journal of Personality and Social Psychology, 75,* 178–197.

Fan, C., & Mak, A. S. (1998). Measuring self-efficacy in a culturally diverse student population. *Social Behavior and Personality, 26,* 131–144.

Gartner, J. W., Larson, D. B., & Allen, G. D. (1991). Religious commitment and mental health: A review of the empirical literature. *Journal of Psychology and Theology, 19,* 6–25.

Gecas, V., & Burke, P. J. (1995). Self and identity. In K. A. Cook, G. A. Fine, & J. S. House (Eds.), *Sociological perspectives on social psychology* (pp. 41–67). Boston: Allyn & Bacon.

Heidrich, S. M. (1996). Mechanisms related to psychological well-being in older women with chronic illnesses: Age and disease comparisons. *Research in Nursing and Health, 19,* 225–235.

Heine, S. J., & Lehman, D. R. (1997). The cultural construction of self-enhancement: An examination of group-serving bias. *Journal of Personality and Social Psychology, 72,* 1268–1283.

Higgins, E. T. (1987). Self-discrepancy: A theory relating self and affect. *Psychological-Review, 94,* 319–340.

Higgins, E. T. (1989). Self-discrepancy theory: What patterns of self-beliefs cause people to suffer? In L. Berkowitz (Ed.), *Advances in experimental social psychology* (Vol. 22, pp. 93–136). San Diego: Academic Press.

Koenig, H. G., Cohen, H. J., Blazer, D. G., Pieper, C., Meador, H. G., Shelp, F., Goli, V., & DiPasquale, B. (1992). Religious coping and depression among elderly, hospitalized medically ill men. *American Journal of Psychiatry, 149,* 1693–1700.

Koenig, H. G., Pargament, K. I., & Nielsen, J. (1998). Religious coping and health status in medically ill hospitalized older adults. *Journal of Nervous and Mental Disease, 186,* 513–521.

Langer, E. J. (1975). The illusion of control. *Journal of Personality and Social Psychology, 32,* 311–328.

Lewisohn, P. M., & Mischel, W. (1980). Social competence and depression: The role of illusory self-perceptions. *Journal of Abnormal Psychology, 89,* 203–212.

McIntosh, D., & Spilka, B. (1990). Religion and physical health: The role of personal faith and control beliefs. *Research in the Social Scientific Study of Religion, 2,* 167–194.

Miller, D. T., & Ross, M. (1975). Self-serving biases in attribution of causality: Fact or fiction? *Personality and Social Psychology Bulletin, 82,* 313–325.

Pargament, K. I. (1997). *The psychology of religion and coping.* New York: Guilford Press.

Pargament, K. I., Olsen, H., Reilly, B., Falgout, K., Ensing, D., & Van Haitsma, K. (1992). God help me: 2. The relationship of religious orientations to religious coping with negative life events. *Journal for the Scientific Study of Religion, 31,* 504–513.

Pargament, K. I., Smith, B. W., Koenig, H. G., & Perez, L. (1998). Patterns of positive and negative religious coping with major life stressors. *Journal for the Scientific Study of Religion, 37,* 710–724.

Pearlin, L. I., Lieberman, M. A., Menaghan, E. G., & Mullan, J. T. (1981). The stress process. *Journal of Health and Social Behavior, 22,* 337–356.

Pollner, M. (1989). Divine relations, social relations, and well-being. *Journal of Health and Social Behavior, 30,* 92–104.

Rosenberg, M. (1979). *Conceiving the self.* New York: Basic Books.

Sanna, I. J., & Pusecker, P. A. (1994). Self-efficacy, valence of self-evaluation, and performance. *Personality and Social Psychology Bulletin, 20,* 82–92.

Schwalbe, M. L. (1985). Autonomy in work and self-esteem. *The Sociological Quarterly, 26,* 519–535.

Sutton, R. I., & Kahn, R. L. (1984). Prediction, understanding, and control as antidotes to organizational stress. In J. Lorsch (Ed.), *Handbook of organizational behavior* (pp. 272–285). Cambridge, MA: Harvard University Press.

Tuckman, B. W., & Sexton, T. L. (1990). The relation between self-beliefs and self-regulated performance. *Journal of Social Behavior and Personality, 5,* 465–472.

Yik, M. S. M., Bond, M. H., & Paulhus, D. L. (1998). Do Chinese self-enhance or self-efface? It's a matter of domain. *Personality and Social Psychology Bulletin, 24,* 399–406.

CHAPTER 2

The Social Foundations of Personal Control in Late Life

Neal Krause

The construct of control has occupied a central place in social and psychological research for decades. In fact, it has become so popular that some investigators argue that a strong sense of personal control is a key marker of successful aging (Rowe & Kahn, 1998). However, as a number of researchers point out, feelings of personal control have been operationalized in many different ways (Ross & Sastry, 1999). Among the specific variables subsumed under this broad rubric are mastery (Pearlin & Schooler, 1978), fatalism (Wheaton, 1983), self-efficacy (Bandura, 1995), and locus of control beliefs (Rotter, 1966). Even though there are differences in the way these variables have been defined and measured, they nevertheless share a common conceptual core. Embedded in each measure is the notion that individuals with a strong sense of control believe that changes in their social world are responsive to and contingent upon their own choices, efforts, and actions. In contrast, people with a weak sense of control believe that events in their lives are shaped by forces outside their influence and that they have little ability to regulate the things that happen to them.

One reason why the construct of control has enjoyed such great popularity may be found by turning to the literature on health and well-being. In particular, this research indicates that strong feelings of personal control are associated with better mental health (Pearlin, Menaghan, Lieberman, & Mullan, 1981), better physical health (Seeman & Lewis, 1995), and the adoption of a wide range of positive health behaviors (Schwarzer & Fuchs, 1995). Given the potential of personal control to enhance the quality of life in this way, it is essential that researchers arrive at a better understanding of how perceptions of control arise.

Unfortunately, the search for causes of control has been hampered by two problems. First, a number of studies rely on global measures that are designed to evaluate control over life as a whole. Although research with this measurement strategy has made many valuable contributions to the literature, it does not fit well with what we know about social life. More specifically, people typically occupy a number of different roles. For example, they are spouses, parents, friends, and members of voluntary associations (e.g., churches). Because global approaches to measuring control are designed to evaluate control over life as a whole, this measurement strategy implicitly assumes that a person is able to exert a roughly equal amount of influence in each domain. Research suggests that this may not be the case. For example, a recent study by Lachman and Weaver (1998) indicates that older adults feel they have more control over financial matters than other life domains, such as relationships with their children (see also McAvay, Seeman, & Rodin, 1996).

The second problem with the literature in this field arises from the fact that the scope of research designed to identify the causes of control is too narrow. In particular, a number of investigators argue that feelings of personal control may be little more than a personality trait (e.g., Cohen & Edwards, 1989). However, as the following discussion provided will reveal, this overlooks the important role played by social factors in shaping feelings of personal control in late life.

Viewed broadly, the current literature on control often focuses on measures that are too broad, whereas the search for factors that shape control is often too narrow. In view of these limitations, the purpose of the discussion that follows is threefold. First, a case is made for devising more focused measures of personal control. In the process, special attention is given to ways of thinking about this construct that have been largely overlooked in the literature. Second, an effort is made to expand the scope of research on the causes of control by highlighting the key role played by social support in this process. Finally, the social basis of control is further explicated by exploring the influence of socioeconomic status.

MEASURING THE CONSTRUCT OF CONTROL

As Bohrnstedt (1983) observed some time ago, "Measurement is a sine qua non of science" (p. 69). Consequently, any attempt to better understand the construct of control must begin with this issue. However, measurement is always based on a set of theoretical assumptions. This point was made some time ago by Blalock (1982), who argued convincingly that all efforts to operationalize a construct ultimately rest on auxiliary measurement theory. Simply put, measurement and theory are inextricably bound. Consistent with this view, the discussion in this section is divided into two main segments. First, recent efforts by Schulz and Heckhausen (1996) to provide an age-based theory of control and adult development are reviewed briefly. Following this, issues in the conceptualization and measurement of control that are embedded in this conceptual framework are elaborated and extended.

An Age-Based Theory of Control

Schulz, Wrosch, and Heckhausen (this volume) set out to derive a life course theory of successful aging by asking how elderly people adjust to the inevitable decline of resources that accompanies old age. Included in this age-related decline in resources is a deterioration of physical and mental functioning. Schulz and colleagues (this volume) turn to the distinction between primary and secondary control to explain how elderly people cope with these losses. Viewed in general terms, primary control refers to efforts aimed at changing the external environment, whereas secondary control is concerned with changing internal cognitions (e.g., one's attitudes, attributions, or perceptions) rather than altering the external social world.

Following the theory of selection, optimization, and compensation (Baltes, 1991), Schulz and colleagues (this volume) argue that as people age and their resources dwindle, they gradually relinquish primary control in some areas of life so available resources can be devoted to maintaining primary control in other domains. This work is thought provoking and makes a number of significant contributions to the literature. Yet, as with many gerontological theories, it is incomplete.

In particular, there are at least three ways to elaborate and extend this conceptual framework. First, because the social world of elderly people can be broken down into a number of different domains (e.g., financial, friendship, and family), it is not entirely clear how older adults select the domains where they will attempt to exercise primary control. Second, there are problems with the way in which secondary control is conceptualized and measured. Finally, the distinction between primary and secondary control does not exhaust all the ways in which control can be exercised in late life. In particular, there is another way of thinking about control that been largely overlooked in social gerontology (i.e., collaborative control). In the discussion that follows, steps will be taken to resolve the three problems identified here.

Determining Where to Exercise Primary Control

The notion that older people cope with declining resources by restricting primary control efforts to select life domains makes a good deal of sense intuitively. However, Schulz and colleagues (this volume) do not identify the factors that lead older adults to select one life domain over another for this purpose. Fortunately, some useful insights may be found in identity theory (Burke, 1991; Thoits, 1991).

Social roles and identities assume a pivotal position in identity theory. According to this perspective, a social role is defined structurally as a position in a group (e.g., father, husband, or provider), whereas identities are self-evaluations that emerge for occupying particular roles. In essence, identities refer to the kinds of information people use when thinking about themselves (e.g., "I am a father"). Associated with each role are clusters of normative or behavioral expectations that guide a person's actions and provide a basis for evaluating the adequacy of role performance. By providing guidance as well as a mechanism for appraising role enactment, the behavioral expectations associated with roles promote a sense of meaning and purpose in life.

But there is an important qualification in identity theory that is especially helpful for elaborating the work of Schulz and colleagues (this volume). Even casual observation suggests that people occupy multiple roles. Consequently, there is a separate identity associated with each of these social positions. A basic tenet of identity theory specifies that individuals attach greater importance to some role-specific identities than others. As a result, individual identities are arrayed in a salience hierarchy reflecting varying levels of commitment to, and investment in, the roles underlying these identities (Stryker, 1987).

Casting the framework devised by Schulz and colleagues (this volume) in the language of identity theory helps to specify the underlying process more clearly: As people grow older, they concentrate diminishing resources in roles that are most salient to them, while devoting fewer resources to roles they value less highly. The key point to emphasize here is that the decision regarding where to exercise primary control is inherently social in nature. In particular, it is made in a social arena where the roles people occupy are socially defined and the system of values used to prefer one role over another is also socially determined (Stryker, 1987). The social thread that runs throughout efforts to influence the environment in late life becomes even more evident when the construct of secondary control is examined closely.

Secondary Control

As noted earlier, secondary control is typically defined and measured by focusing on internal cognitions aimed at altering one's view of the external world. Schulz and colleagues (this volume) are by no means the only investigators to think about secondary control in this way (see, for example, Chipperfield, Perry, & Menec, 1999). The emphasis on internal cognitions is readily apparent in the following secondary control item, which was developed by Peng and Lachman (1995): "When I can't get what I want, I assume my goals must be unrealistic." But, as Skinner (1997) argues persuasively, these internal cognitions do not really capture efforts to gain control at all. Instead, they emphasize passivity and helplessness, culminating in the relinquishment of control efforts.

A central premise in this chapter is that there is a better way to approach the study of secondary control that is intrinsically social in nature. This alternative view of secondary control is perhaps best approached through an example. Assume that an older woman is having difficulty managing her financial affairs, so she turns these matter over to her son. He subsequently manages her money in a very efficient manner. As a result, the older woman feels as though her financial affairs are under control. But she has little to do with them directly, and as a result, it is difficult to see why she would feel that she is personally in control of her financial situation. Instead, her son is. In essence, this social view of secondary control suggests that it is a sense of confidence that the demands arising in a specific domain will be handled smoothly and that one's needs will be met, because significant others are working to ensure that things will turn out in one's own best interests. The essence of this approach to thinking about secondary control is illustrated in the following hypothetical survey item: "The members of my family can take care of any financial problem that may arise in my life."

The notion of secondary control that is developed here is not without precedence in the literature. Similar principles were espoused some time ago by Bandura (1982), who introduced the construct of proxy control (see also Baltes & Carstensen, 1999). Even so, research on proxy control is incomplete because the social basis of this form of control has not been explored fully.

Before turning to a discussion of collaborative control, it is important to examine an important issue having to do with the scope of secondary control. As defined here, secondary control involves turning over all responsibility for a life domain to a trusted other. However, there are some circumstances where this may not always be possible. For example, friendships represent a vitally important domain in late life (Adams & Blieszner, 1989). Yet it is clear that the obligations and responsibilities associated with this role cannot be turned over entirely to someone else. Simply put, there is no such thing as a proxy friendship. This does not, however, diminish the importance of secondary control. Instead, it sharpens our understanding of this construct by calling our attention to the fact that it is possible to exercise secondary control in some domains of life but not others.

Collaborative Control

Although the dichotomy between primary and secondary control is useful, it does not exhaust all the ways that older adults may attempt to influence the world in which they live. The problem arises because the distinction between these constructs is framed in terms of two extreme positions: Elderly people either try to exercise control solely on their own, or someone else takes over completely and manages things for them. This overlooks the fact that there is another option that falls midway between the two. More specifically, elderly people may work together with significant others to jointly influence the problems that confront them. This is what is meant by collaborative control.

The value of considering collaborative control can best be illustrated by returning to the stress process. Although some of the difficulties that confront older adults are personal events that primarily involve them alone, many of the stressors they encounter are experienced by their social network members as well (Hobfoll, 1998). For example, if an older woman is married and experiences financial difficulty, it is almost certain these economic problems are shared by her husband too. As a result, it is likely that both the husband and the wife will make an effort to respond to the fiscal crisis. For example, the husband may decide to reenter the labor force, and the wife may make a concerted effort to better manage their household finances by restricting expenditures on nonessential items. Simply put, they face the crisis as a team. Consequently, any attempt to measure control under these circumstances must reflect these collaborative efforts. In this case, the wife is not in control of the situation entirely on her own, nor is her husband. Instead, they are jointly or collaboratively in control. The essence of this view is captured in the following hypothetical survey question: "Together, my family members and I can take care of any financial problem that may arise in my life."

Cast within the context of the framework devised by Schulz and colleagues (this volume), the collaborative control construct suggests that older adults may deal with declining resources not by relinquishing control in select domains entirely, but by working together with significant others to jointly ensure that problems and role obligations are met.

It should be emphasized that the contributions made by two parties in the collaborative control process may vary greatly. This suggests that collaborative control is a matter of degree or balance. The contributions made by each party are likely to be a complex function of a number of factors, including the resources available to each individual, as well as the nature of the relationship between them.

The notion that people may work together to jointly solve mutual problems is hardly a new one. Evidence of this may be found, for example, in three largely unrelated bodies of research. The first involves married couples. Consistent with the example provided above, Conger, Rueter, and Elder (1999) explored how some married couples jointly identify solutions to economic problems they face, then work together until a resolution is reached. However, this research is couched in terms of specific coping responses, and not the feelings of control that are associated with them.

The second body of research deals with empowerment. Here, efforts are made to enhance an individual's sense of control by encouraging one to work with social network members, such as neighbors, to make changes in the social (and especially the political) environment (Zimmerman, 2000). But the scope of empowerment research differs from collaborative control in the following way. In particular, empowerment deals with the concerted efforts of a relatively large number of people to exercise control by altering the social system. In contrast, collaborative control is concerned primarily with the alleviation of personal problems without the concerted action needed to bring about systemic change.

Bandura's (1995) work on collective self-efficacy represents the third body of research dealing with the notion that people work together jointly to solve mutual problems. However, like empowerment theory, the scope of collective self-efficacy is quite broad. In particular, Bandura (1995) is interested in specifying how the quality of a nation's health can be improved when societal members recognize that change can be brought about through unified effort (see Weisz, Rothbaum, & Blackburn, 1984, for a discussion of another societal-level notion of control).

Although there are differences between collaborative control and previous work in this area, embedded in these perspectives is the notion that people can enhance their sense of control by working collaboratively with others. Unfortunately, these valuable insights do not seem to have been integrated into the mainstream gerontological literature on feelings of personal control.

It seems especially important to focus on collaborative control when studying older adults because it may be a more desirable alternative for elderly people to pursue. Taken at face value, secondary control means turning over complete responsibility for a life domain to a trusted other. However, doing so may foster feelings of dependence. There is some evidence that older adults would prefer to avoid being overly dependent on their social network members. More specifically, research reviewed by Lee (1985) reveals that older adults value independence highly and prefer to take care of things on their own instead of relying solely on others. In fact, this predilection for autonomy appears to be part of a wider historical trend toward an increasing preference for independence in successive cohorts (Hareven, 1994).

Taken as a whole, the discussion provided in this section leads to two key points. First, control in late life may be best represented by a continuum that is anchored by primary control on one end and secondary control on the other. Falling somewhere between the two is collaborative control. Second, the different types of control are distinguished by the extent to which significant others are involved. This is important because it highlights the social foundations of personal control in late life. However, the social basis of control is still not explicit enough because the specific things that social network members do to enhance an older person's sense of control have not been spelled out clearly. The goal of the next section is to address this issue by turning to the literature on social support.

SOCIAL SUPPORT AND FEELINGS OF PERSONAL CONTROL

The relationship between feelings of personal control and social support is perhaps best understood when it is examined within the context of stressful life events. A number of studies reveal that stressful events exert a noxious effect on health and well-being by eroding an individual's sense of personal control (Pearlin et al., 1981). Presumably, this occurs because major life events compromise a person's usual cognitive and problem-solving abilities (Caplan, 1981). However, research further reveals that assistance from significant others helps to replenish and restore feelings of control that have been eroded by these stressful experiences (Krause, 1987a). Caplan (1981) provides a succinct overview of how this takes place. In particular, he argues that social network members help to define the problem situation, develop a plan of action, assist in implementing the plan, and provide feedback and guidance as the plan is being executed. Because of this assistance, the stressed individual comes to believe the problem situation can be controlled and overcome. As this brief overview of the stress process reveals, it is social factors that erode feelings of personal control (i.e., stressful events), and it is social factors that build it back up again (i.e., social support).

Although research on the interface between social support and personal control has provided a number of valuable insights, work in this field suffers from two major limitations. First, most studies focus solely on global measures of personal control. As discussed earlier, this may not be the best approach. Second, social support is a complex domain in its own right because significant others provide assistance in a number of different ways. If further strides are to be made in this area, then researchers must try to link specific types of support with particular dimensions of control. The purpose of the discussion in this section is to tackle this challenge. After briefly reviewing different dimensions of social support, an effort will be made to show how they may be linked to primary control, secondary control, and collaborative control. This discussion takes recent work by Krause (2001) as a point of departure.

Although there are a number of ways to classify or categorize different types of social support, Barrera's (1986) straightforward classification scheme provides a useful way of getting a handle on this literature. He proposes that there are three kinds of informal social support measures: (1) measures of social embeddedness (e.g., indicators assessing the frequency of contact with others), (2) received or enacted support (e.g., measures of the amount of tangible help actually provided by social network members), and (3) perceived support (i.e., subjective evaluations of support exchanges, such as satisfaction with support). One type of perceived support that appears to play an especially important role in promoting health and well-being in late life is anticipated support (Krause, 1997a). Anticipated support is defined as the belief that significant others will provide assistance in the future should the need arise (Wethington & Kessler, 1986).

In the discussion that follows, an effort will be made to show how anticipated support affects feelings of primary control, enacted support shapes secondary control, and collaborative control is influenced by enacted support that is both received and given (i.e., exchanged) by elderly people.

Anticipated Support and Primary Control

The relationship between anticipated support and primary control is best illustrated by returning once again to the stress process. Here, research consistently shows that anticipated support tends to offset the noxious effects of stress, and that it may be a more effective coping resource than assistance that has actually been provided by social network members (Krause, 1997a). To see why this may be so, it is helpful to first consider how people typically attempt to cope with stress.

Although the selection of a particular coping response is undoubtedly shaped by many factors (Aldwin, 1994), research reviewed by Eckenrode and Wethington (1990) indicates that instead of immediately turning to significant others for assistance, individuals often try to resolve problems on their own. After this, they may seek help from others, but only if their own personal resources prove to be ineffective (Wethington & Kessler, 1986). It is for this reason that some investigators view received support as a marker of failed individual coping efforts (Wethington & Kessler, 1986).

Initially, this view of individual responses to stress would appear to suggest that social support assumes a secondary role in helping older people deal with the effects of adversity. This may not be true. Instead, anticipated support may figure prominently in this respect. As Wethington and Kessler (1986) point out, the realization that others stand ready to help if the need arises constitutes a social safety net that promotes risk taking and encourages people to resolve problems on their own. Doing so should either promote the acquisition of new coping responses or strengthen existing ones. By fostering the development of personal coping responses in this way, an older person is likely to develop the sense that he or she is better able to control the crises they face. It is for this reason that anticipated support should be especially likely to increase feelings of primary control.

Enacted Support and Secondary Control

The notion that enacted support is just a marker of failed individual coping efforts tends to downplay the value of receiving assistance from others. In effect, this perspective amounts to portraying enacted support as little more than a scarlet letter. This flies in the face of common sense. If enacted support was viewed solely in this way, it would not be such a central factor in the lives of elderly people. In fact, they would avoid it. However, this is clearly not the case. Instead, even casual observation reveals that older adults actively seek out and gratefully receive assistance from the people who are close to them. This simple realization points to a gap in our understanding of the social support process in late life.

One way to address this shortcoming is to return to the work of Schulz and colleagues (this volume). As noted earlier, they maintain that as resources dwindle in late life, elderly people give up primary control in some domains so that they can focus their efforts on maintaining primary control in other areas of life that are more important to them (see also Brandtstadter, Wentura, & Greve, 1993). A central premise in the present discussion is that elderly people do this by turning over role responsibilities in less salient life domains to significant others. Under these circumstances, the efforts of significant others ensure that needs and responsibilities are met and that, as a result, the situation in the delegated life domain is under control.

It is important to emphasize two key issues that emerge from this perspective. First, feelings of secondary control arise from the direct action taken by others (i.e., the enacted support they actually provide). Second, because of this, it is not at all clear why turning the situation over to a trusted other would lead an older adult to feel that he or she is personally in control of a domain. Stated simply, it is not evident why enacted support would bolster feelings of primary control. Instead, support provided by a social network member should promote the sense that the trusted other is in control and is operating with the best interests of the focal elder in mind.

Although the rationale for linking enacted support with secondary control is plausible, one might challenge this perspective by arguing that the two constructs are indistinguishable and that they essentially represent the same thing. Consequently, it is important to show how enacted support and secondary control are distinct conceptual domains. Enacted support refers to the specific behaviors or tangible goods provided by significant others. In contrast, secondary control represents the impact that support has on the recipient's appraisal of the extent to which the social world is responsive to the efforts of those who are acting on their behalf.

One way to highlight the distinction between enacted support and secondary control is to argue that there is not always a one-to-one correspondence between the two. This can happen for a number of reasons. For example, support may be provided, but it may not be effective because it does not meet the needs of the support recipient. This may happen, for example, when well-intentioned others feel they are helping a cancer victim by discussing only pleasant matters while failing to provide an opportunity for them to express concerns about their medical problems (Wortman, 1984). In addition, there are times when significant others may help too much and provide an excessive amount of assistance. This is illustrated clearly in the work of Margaret Baltes on the dependency-support script (Baltes & Wahl, 1992; see also Krause, 1987b). Instead of bolstering an older person's sense of control, excessive support is likely to make elders feel they are being smothered by, and are overly dependent upon, their social network members. Viewed more broadly, the slippage between enacted support and secondary control points to the tenuous balance between the two and illustrates the intricate role played by these social factors in facilitating adjustment in late life.

Exchanged Support and Collaborative Control

The literature on social support in late life has been largely concerned with assistance that elderly people receive from others. In contrast, less attention has been given to the support that older people may provide to the people who are close to them (but see Ikkink & van Tilburg, 1998). This oversight can be addressed by turning to the construct of collaborative control because it encompasses both giving and receiving assistance. In particular, both parties must contribute something toward the resolution of a common stressor to enhance the feeling they are jointly in control of a situation.

However, there are two reasons why the mutual exchange of assistance in the context of collaborative control is relatively unique. First, most discussions of how people help each other involve support that is directed toward the eradication of problems or needs that are not shared by both parties. For example, research by Kulis (1992) reveals that children tend to help their aging parents by performing household chores, and parents may reciprocate by providing financial assistance to their children. However, collaborative control is geared toward the eradication of a common or mutual problem facing both parties involved in the social exchange process.

Second, when support is exchanged within a collaborative control setting, the underlying motive for helping is not the same as we have seen previously in the literature. In most cases, one person helps another out of a sense of duty, repayment of past debt, or for altruistic reasons. In contrast, when two people work together to resolve a joint problem, the help that is given enhances the situation of the support provider as much as that of the support recipient. This may have an important bearing on the quality of assistance that is exchanged. In particular, a support provider may be more likely to invest resources in eradicating a problem when they have a personal stake in the resolution of the event. Moreover, they may be more persistent in striving toward the resolution of a problem when they know they will benefit personally from doing so.

Viewed broadly, the discussion provided up to this point serves to highlight the social basis of control in late life. By identifying different types of control and linking them with particular kinds of social support, it is possible to show more clearly how significant others shape and maintain feelings of control among older adults. In some instances, the influence of social network members is more subtle, as in the relationship between anticipated support and primary control. In other cases, the role played by significant others is more overt, such as the relationship between enacted support and secondary control. Still, in each case, it is evident that feelings of personal control arise from the relationships that elderly people have with those who are close to them.

Although this simple framework underscores the social foundations of control, it does not go far enough. Too much emphasis is placed on micro-level factors, such as informal support networks or dyadic relationships. To more fully understand this process, we must also consider macro-level factors that may come into play. As the discussion in the following section will reveal, socioeconomic status (SES) is a critical macro-level factor in this respect.

SOCIOECONOMIC STATUS, SOCIAL SUPPORT, AND FEELINGS OF PERSONAL CONTROL

The discussion in this section begins with a brief review of why it is important to examine socioeconomic status in the context of studies on social support and feelings of personal control in late life. Then, the theoretical framework that has been developed up to this point is further enhanced by exploring the role that SES may play in shaping feelings of personal control among older adults.

Impact of Socioeconomic Status on Support and Control

Income and education are typically used to measure SES. Research consistently shows that these markers of SES are related to global feelings of personal control. This is true regardless of how control is operationally defined. For example, research indicates that a higher SES standing is associated with greater feelings of personal mastery (Pearlin et al., 1981), self-efficacy (Gecas, 1989), and internal locus of control beliefs (Ross & Sastry, 1999).

Although most studies in this area rely on global measures of control, there is some evidence that domain-specific feelings of control may also vary by SES. In particular, the widely cited work of Kohn and Schooler (1983) reveals that control over the work process is inversely related to SES as well.

The literature also indicates that SES may be related to social support, but the findings are less consistent. More specifically, there is some evidence that high SES individuals tend to receive more social support than their lower SES counterparts (Turner & Marino, 1994). Although Krause and Borawski-Clark (1995) also report SES variations in social support, their study of older adults reveals that SES differences tend to emerge only in some dimensions of support (e.g., satisfaction with support), but not others (i.e., support received from social network members).

The theoretical rationale that has been developed so far suggests that social support influences feelings of personal control in late life. If SES is related to both social support and control, it follows that SES may shape the relationship between these key constructs as well. The purpose of the discussion that follows is to examine this issue in detail. In particular, potential SES variations are explored in the relationship between anticipated support and primary control, enacted support and secondary control, and social exchange and collaborative control.

Socioeconomic Status, Anticipated Support, and Primary Control

In essence, the study of SES is a study of the distribution of resources. This, in turn, has important implications for evaluating the relationship between anticipated support and primary control. In particular, there are at least two ways in which SES may affect the relationship between these constructs. First, according to the theoretical rationale developed earlier, anticipated support operates in part by encouraging older adults to resolve problems on their own. This involves an element of risk taking that is associated with pursuing novel ways of resolving stressful situations. However, elderly people will only be able to follow through on this, and pursue novel self-initiated coping responses, if they have adequate resources at their disposal. Unfortunately, this is not likely to be the case for lower SES elders.

But pointing out that lower SES elders lack adequate resources does not do justice to the complex process that may be at work. Fortunately, it is possible to get a better feel for the underlying process by turning to the work of Hobfoll (1998). In devising his conservation of resources theory, he argues that "those who lack resources are likely to adopt defensive patterns to guard their resources" (Hobfoll, 1998, p. 83). This defensive approach involves holding a maximum of resources in reserve so that a person can deal with further losses that may arise in the future. But if too much is held in reserve, then too little is invested in the kind of risk taking fostered by anticipated support. Instead of taking chances and trying out new ways of dealing with the problems that confront them, lower SES elders may assume a more defensive posture in an effort to hold on to the little they have. However, because a more proactive stance toward problem resolution is not taken, the opportunity for growth, and ultimately primary control, is lost. Simply put, if nothing is invested, then nothing is gained. It is in this social psychological sense that the rich truly do get richer.

The second way that SES may influence the relationship between anticipated support and primary control may be found by returning to the definition of anticipated support. It is the belief that others will help out in the future if the need arises. Social networks tend to be homogeneous with respect to resources and SES (Lin, 1982). If respondents lack adequate resources, there is a good chance their significant others will too. Undoubtedly, lower SES elders are well aware of this fact. Unfortunately, this awareness may undermine an older person's confidence in the ability of others to provide assistance in the future, resulting in an insecure or tenuous sense of anticipated support. It is hard to see how anticipated support could bolster feelings of primary control under these circumstances.

Taken together, the discussion in this section suggests that the unwillingness to assume risk coupled with the uncertainty about the ability of others to help in the future may compromise the ability of lower SES elders to exercise primary control. Perhaps this is one reason why Krause (1997b) found that anticipated support was associated with a greater mortality risk in the lower social classes while enhancing longevity among the more well-to-do.

Socioeconomic Status, Enacted Support, and Secondary Control

Although SES may affect the relationship between anticipated support and primary control, it may influence the link between enacted support and secondary control as well. This can be seen by again returning to the notion that lower SES elders, as well as their significant others, are not likely to have adequate resources at their disposal. Hobfoll's (1998) research on the pressure cooker effect helps to show how the lack of resources across an entire social network may ultimately inhibit the development of secondary control. In particular, he maintains that, because "no one in the system is free of threat, individuals who themselves have great need to depend on others must serve as supporters and lose precious resources that they themselves require at the time" (Hobfoll, 1998, p. 208). These insights have important implications for the theoretical rationale developed in this chapter. A major premise in this conceptual framework is that as people grow older and their own resources decline, they turn over control in less salient domains to trusted others, who then take care of things on their behalf. This assumes, however, that significant others have the resources that are needed to take on these responsibilities. This may not be true in lower SES networks.

The lack of adequate personal and social network resources sets up three potential scenarios, none of which bodes well for lower SES elders. First, when significant others lack adequate resources, a focal elder may be unable to pursue secondary control strategies because significant others cannot assume additional responsibilities. As a result, lower SES elders may have to struggle to maintain primary control in more roles than they are capable of handling. This leads to a more refined way of thinking about role overload. In this context, overload arises from having to use scarce resources to maintain primary control in an excessive number of roles.

The second scenario holds that lower SES network members may endeavor to provide the necessary assistance, but do so at some personal expense because their own meager resources are taxed excessively in the process. There are two ways in which this may affect the quality, but not necessarily the quantity, of support that is provided. To begin with, when support is provided at some sacrifice, older support recipients may feel they are a burden to others and that assistance has been provided out of a sense of obligation or duty. Alternatively, significant others may convey a sense of resentment for having to help out when they lack the means to do so. Either way, the provision of support under these circumstances is not likely to enhance feelings of secondary control because a key element in this process is missing. As defined earlier, secondary control involves a sense of confidence that arises from knowing that social network members are watching out for one's own best interests. However, it is hard to see how feelings of confidence would arise in situations where the support provided by others is accompanied by feelings of guilt, dependence, and resentment.

A third scenario suggests that lower SES elders may simply withdraw from social roles if they lack the adequate resources to exercise primary control, and their social network members prove to be of little help. The loss of social roles is important because some researchers argue that having a large number of roles promotes health and well-being by providing older adults with alternative sources of life satisfaction and self-enhancement (Barnett, 1993).

Socioeconomic Status, Exchanged Support, and Collaborative Control

The discussion provided up to this point paints a rather bleak picture of lower SES life. However, it is unlikely that these views adequately depict the situation of all elderly people in lower SES groups. Fortunately, a more balanced perspective of the interface between SES, support, and control may be developed by turning to the notion of collaborative control. As discussed earlier, collaborative control involves the pooling of mutual resources and efforts to confront common problems and stressors. There is some evidence that this strategy is employed by lower SES elders, but only under certain circumstances. The purpose of the discussion in this section is to bring these issues to the foreground.

Initially, the work of Hobfoll (1998) and others may create the impression that lower SES elders are unwilling and unable to engage in collaborative control efforts. This may happen for two reasons. First, as discussed above, they may lack adequate resources to do so. Second, the defensive posture that is assumed by those who have little is not likely to foster the mutual exchange of support necessary for the development of collaborative control. In fact, there is some evidence that the mutual exchange of assistance is a source of distress, rather than control, in lower SES networks. Based on her work with women living in poverty, Belle (1982) notes that helping others may lead lower SES women to experience "betrayal, burdensome dependence, and vicarious pain" (Belle, 1982, p. 142). Even though lower SES women do help each other out, Belle (1982) argues that they were "essentially coerced . . . into relationships which they might otherwise avoid" (p. 142) (see also Hughes, Tremblay, Rapoport, & Leighton, 1960; Rubin, 1976; Stephens, 1976). Clearly, exchanging assistance under these circumstances is not likely to foster a sense of collaborative control. Instead, it is likely to promote the opposite.

Even though the work of Belle (1982, 1990) and others highlights significant problems in lower SES support networks, it may not adequately depict the circumstances of all who are poor. Instead, some lower SES elders may be able to exercise collaborative control by turning to formal organizations, especially the church. Research consistently shows that people tend to become more religious as they grow older and that lower SES individuals are more involved in religion than those in upper SES groups (Pargament, 1997). This has led some researchers to conclude that the purely spiritual aspects of religion are an important coping resource for the socially disenfranchised (Pargament, 1997). Although this may be true, there is some evidence that the church also serves as an important conduit for social and community services in lower SES neighborhoods (Chatters, Taylor, & Lincoln, 2001). In particular, these institutions often provide food, clothing, and home maintenance, and even assist church members in finding employment. It is important to emphasize that these services are often delivered by fellow parishioners who are faced with similar economic problems. The key point here is that by pooling their efforts and resources, members of churches in lower SES neighborhoods are able to help each other confront the problems they mutually encounter. Although it is not typically discussed in these terms, the deep sense of community that is fostered under these circumstances is very consistent with the notion of collaborative control.

The idea that collaborative control can arise within churches in lower SES settings does not invalidate the work of Belle (1990) and others. Instead, both perspectives may be valid but describe different segments of the lower SES population. This may happen because even though the means for collaborative control are accessible to many, some lower SES elders may not elect to take advantage of them.

The notion that collaborative control may arise within the context of formal organizations points to a significant gap in the literature on the sources of control in late life. There are two ways in which the perspective developed above helps to address this limitation. First, virtually every study on social support and control traces the genesis of control to assistance arising solely in informal social networks. By bringing mutual support in church settings to the foreground, the perspective developed here provides a way to bridge feelings of personal control with formal, as well as informal, sources of assistance. Second, in the process of doing so, it is possible to show yet another way in which social factors promote feelings of personal control in late life.

CONCLUSION

The purpose of this chapter has been to identify and describe the social foundations of personal control among older adults. However, in order to accomplish this task, it was first necessary to think more carefully about how control is conceptualized and measured. Using the work of Schulz and colleagues (this volume) as a point of departure, three types of control were identified: primary control, secondary control, and collaborative control. The three types of control were differentiated by the extent to which social network members are involved in this process. More specifically, the locus of primary control resides solely within the focal elder, whereas secondary control arises entirely from the efforts of significant others. In contrast, collaborative control was viewed as a joint effort to influence the social world that is undertaken by an older adult in junction with their social network members.

Although the social basis of control was fairly evident when this three-part scheme was introduced, an effort was made to develop the social foundations of control even further by linking each type of control with a particular facet of social support. More specifically, it was proposed that anticipated support affects primary control, enacted support gives rise to feelings of secondary control, and the mutual exchange of assistance helps promote feelings of collaborative control.

Finally, this emerging theoretical perspective was embedded in an even wider social context by considering the key role played by socioeconomic status in the relationship between social support and feelings of personal control in late life. In essence, it was argued that upper SES elders may enjoy greater success than their lower SES counterparts in deriving and exercising feelings of primary, as well as secondary, control. In contrast, the construct of collaborative control was extended to show how lower SES elders might, nevertheless, be able to influence the course of events in their lives by working together with others to confront mutual problems. The role of the church figured prominently in this respect.

The notion that control can be exercised in at least three different ways (primary, secondary, and collaborative) raises the question as to which is best for successful aging. Initially, it would be tempting to say that primary control is the most desirable because a good deal of emphasis is placed on self-reliance in American culture (Weisz et al., 1984). But further reflection on this matter suggests this may not be the most accurate conclusion. Instead, it seems more reasonable to propose that no one type of control is inherently better than another, and that the value of any one type of control depends on the social environment in which it is exercised. More specifically, primary control may be the most effective means of influencing the social world when an older adult has at his or her disposal the resources necessary to engage in self-initiated coping responses. However, in the absence of sufficient resources, efforts at exercising primary control may be ill-advised, and may even lead to maladaptive outcomes (Krause & Stryker, 1984). Instead, when resources are scarce, collaborative control may be the method of choice for confronting personal problems.

Two important conclusions follow from the notion that the value of a particular control strategy arises from the social environment in which it is exercised. First, because social factors influence the distribution of resources and therefore the type of control that is possible, this postulate provides yet another way of showing how the genesis of control resides in the social realm. Second, this hypothesis has important data analytic implications. If a researcher were to evaluate, for example, whether the different types of control affect health and well-being, great care would be needed to make sure the model is correctly specified. Rather than looking for additive effects of primary, secondary, and collaborative control, a more appropriate strategy would be to test for the statistical interaction between each type of control and select resources on health and well-being.

Those investigators wishing to further evaluate the perspective developed in this chapter would be well advised to pay careful attention to the limitations in this work. Three are reviewed here briefly. First, the discussion has been framed in terms of ideal types (Weber, 1925). This means that in reality, primary control is probably not determined solely by anticipated support, nor is secondary control purely a function of enacted support. Instead, both types of control are likely to reflect the influence of anticipated and received support, but differ only in the relative influence of each dimension of social support. More specifically, anticipated support may play a larger role in shaping primary control, whereas enacted support may be a greater factor in the genesis of secondary control. Even so, the conceptual scheme developed in this chapter helps to simplify the complex processes that are at work, thereby allowing the predominant forces shaping control in late life to be grasped more easily.

The second shortcoming in the perspective developed here has to do with assumptions that have been made about the direction of causality between social support and feelings of control. For example, some psychologists might argue that instead of being caused by social support, individuals with a strong sense of personal control are subsequently able to utilize their support networks more effectively than people who believe the environment is less responsive to their demands (e.g., Sandler & Lakey, 1982). The resolution of this complex issue awaits rigorous empirical tests with data that have been gathered at multiple points in time. Until then, the utility of the framework developed here rests solely on conceptual or theoretical grounds.

The third limitation has to do with the scope of the collaborative control construct. As defined here, it refers to the efforts made by older adults and their social network members to deal with common problems. However, it is likely that older adults work together with significant others to resolve stressors that affect only the focal elder. Even so, only joint efforts aimed at eradicating mutual problems were considered in this chapter because this is where the social foundations of collaborative control are most evident.

Although a good deal of work remains to be done before we have a firm grasp on how feelings of control arise in late life, the main intent of this chapter has been to make sure that social factors are not overlooked. This objective was best expressed decades ago by George Herbert Mead, who argued, "What I want particularly to emphasize is the temporal and logical pre-existence of the social process to the self-conscious individual that arises in it" (Mead, 1934, p. 186).

ACKNOWLEDGMENTS

This research was supported by two grants from the National Institute on Aging: RO1 AG09221 and RO1 AG14749. Address all communications to Neal Krause, Department of Health Behavior and Health Education, School of Public Health, University of Michigan, 1420 Washington Heights, Ann Arbor, MI 48109-2029; e-mail: nkrause@umich.edu.

REFERENCES

Adams, R. G., & Blieszner, R. (1989). *Older adult friendship: Structure and process.* Newbury Park, CA: Sage.

Aldwin, C. M. (1994). *Stress, coping, and development.* New York: Guilford.

Baltes, M. M., & Carstensen, L. L. (1999). Social-psychological theories and their applications to aging: From individual to collective. In V. L. Bengtson & K. W. Schaie (Eds.), *Handbook of theories of aging* (pp. 209–226). New York: Springer.

Baltes, M. M., & Wahl, H. W. (1992). The dependency-support script in institutions: Generalization to community settings. *Psychology and Aging, 7*, 409–418.

Baltes, P. B. (1991). The many faces of aging: Toward a psychology of old age. *Psychological Medicine, 21,* 837–854.

Bandura, A. (1982). Self-efficacy mechanism in human agency. *American Psychologist, 37,* 122–147.

Bandura, A. (1995). Exercise of personal and collective efficacy in changing societies. In A. Bandura (Ed.), *Self-efficacy in changing societies* (pp. 1–45). New York: Cambridge University Press.

Barnett, R. C. (1993). Multiple roles, gender, and psychological distress. In L. Goldberger & S. Breznitz (Eds.), *Handbook of stress: Theoretical and clinical aspects* (pp. 427–445). New York: Free Press.

Barrera, M. (1986). Distinctions between social support concepts, measures, and models. *American Journal of Community Psychology, 14,* 413–445.

Belle, D. (1982). *Lives in stress: Women and depression.* Beverly Hills, CA: Sage.

Belle, D. (1990). Poverty and women's mental health. *American Psychologist, 45,* 385–389.

Blalock, H. M. (1982). *Conceptualization and measurement in the social sciences.* Beverly Hills, CA: Sage.

Bohrnstedt, G. W. (1983). Measurement. In P. H. Rossi, J. D. Wright, & A. B. Anderson (Eds.), *Handbook of survey research* (pp. 70–122). New York: Academic Press.

Brandtstadter, J., Wentura, D., & Greve, W. (1993). Adaptive resources of the aging self: Outlines of an emergent perspective. *International Journal of Behavioral Development, 16,* 323–349.

Burke, P. J. (1991). Identity process and social stress. *American Sociological Review, 56,* 836–849.

Caplan, G. (1981). Mastery of stress: Psychosocial aspects. *American Journal of Psychiatry, 138,* 413–420.

Chatters, L. M., Taylor, R. J., & Lincoln, K. D. (2001). Advances in the measurement of religiosity among older African-Americans: Implications for health and mental health researchers. *Mental Health and Aging, 7,* 181–200.

Chipperfield, J. G., Perry, R. P., & Menec, V. H. (1999). Primary and secondary control-enhancing strategies: Implications for health in later life. *Journal of Aging and Health, 11,* 517–539.

Cohen, S., & Edwards, J. R. (1989). Personality characteristics as moderators of the relationship between stress and disorder. In R. W. Neufeld (Ed.), *Advances in investigations of psychological stress* (pp. 235–283). New York: Wiley.

Conger, R. D., Rueter, M. A., & Elder, G. H. (1999). Couple resilience to economic pressure. *Journal of Personality and Social Psychology, 76,* 54–71.

Eckenrode, J., & Wethington, E. (1990). The process and outcome of mobilizing social support. In S. Duck (Ed.), *Personal relationships and social support* (pp. 83–103). Newbury Park, CA: Sage.

Gecas, V. (1989). The social psychology of self-efficacy. In W. R. Scott & J. Blake (Eds.), *Annual review of sociology* (Vol. 15, pp. 291–316). Palo Alto, CA: Annual Reviews.

Hareven, T. K. (1994). Aging and generational relations: A historical and life course perspective. In J. Hagen & K. S. Cook (Eds.), *Annual review of sociology* (Vol. 20, pp. 437–461). Palo Alto, CA: Annual Reviews.

Hobfoll, S. E. (1998). *Stress, culture, and community.* New York: Plenum.

Hughes, C. G., Tremblay, M. A., Rapoport, R. N., & Leighton, A. H. (1960). *People of cove and woodlot.* New York: Basic Books.

Ikkink, K. K., & van Tilburg, T. (1998). Do older adults' network members continue to provide instrumental support in unbalanced relationships? *Journal of Personal and Social Relationships, 15,* 59–75.

Kohn, M. L., & Schooler, C. (1983). *Work and personality: An inquiry into the impact of social stratification.* Stamford, CT: Ablex.

Krause, N. (1987a). Chronic strain, locus of control, and distress in older adults. *Psychology and Aging, 2,* 375–382.

Krause, N. (1987b). Understanding the stress process: Linking social support with locus of control beliefs. *Journal of Gerontology, 42,* 589–593.

Krause, N. (1997a). Anticipated support, received support, and economic stress among older adults. *Journal of Gerontology: Psychological Sciences, 52B,* P284–P293.

Krause, N. (1997b). Received support, anticipated support, social class, and mortality. *Research on Aging, 19,* 387–422.

Krause, N. (2001). Social support. In R. H. Binstock & L. K. George (Eds.), *Handbook of aging and the social sciences* (5th ed., pp. 272–294). San Diego: Academic Press.

Krause, N., & Borawski-Clark, E. (1995). Social class differences in social support among older adults. *The Gerontologist, 35,* 498–508.

Krause, N., & Stryker, S. (1984). Stress and well-being: The buffering role of locus of control beliefs. *Social Science and Medicine, 28,* 783–790.

Kulis, S. S. (1992). Social class and the locus of reciprocity in relationships with adult children. *Journal of Family Issues, 13,* 482–504.

Lachman, M. E., & Weaver, S. L. (1998). Sociodemographic variations in the sense of control by domain: Findings from the MacArthur Studies of Midlife. *Psychology and Aging, 13,* 553–562.

Lee, G. (1985). Kinship and social support of the elderly: The case of the United States. *Ageing and Society, 5,* 19–38.

Lin, N. (1982). Social resources and instrumental action. In P. V. Marsden & N. Lin (Eds.), *Social structure and network analysis* (pp. 131–145). Beverly Hills, CA: Sage.

McAvay, G. J., Seeman, T. E., & Rodin, J. (1996). A longitudinal study of change in domain-specific self-efficacy among older adults. *Journal of Gerontology: Psychological Sciences, 51B,* P243–P253.

Mead, G. H. (1934). *Mind, self, and society from the standpoint of a social behaviorist.* Chicago: University of Chicago Press.

Pargament, K. I. (1997). *The psychology of religion and coping: Theory, research, and practice.* New York: Guilford.

Pearlin, L. I., Menaghan, E. G., Lieberman, M. A., & Mullan, J. T. (1981). The stress process. *Journal of Health and Social Behavior, 22,* 337–356.

Pearlin, L. I., & Schooler, C. (1978). The structure of coping. *Journal of Health and Social Behavior, 19,* 2–21.

Peng, Y., & Lachman, M. (1995). Scale to measure primary and secondary control. In J. Haidt & J. Rodin (Eds.), *Control and efficacy: An integrative review—A report to the John D. and Catherine T. MacArthur Foundation* (appendix p. 14). Philadelphia: University of Pennsylvania Press.

Ross, C. E., & Sastry, J. (1999). The sense of personal control: Social-structural causes and emotional consequences. In C. S. Aneshensel & J. C. Phelan (Eds.), *Handbook of the sociology of mental health* (pp. 369–394). New York: Plenum.

Rotter, J. B. (1966). Generalized expectancies for internal versus external control of reinforcement. *Psychological Monographs: General and Applied, 80*(Whole No. 609), 1–28.

Rowe, J. W., & Kahn, R. L. (1998). *Successful aging.* New York: Pantheon.

Rubin, L. B. (1976). *Worlds of pain: Life in the working-class family.* New York: Basic Books.

Sandler, I. N., & Lakey, B. (1982). Locus of control as a stress moderator: The role of control perceptions and social support. *American Journal of Community Psychology, 10,* 60–80.

Schulz, R., & Heckhausen, J. (1996). A life-span model of successful aging. *American Psychologist, 51,* 702–714.

Schwarzer, R., & Fuchs, R. (1995). Changing risk behaviors and adopting health behaviors: The role of self-efficacy beliefs. In A. Bandura (Ed.), *Self-efficacy in changing societies* (pp. 259–288). New York: Cambridge University Press.

Seeman, M., & Lewis, S. (1995). Powerlessness, health, and mortality: A longitudinal study of older men and mature women. *Social Science and Medicine, 41,* 517–525.

Skinner, E. A. (1997). A guide to the construct of control. *Journal of Personality and Social Psychology, 71,* 549–570.

Stephens, J. (1976). *Loners, losers, and lovers: Elderly tenants in a slum hotel.* Seattle: University of Washington Press.

Stryker, S. (1987). Identity theory: Developments and extensions. In K. Yardley & T. Honess (Eds.), *Self and identity: Psychosocial perspective* (pp. 83–103). New York: Wiley.

Thoits, P. A. (1991). On merging identity theory with stress research. *Social Psychology Quarterly, 54,* 101–112.

Turner, R. J., & Marino, F. (1994). Social support and social structure: A descriptive epidemiology. *Journal of Health and Social Behavior, 35,* 193–212.

Weber, M. (1925). *From Max Weber: Essays in sociology* (H. Gerth & C. W. Mills, Eds.). New York: Oxford University Press.

Weisz, J. R., Rothbaum, F. M., & Blackburn, T. C. (1984). Standing out and standing in: The psychology of control in America and Japan. *American Psychologist, 39,* 955–969.

Wethington, E., & Kessler, R. C. (1986). Perceived support, received support, and adjustment to stressful life events. *Journal of Health and Social Behavior, 27,* 78–89.

Wheaton, B. (1983). Stress, personal coping resources, and psychiatric symptoms: An investigation of interactive models. *Journal of Health and Social Behavior, 24,* 208–229.

Wortman, C. B. (1984). Social support and the cancer patient. *Cancer, 53,* 2339–2362.

Zimmerman, M. A. (2000). Empowerment theory: Psychological, organizational, and community levels of analysis. In J. Rappaport & E. Seidman (Eds.), *Handbook of community psychology* (pp. 43–63). New York: Plenum.

Commentary

Perceived, Generalized, and Learned Aspects of Personal Control

Scott Schieman

A rich collection of social-psychological research documents the social causes of perceptions, feelings, and behaviors. In harmony with that tradition, Neal Krause's thoughtful and stimulating chapter (this volume) asks how do perceptions of personal control arise in late life? His contributions deserve credit for explicating the social aspects of secondary control, a concept often described in the literature in individualistic and cognitive terms. Citing limitations related to the global sense of control, Krause develops his ideas in congruence with Schulz and Heckhausen's (1996) more realm-specific conceptualizations of primary and secondary control. I am in essential agreement with these authors concerning the importance of realm-specific control. However, their emphasis, I believe, should not be at the expense of the perceived, generalized, and learned aspects of personal control. As I will argue, these are at least of equal importance in our efforts to understand individuals' attempts to solve problems and adapt to life course changes.

THE GENERALIZED SENSE OF CONTROL VERSUS REALM-SPECIFIC ACTUAL CONTROL

Global measures of personal control, in contrast to the realm-specific, are generalized. Such beliefs or expectancies are comprehensive in scope and span across a range of domains, collectively representing something akin to a worldview (Skinner, 1996). Krause criticizes global measures of perceived control for assuming that individuals can exert a similar degree of influence across domains—an assumption he claims is incompatible with reality. As a consequence, he devotes substantially more attention to realm-specific control. Conversely, the generalized sense of personal control appears to be diminished as something meriting our consideration.

Why is realm-specific control so important? According to Schulz and Heckhausen (1996), aging individuals—who are also experiencing declining resources—decide to surrender primary control in specific realms in order to allocate their efforts for primary control to other domains. Krause adopts similar language by claiming that older people choose the specific realms in which they "exercise" primary control. In my view, the language used to conceptualize personal control in that manner often blurs the distinctions between the behaviors designed to manage realm-specific responsibilities and the perceptions of personal control that one has over the events and outcomes within specific domains. That is, the language better fits possible differences between the execution of tasks and the perceptions of control over outcomes. Many scholars, some included in this volume, have discussed in detail the differences between realm-specific (enacted) and global feelings of personal control. General beliefs about control shape action and affect, independent of the specific, objective conditions of personal control that influence those perceptions (Skinner, 1996). Moreover, it cannot be presumed that the beliefs about control and the "realistic perceptions of objective conditions" are unrelated (Ross & Sastry, 1999, p. 376). The following sections further explore the potential utility of considering the generalized sense of personal control together with realm-specific control.

SECONDARY CONTROL, COLLABORATION, AND THE GENERALIZED SENSE OF CONTROL

According to Schulz and Heckhausen (1996), humans possess the desire for behavior–outcome contingencies in their everyday affairs, which, in turn, stimulates the motivation for primary control. In that context, Krause suggests that aging adults who encounter diminishing resources and capacities for primary control are motivated to exercise other forms of control, such as secondary or collaborative control. He summarizes a continuum, arranged with primary and secondary control at the poles and collaborative control in the middle, as an accurate reflection of control in later life. Secondary control "targets the self and attempts to achieve changes directly within the individual" (Schulz & Heckhausen, 1996, p. 708). However, Krause approaches secondary control from a different angle by stressing its "inherently social nature."

At that juncture, Krause draws attention to the social foundations of control by illustrating the involvement of significant others in realm-specific responsibilities. For example, he describes a woman who encounters problems (stressors) within the financial domain. Although he does not specify what financial problems are at issue, the woman's difficulties may result from declining competency. Whatever the reason, in order to cope with the stressor, she turns financial matters over to her son and relinquishes those duties at some level. Does she relinquish total "control" of her finances to her son? Is "secondary control," in the sense described by Krause, realistically likely? Unless she is totally impaired or incapacitated, the mother in that scenario would probably maintain some form of finance-related activity. For example, her son may manage her bill payments and sustain the balance of responsibilities; however, she may still make some decisions about expenditures on minor purchases as well as on major matters, such as how her assets should be distributed at her death. Conversely, in collaborative control, older adults act jointly to solve problems and satisfy obligations. Krause portrays a couple that encounters economic hardship and "faces the crisis as a team." Taken together, secondary and collaborative controls are aimed at mitigating difficulties—so they appear to reflect problem-solving and coping behaviors more than the yielding of control.

How might the generalized sense of personal control fit into Krause's conceptual scheme? Global feelings about control may provide a motivational source for the realm-specific acts aimed at the management of responsibilities. An individual's broad sense that behavior–outcome contingencies tend to sway (favorably) in his or her direction may promote incentives to "exercise control" within a specific realm and foster perceptions of realm-specific control. Some evidence indirectly supports that contention by showing that the generalized sense of control predicts problem-solving behavior (Ross & Mirowsky, 1989). In addition, a high sense of personal control fosters active and constructive engagement with the social and physical world (Skinner, 1996); conversely, a low sense of control facilitates the slide into feelings of helplessness and concurrent forms of behavior (Seligman, 1975). Individuals with a generalized sense of control may have more flexible options that allow them to shift interest in realm-specific control. The wealthy, for example, may possess more economic resources that allow them to afford professional assistance with finances during the later years. In sum, if we hope to understand individuals' awareness, desires, and decisions about control-type behavior within domains, we should consider the generalized control orientation that one brings to various situations. The general sense of control might very well serve as a spur for people to employ, in Krause's terms, secondary controls. One augments rather than replaces the other. Moreover, that generalized disposition is learned within recurring role performances and exchanges in institutions such as family, school, work, and religion. Thus, accumulation and continuity processes across the life course may further contribute to our understanding of the social foundations of control in late life.

LEARNING A SENSE OF CONTROL: ACCUMULATION, CONTINUITY, AND THE LIFE COURSE

A starting point for Krause is that elderly individuals who encounter problems within particular realms actively decide to shift responsibilities for processes and outcomes. The "active" element within that argument implies something about the problem-solving orientation of the individual. Problem solving is "nonroutine mental and/or motor activity actively undertaken under conditions of uncertainty and oriented toward overcoming an impediment to goal attainment by circumventing, eliminating, or removing a barrier and/or restoring previously established routes to goal attainment" (Tallman, Leik, Gray, & Stafford, 1993, p. 159). It is critical to reinforce that a learned global sense of control shapes how actively or passively an individual engages new problems—across the entire age span and in late life. Recognizing the learned aspect of control reiterates the developmental sources and nature of perceived control, as well as the significance of continuity that spans over the life course.

How does a 67-year-old individual think, feel, and act when faced with a problem? Long ago, James (1890) argued that individuals enact ingrained "habits" of mind to think about and act toward their social world. The learning of those habits occurs at all life stages. In childhood, parents' socioeconomic status (SES), dispositions, and cognitive orientations about the sense of control reflect the fundamental social sources of the generalized beliefs about control and other personal qualities, such as self-esteem. The experiences within roles during young adulthood and middle age continue to shape perceptions of control. The persistence of general patterns of thought, feeling, and behavior reflect a continuity that links the younger, middle, and later years of one's life (Atchley, 1999). As development progresses and role transitions transpire, personal dispositions evolve and solidify. Thus, when faced with adversity, an elder individual may think, feel, or act in ways akin to earlier ages. The problems and stressors may differ, but control-related cognitive and behavioral processes are likely to be fairly consistent. In sum, established patterns accumulate over time and persist into late life as relatively stable control orientations.[1]

There are notable parallels between research that explicates the social causes of distress across the life course (Mirowsky & Ross, 1986) and the study of the social influences on perceived control in later life. Research documents the correlation of emotional distress with objective conditions (i.e., educational attainment, income, and the quality of work and family roles). Many of those social patterns may also be replicated when, in place of emotions, we look at the generalized sense of control (see Ross & Sastry, 1999, for a review). One social factor in particular, education, may have unique economic, occupational, and psychosocial benefits that accumulate with age and yield divergent trajectories of personal control in late life. "Human capital" theory (Becker, 1993) asserts that education can foster personal qualities like persistence and a sense of effectiveness—qualities acutely relevant given the focus on problem solving in late life. Education develops cognitive skills that can cultivate the belief that one actively determines life outcomes (Ross & Van Willigen, 1997). Moreover, education "increases learned effectiveness; its absence produces learned helplessness" (Mirowsky & Ross, 1998, p. 420). Blending issues of aging, the "cumulative advantage" thesis implies that education (and other indicators of SES) can buffer against health decline in late life (Ross & Wu, 1996). In reference to the sense of control, elders who have had the advantage of lifelong returns from education may maintain a higher perceived control even in the face of decline (Schieman, 2001). That fundamentally social and structural source of personal control may well affect elders' desires and choices about realm-specific control.

STRUCTURAL CONTEXTS OF CHOICES
ABOUT CONTROL, SUPPORT, AND
PROBLEM-SOLVING BEHAVIOR

The sense of control involves "a view of the self as competent and efficacious and a view of the world as structured and responsive" (Skinner, 1996, p. 559). Thus, an older individual who possesses feelings of generalized control may also hold fairly positive views about his or her capacity to solve problems, regardless of the actual or anticipated instrumental support of others. However, at times blending themes from the stress process and coping, Krause claims that individuals who are embedded within social networks can draw upon the resources of others to help define and solve problems. Such assistance, or the awareness of its existence and availability, purportedly fosters the stressed individual's sense that problems can be controlled. In this section, I reflect on the utility of the sense of control in support and problem-solving processes.

Individuals with the means and access to conditions that foster a high rate of behavior–outcome contingencies are likely also to have high levels of subjective and objective control. Such conditions, however, are differentially distributed by social characteristics. Following the ideas of Merton (1957), who described the emotional consequences of conflicts between goal-related ambitions and structural constraints, it is essential to consider the ways that opportunity structures impinge upon individuals' sense of the possible. This is particularly important if conceptual and theoretical emphasis is placed on individuals' desires for behavior–event contingencies and their choices about where to exercise primary control. Such a depiction suggests that individuals have the capacity to think about, and actually execute, decisions about control; that is, they have active control over how, where, and what they desire to control. However, in my view, that assertion discounts the unequal social distribution of the awareness, quality, and plausibility of choices about different forms of enacted control. Objective conditions contribute to the belief that outcomes or situations are determined by forces external to the self (i.e., powerful others, luck, and fate) (Rotter, 1966). That fact extends to choices about control-related actions. Thus, theoretical assertions about individuals' active choices to shift between types of control should consider social sources of the generalized sense of control, as well as the personal and social inequities that restrict or encourage choice.

Perceptions about support influence the choices about control. For example, Krause identifies anticipated social support as a distinct social source of personal control: It affects choice about the enactment of control largely because it encourages older people to resolve problems on their own (i.e., maintain primary control). With greater anticipated support, elders take more risks and enact novel problem-solving approaches. In that context, Krause delineates the effects of social class: Lower SES elders are less able to "follow through" on problem-solving methods because they lack resources. However, the exact meaning of "resources" in that suggestion is unclear. Are they cognitive, personal, or social? Older adults with lower SES may have a personal history of successes and failures that foster a low generalized sense of control. That orientation, in turn, might obstruct the motivation for risk taking and the performance of novel problem-solving techniques. Moreover, elders who have fewer years of education and income probably held social positions during the earlier periods of life that provided fewer opportunities for control. For example, research shows that homemakers tend to report a lower sense of personal control relative to individuals in paid employment. In addition, substantively complex jobs with freedom and autonomy increase the sense of personal control (Ross & Sastry, 1999). An individual may spend most of his or her life with low education, few credentials, high job insecurity, little mobility (geographic and occupational), unstable family life, poor housing, and disorderly neighborhoods. Those conditions are structural sources of the generalized sense of control that affect processes of desire, choice, and enactment of objective realm-specific control during the later years.

COLLABORATING WITH "THE" POWERFUL OTHER OR RELINQUISHING CONTROL?

In a reference to problem solving among elders in lower SES neighborhoods, Krause describes opportunities for collaborative control within the religious domain; that is, fellow members of one's congregation can provide supportive ties that enhance problem solving and feelings of collaborative control. I offer another perspective: a focus on one's relationship with a specific Powerful Other—God—and how that influences the generalized sense of personal control. Over time, socialization within religious institutions teaches that most, if not all, of the fundamental features of life are beyond our control. A "higher being" controls the events and outcomes of our lives. However, if an individual agrees with the statement "What happens to me in the future mostly depends on God," then does he or she possess a low sense of personal control? An individual who agrees with that statement may still feel in control if he or she believes in a God who acts with his or her best interests in mind. That may well be one of the few scenarios in which an individual may relinquish total global control to a powerful other. In addition, an external locus of control, or the mind-set that God molds one's fate, will determine the form and degree of desires, choices, and enactment of control within any particular realm of life (e.g., finances, health, and interpersonal relationships).

An alternative view involves the perception that one can act jointly with God—as a partner—to solve problems or to cope with stressors, and thus maintain global feelings of control over life events and outcomes. Some evidence supports the contention that Americans hold such beliefs and that those perceptions vary by age. For example, a general statement in the 1998 General Social Survey (Davis & Smith, 1999) asks respondents the following: "Think about how you try to understand and deal with major problems in your life." This is followed by a specific item asking about the extent to which they cope by working "together with God as partners." Results shown in Table 2.1 indicate that less than 20% of adults responded "not at all." Moreover, older people are more likely to report that they work together with God as

TABLE 2.1 Age and Perceptions of Respondents' Partnership with God

Item and Response Choices	Age Categories			
"I work together with God as partners."	18–39 years	40–64 years	65 years plus	Total
Not at all	140 (23.18%)	95 (17.06%)	32 (13.56%)	267 (19.11%)
Somewhat	236 (39.07%)	191 (34.29%)	75 (31.78%)	502 (35.93%)
Quite a bit	121 (20.03%)	135 (24.24%)	60 (25.42%)	316 (22.62%)
A great deal	107 (17.72%)	136 (24.42%)	69 (29.24%)	312 (22.33%)
Total	604	557	236	1397

Note: Chi-square = 28.61, $p < .001$

partners a great deal or quite a bit, relative to younger adults. About 29% of elders age 65 and older report that they work with God as partners a great deal, compared to about 23% of adults age 40 to 64 and about 17% of adults age 39 and younger. Thus, there is some indication that, to a greater extent, older adults report working with God as partners in the effort to understand and cope with major problems in their own life. That particular form of control may be critical for elders who face increasing physical impairment. It is not "collaborative" in the sense that Krause describes (i.e., two individuals jointly have a problem and jointly enact solutions); rather, it focuses on a generalized sense that one has a potent resource that cannot be taken away. Moreover, an individual does not have to attend a place of worship in order to develop ties with that omnipresent Powerful Other. Future research might examine if the sense that God is in control of events and outcomes influences both generalized perceptions of personal control and realm-specific control.

CONCLUSION

How does the sense of control "arise in late life"? Krause's "Social Foundations of Personal Control in Late Life" (this volume) focuses on realm-specific beliefs and actions that relate to control among the elderly. With his contribution, Krause deserves a great deal of credit for giving social meaning to secondary control. Social exchanges and expectations about supportive interactions shape the ways older adults approach problems and stressors in their everyday life. In my commentary, I contend that the generalized sense of personal control—which is learned and developed over an entire life course—has a central role in the opportunities, desires, choices, and ultimate enactment of realm-specific types of control during the elder years. Micro-level experiences with control during late life are shaped by a personal history of successes and failures within salient role domains and broader institutions such as the family, school, economy, and religion. From a life course perspective, predictions about the ways that realm-specific forms of control emerge in later life are likely determined by the generalized sense of personal efficacy, mastery, and control that carries over from earlier years. The problems may be new, but the feelings, thoughts, and actions occur within a generalized control orientation that has developed over a lifetime of encounters with challenge and adversity.

NOTE

1. Although several recent surveys using cross-sectional designs find that older people tend to report a lower sense of personal control (Mirowsky, 1995; Schieman, 2001), our reviews of the literature reveal rather mixed results regarding cross-sectional and longitudinal findings about age and the sense of control (Clark-Plaskie & Lachman, 1999; Lachman, 1986).

REFERENCES

Atchley, R. C. (1999). Continuity theory, self, and social structure. In C. D. Ryff & V. W. Marshall (Eds.), *The self and society in aging processes* (pp. 94–121). New York: Springer.

Becker, G. S. (1993). *Human capital* (3rd ed.). New York: Columbia University Press.

Clark-Plaskie, M., & Lachman, M. E. (1999). The sense of control in midlife. In S. L. Lewis & J. D. Reid (Eds.), *Life in the middle: Psychosocial and social development in middle age* (pp. 181–208). San Diego: Academic Press.

Davis, J., & Smith, T. (1999). *General social surveys, 1972–1998: Cumulative codebook and data file.* Chicago: National Opinion Research Center and the University of Chicago.

James, W. (1890). *Principles of psychology* (Vol. 1). New York: Norton.

Lachman, M. E. (1986). Personal control in later life: Stability, change, and cognitive correlates. In M. M. Baltes & P. B. Baltes (Eds.), *The psychology of control and aging* (pp. 207—236). Hillsdale, NJ: Erlbaum.

Merton, R. (1957). *Social theory and social structure.* New York: Free Press.

Mirowsky, J. (1995). Age and the sense of control. *Social Psychology Quarterly, 58,* 31–43.

Mirowsky, J., & Ross, C. E. (1986). Social patterns of distress. *Annual Review of Sociology, 12,* 23–45.

Mirowsky, J., & Ross, C. E. (1998). Education, personal control, lifestyle and health. *Research on Aging, 20,* 415–449.

Ross, C. E., & Mirowsky, J. (1989). Explaining the social patterns of depression: Control and problem solving—or support and talking? *Journal of Health and Social Behavior, 30,* 206–219.

Ross, C. E., & Sastry, J. (1999). The sense of personal control: Social-structural causes and emotional consequences. In C. S. Aneshensel & J. C. Phelan (Eds.), *Handbook of the sociology of mental health* (pp. 369–394). New York: Kluwer Academic/Plenum.

Ross, C. E., & Wu, C. (1996). Education, age, and the cumulative advantage in health. *Journal of Health and Social Behavior, 37,* 104–120.

Ross, C. E., & Van Willigen, M. (1997). Education and the subjective quality of life. *Journal of Health and Social Behavior, 38,* 275–297.

Rotter, J. B. (1966). Generalized expectancies for internal vs. external control of reinforcements. *Psychological Monographs, 80,* 1–28.

Schieman, S. (2001). Age, education, and the sense of control: A test of the cumulative advantage hypothesis. *Research on Aging, 23,* 153–178.

Seligman, M. (1975). *Helplessness.* San Francisco: Freeman.

Schulz, R., & Heckhausen, J. (1996). A life-span model of successful aging. *American Psychologist, 51,* 702–714.

Skinner, E. A. (1996). A guide to constructs of control. *Journal of Personality and Social Psychology, 71,* 549–570.

Tallman, I., Leik, R. K., Gray, L. N., & Stafford, M. C. (1993). A theory of problem-solving behavior. *Social Psychology Quarterly, 56,* 157–177.

CHAPTER 3

Cultural Variations in Meaning of Control

Marilyn McKean Skaff and Phillip Gardiner

John Wayne gets a determined look on his face, mounts his powerful steed, and heads off to make things right. This is a man in control. We can assume that his scores on measures of control would reflect his beliefs that what happens to him lies in his big, strong hands, that he has the abilities necessary for what he needs to do, and that, in general, he is a person who is in control of his life. Although few of us would admit to identifying with John Wayne, the majority of the extant inquiries into control reflect the same set of beliefs and values represented by this American cultural icon. The ideal setting the standard for these inquiries rests on the beliefs that you are in the saddle (or driver's seat), that you have the capabilities to do what is required to control your life, and that all you have to do is act and things will happen as you wish. This assumes, of course, that the environment will be responsive (and has been in the past) to your attempts to control it.

Now, we switch from the image of John Wayne to that of a fish tank. There is an ancient proverb that states that the fish is always the last one to discover water (Weisz, Rothbaum, & Blackburn, 1984). This chapter begins with the proposal that it is time for scientists who study control to pay attention to the water. This "water" contains the basic but unquestioned assumptions about the way things are. As a place to begin, we believe that the study of sense of control will benefit from a more contextual perspective on sense of control. Such a perspective suggests not only a greater awareness of the predominant cultural values and beliefs that have heavily influenced work on sense of control, but also an understanding of how control can have different cultural meanings and manifestations across diverse racial and ethnic groups. In other words, we need to question existing ethnocentric views about control and broaden the theories of control to incorporate cultural variations in meaning and mechanisms of control (Brown, Sellars, Brown, & Jackson, 1999; Rogler, 1999; Schooler, 1990). It is a basic premise of this chapter that culture exerts a major influence on the beliefs and values that people carry around with them regarding their relationship to the environment and what is desirable and possible in terms of their personal control.

The time has never been more right for incorporating cultural differences into the existing theories of control. Massive demographic changes are sweeping across the United States, bringing increasing numbers of people from around the world who do not share the same assumptions about personal control as many in the United States. Indeed, by mid-century, the European American majority will have given way to a new multicultural majority. Along with African Americans, Native Americans, and Alaska Natives, peoples of Asia, Africa, and Latin America harbor shared assumptions about how the world works, which are often distinct from those of the dominant culture in the United States (Brown et al., 1999; Markus & Kitayama, 1991; Rogler, 1999; Schooler, 1990; Weisz et al., 1984). It is this diversity in worldviews as well as the distinct social realities that many people of color face that, of necessity, should force social scientists to question their present frameworks, reexamine their assumptions, and ultimately broaden and change existing constructs.

Although there is ample literature on control and on culture, there is relatively sparse literature examining the intersection of these two areas. (There are a couple of notable exceptions to this that will be discussed later.) The goal of this chapter is to begin to bring together the literature in these two areas and to examine the ways in which culture can inform and enrich theories of sense of control. What we are proposing here may be seen as heretical by some traditional scholars who believe that there are universal traits that stand (usually without scrutiny) across time and cultures. Much of the previous research on control has followed a "one size fits all" model, resulting in the indiscriminate measurement of control across different groups, with the western model of control being held as the gold standard to which others are compared (Brown et al., 1999; Rogler, 1999; Vega, 1992). Here we argue for a much more flexible and contextual view of control that does not judge all by the John Wayne model, but looks to expand and differentiate the ways we conceptualize and measure sense of control.

CULTURE AS CONTEXT

Culture as it is used here refers to social norms, rituals, language, beliefs, and values that influence how people think about themselves and the world (Betancourt & Lopez, 1993; Brown et al., 1999; Triandis, 1995, 1997). *Ethnicity* generally refers to a grouping of individuals on the basis of shared geographic, national, or cultural heritage (Betancourt & Lopez, 1993; Brown et al., 1999). *Race* is a socially constructed term that has its origins in the special oppression of African Americans and other peoples of color in this country (Davis, 1991) and elsewhere. Along with their oppression, people of color have historically been assigned to the lowest rungs of the class structure, including slavery, the system of share cropping, and positions as service workers, farmworkers, and domestic laborers.

There are two caveats that need to be stated before we can proceed. First, although most of the cultural influences on sense of control that we will be considering here are related to race and ethnicity, we acknowledge the additional differentiation within and across groups due to gender, socioeconomic status (SES), geographic location, immigration history, acculturation, wealth, oppression, and power (Vega, 1992). There is considerable variability within groups, and we do not wish to contribute to any stereotypical perceptions of diverse ethnic and racial groups; however, given intragroup variability, we still suggest that there are important cultural influences that can inform differences in sense of control across groups.

Second, any discussion about culture and control must address the historical and social implications of culture in American society. It is impossible to address beliefs about control separate from the sociopolitical context in which people live. The objective differences in power and control that exist cannot be ignored. How these imbalances in actual control relate to subjective perceptions of control is one of the questions that we can only begin to address here. There is ample evidence that control varies by SES and political system, as well as with ethnicity (Mirowsky & Ross, 1984; Oettingen & Maier, 1999; Ross & Sastry, 1999; Sastry & Ross, 1998).

CULTURE AS A CONTEXT OF CONTROL

Mirowsky and Ross (1984) define *sense of control* as "a socially transmitted and thus socially structured conception of reality," thus suggesting that control beliefs should reflect their cultural context. The relationship between culture and control is stated even more strongly by Fung, Abeles, and Carstensen (1999), who propose that "[c]ultures provide elaborate belief systems (e.g., science, religion) for explaining how both the social and physical worlds operate and about the appropriate means for achieving desired outcomes including whether particular outcomes are contingent or noncontingent upon people's behavior" (p. 349). To begin to address how culture might affect control, we consider three broad areas related to culture: history unique to particular racial and ethnic groups; the relationship between SES and race/ethnicity; and variations in beliefs, attitudes, and values.

History

The history of any racial, ethnic, or cultural group will have a long-lasting impact on cultural beliefs and attitudes, as well as behaviors. In the United States, some examples include the effects of the virtual genocide of Native Americans, the importation and imprisonment of Asians, the confiscation of land from Mexican Americans, and the forced importation and enslavement of African Americans. These aspects of history have left a legacy that cannot be overestimated. Real experiences of lack of control and powerlessness have had a lasting impact on attitudes about who is in control, what can and cannot be controlled, and what kinds of control are possible given the circumstances and the context. Transmission across generations of powerlessness and structured conditions are reinforced by such experiences in people's everyday lives.

Experiences of immigration can also have a complex effect on feelings of control involving issues such as acculturation, generation, language, SES, and degree of difference between country of origin and host country (Vega, 1992). The immigration experience will vary also by the conditions driving that immigration. For example, the experience will be different for those who were drawn to the United States by a promise of riches or reconciliation with family, those who were forcibly brought here and enslaved, and those who were fleeing conditions in their country of origin. These immigration experiences are expected to have a direct impact on ongoing objective conditions of everyday life, as well as a lasting impact on values, beliefs, and attitudes about control.

Socioeconomic Status

The pervasive effects of SES cannot be left out of a discussion of culture and control. Along with discrimination based on race and ethnicity, many of the diverse cultural groups in the United States are also at a socioeconomic disadvantage. Because there is a strong relationship between multiple indicators of SES (income, education, work status, social class, and accumulated wealth) and racial/ethnic group membership, it is difficult to disentangle the effects of SES on sense of control from those of race and ethnicity. However, although they may be difficult to separate statistically, this does not mean that one is a proxy for the other and that we should give up on the effort to understand their unique contributions to variations in control.

For many people who have been marginalized on the basis of race and ethnicity, a diminished sense of control would appear to be a realistic assessment of opportunity (Bastida, 1987). When controlling for SES, the racial and ethnic differences in sense of control sometimes disappear; however, one must ask whether it makes sense to statistically remove what is an important reality in the lives of many people, what in a sense has become part of the culture of some groups. Culture and its structural underpinnings go hand in hand in shaping values and meaning. The real challenge is to try to understand the unique contributions of SES and race/ethnicity by identifying the mediators that connect both of these with sense of control.

Beliefs, Attitudes, and Values

It is a basic premise of this chapter that culture exerts a major influence on the schemas or cognitive structures that people carry with them regarding their relationship to the environment and what is desirable and possible in terms of their control beliefs (Abeles, 1990). In addition to the influence of the historical background of racial and ethnic groups and their location in the social class system, there are several dimensions that can be used to characterize cultural belief systems.

One of the more common dimensions along which cultures and their worldviews vary is that of individualism-collectivism (Markus & Kitayama, 1991; Sastry & Ross, 1998; Schooler, 1990). Individualism, or the independent view of the self, is defined by an emphasis on a view of the self as separate from others and detached from the context. On the other hand, collectivism, or an interdependent view of the self, is one in which the self is defined by relationships or groups and reflects an interrelationship between self and context. Large portions of the world's population are characterized by collectivist views, including Asian/Pacific Islander, African, Latin American, and Southern European cultures. Northern European and European American culture emphasizes a more individualistic view of the self. Although from a Eurocentric perspective there may be a tendency to see a collectivist view of control as "less than," Markus and Kitayama (1991) emphasize that such a worldview requires a high degree of self-control and agency to adjust oneself to interpersonal requirements.

A second dimension on which cultures have been described involves the relative emphasis on primary or secondary control (Azuma, 1984; Kojima, 1984; Weisz, 1990; Weisz et al., 1984). Briefly, primary control is defined as control aimed outside the individual that intends to make a change in the environment. Secondary control, on the other hand, has as its target the actor; that is, the intent is to control the self's reaction to the conditions or situations confronted and to alter the self rather than the environment. Although Skinner (1996) challenges the use of this dimension as a control construct and likens it instead to coping or reactions to challenges to control, Markus and Kitayama (1991) and Weisz and colleagues (1984) make a convincing argument for its use in understanding cultural variations of the meaning of control. Thus, Weisz and colleagues (1984) distinguished between Japanese and European American perspectives on the pathways to control: the Japanese preference for secondary control in which people accommodate to conditions as they are, and the European American tendency to exert primary control, that is, to influence or change existing realities. Similarly, among Latinos, *controlarse,* or control of the self, is highly valued (Cohen, 1985). The origins of the self as target of control may lie in a combination of realistic assessment of possibility and cultural values, a theme to which we return below.

Both primary and secondary control have been differentiated into subcategories that reflect different means of exerting control, whether over the self or the environment. These include vicarious, illusory, predictive, and interpretive control (Azuma, 1984; Weisz, 1990). Kojima (1984) further distinguishes between direct and indirect primary control. By indirect primary control, he refers to the modification of conditions, not through direct confrontation, but through methods that are expected to modify the behaviors of others. Both primary and secondary control have deep cultural roots that are influenced by SES, history, and other powerful social forces that we discussed above.

As a parallel, there is a growing literature applying the primary-secondary control distinction to the study of aging (Brandtstadter & Rothermund, 1994; Schulz & Heckhausen, 1999). Here the assumption is that the ratio of primary to secondary control shifts from primary control in young and middle adulthood to secondary control as people age and can do less about controlling what happens to them and more about how they respond to challenges of aging. Inherent in this discussion is a value judgment that makes primary a superior form of control compared to secondary, without considering variations in realistic control and matching control to context. There is also a dominant culture bias that overlooks the interaction between aging and race/ethnicity and continuing disparities in access to wealth. Still another potential source of variability that has been overlooked is the difference in domains of control. It is possible that individuals across cultures and across the life span may focus on particular domains that are more accessible to them or more valued in their context. As people age, they may shift domains, emphasizing those in which control is possible and deemphasizing the less controllable (Fung et al., 1999).

Finally, an important source of beliefs and values regarding control can be found in the religious heritage of diverse racial and ethnic groups (Fung et al., 1999). Beliefs in a powerful deity that is actively involved in quotidian activities can influence the degree to which a group centers control in an external source. Beliefs about prescribed fate can contribute toward a view that control is not in the hands of the individual, but unfolds as written. Although there is considerable variability within cultural groups in religious involvement and beliefs, many of these beliefs are part of the general cultural beliefs and attitudes about the individual and the environment. These beliefs often generalize from a strictly religious context to the daily lives of individuals and are incorporated into their language, their activities, and their views of the world. For example, in Spanish, conversation is often filled with references to God's will; for example, "If God permits" or "God forbid."

DEFINING SENSE OF CONTROL

Although it is not within the scope of this chapter to review the myriad theories and constructs of control, it is difficult to understand the connections between culture and control beliefs without defining them. Constructs of control have grown out of different disciplinary and theoretical traditions and, thus, vary in at least three critical ways: the desired outcomes or ends of control, the means of achieving control, and the characteristics or abilities of individuals or groups who seek control (Skinner, 1996). As a starting place in our discussion of cultural variations in meaning of control, we consider three of the most common conceptualizations of control that vary with regard to their emphasis on and approach to these three aspects of control. These conceptualizations are represented by locus of control, self-efficacy, and sense of control.

Having its origins in social learning theory, locus of control (LOC) theory differentiates between internal and external control over outcomes. LOC reflects the degree to which people believe that their outcomes are due to internal or personal influence or to external influences, either powerful others or luck/chance. Thus, locus of control focuses on who or what is in charge. Self-efficacy theory proposes that people's beliefs about their own abilities to take certain courses of action will have an influence on their outcome expectancies and subsequently on their actions. Thus, individuals' beliefs about whether they possess the competence, and therefore have access to the means to achieve a desired end, determine which goals they will pursue and how much effort they will put into that pursuit.

In our model of culture and control, we have chosen to focus on a broader construct: sense of control. Sense of control includes beliefs about both the self and the environment. In Skinner's (1996) definition, "A sense of control includes a view of the self as competent and efficacious and a view of the world as structured and responsive" (p. 559). It is akin to such general constructs as personal control, mastery, and so on (Abeles, 1990; Fung et al., 1999; Pearlin & Schooler, 1978; Rodin, 1990; Skinner, 1996), having roots in both psychology and sociology and reflecting the individuals' assessment of control over their life in general. It is a global assessment, much in the same way self-esteem is a general assessment of one's worth as a person, and as such may represent a summing across domains of control (Abeles, 1990). However, Abeles' model suggests that there are both domain-specific components and a global or general sense of control, a distinction that may prove useful in considering variations in meaning of control.

As a foundation for our model of culturally sensitive control, we return to Skinner's (1996) three dimensions on which control may vary. These include the agents of control, the means and mechanisms of control, and the ends or targets of control. Starting with the agent of control, control may be viewed as residing within an individual or a group with which an individual identifies (Markus & Kitayama, 1991). This makes a distinction within what has typically been viewed as an internal locus of control but extends the notion of internal locus by acknowledging that the controlling self is not always an individual actor (I), but may be a collective (we). Consistent with the internal/external distinction, control may also be seen as lying outside the actor, in the hands of powerful others or written into a prescripted fate or at the whims of chance.

Beliefs about control may vary according to the means or mechanisms by which control is exercised. Control may take place by means of action, in the form of either behavior or cognition. Control may be achieved actively or passively. Sometimes, control is exerted by means of accessing others who have the means or access to control. For example, seeking the help of a powerful person in the neighborhood or calling upon a powerful deity may be viewed as exercising control by accessing the power of others. When considering the mechanisms by which control is exerted, it is essential to consider the objective realities of the environment in which the individual resides, that is, the degree to which individuals or groups have access to means of control as well as the barriers that may block control efforts.

The final element of control in our model involves the ends or targets of control. There are at least two ways of thinking about the targets of people's control efforts. First, individuals may vary in the degree to which they direct control efforts toward the environment or toward the self. That is, the target of control efforts may be inner attributes, "such as desires, personal goals, and private emotions that might disturb the harmonious equilibrium of interpersonal transaction" (Markus & Kitayama, 1991, p. 228). A similar distinction was also made by Skinner (1996), differentiating between control over the occurrence of events and over one's reactions to the repercussions of such events.

An additional important distinction among individuals and groups lies in the differences in the domains in which they are more likely to target their efforts. The emphasis placed on such domains as health, interpersonal relations, work, and so on, may vary both across the life span and across diverse groups (Fung et al., 1999).

FATALISM: AN EXAMPLE OF CULTURE AND CONTROL

Fatalism is a control belief whose cultural basis has received considerable attention. We discuss it in detail here because it suggests a number of linkages between control and culture. This construct represents both the potential and the dangers in applying a construct across diverse groups. Consistent with the conceptual fuzziness rampant in this area in general, there are a number ways in which fatalism has been defined and operationalized (Bastida, 1987). For example, it is often defined and measured as external locus of control (Ross, Mirowsky, & Cockerham, 1983), as low control (Varghese & Medinger, 1979; Wheaton, 1983), or as a belief in preordained fate (Bastida, 1987). The concept has been identified most frequently with Latinos (in particular, Mexican Americans), but also with people of low socioeconomic status, women, African Americans, and Asians (Mirowsky & Ross, 1984; Mizell, 1999; Neff & Hoppe, 1993; Ross & Sastry, 1999; Sastry & Ross, 1998).

Regardless of definition, in research comparing ethnic and racial groups, both Latinos and African Americans have been found to have a greater sense of fatalism in comparison to European Americans (Mirowsky & Ross, 1984; Neff, 1993; Neff & Hoppe, 1993; Rini, Dunkel-Schetter, Wadhwa, & Sandman, 1999). Likewise Sastry and Ross (1998) reported that Asians and Asian Americans were more fatalistic than European Americans. Studies consistently demonstrate a strong negative relationship between SES and fatalism (Pill & Stott, 1987; Ross & Mirowsky, 1989). For example, Pill and Stott (1987) examined the "working-class fatalism" among British women and found these beliefs to be a realistic assessment of their life conditions. The evidence in the above-mentioned studies is mixed regarding whether controlling for SES accounts for differences in fatalism.

There is little empirical evidence regarding the sources of fatalism, but they are likely to include the cultural attitudes and beliefs transmitted through child-rearing practices, as well as objective encounters with the environment (Weisz et al., 1984). Religious beliefs, too, can make a strong contribution to beliefs about individuals' ability to control their environment. Across religious groups, there are beliefs that control lies in the hands of a deity. Varghese and Medinger (1979) also point to cultural beliefs about individuals' relationship to nature that support a sense of fatalism, such as those found among some Native American tribes.

Perhaps one of the strongest influences on fatalistic control beliefs is to be found in the intractability of people's environments; that is, the belief that control does not lie in one's own hands may reflect more realism than fatalism (Bastida, 1987). People with low levels of income and education have less access to resources that allow one to control the environment (Varghese & Medinger, 1979). Likewise, research has demonstrated a relationship between autonomy on the job and individuals sense of control (Kohn & Schooler, 1982). In addition to their relationship to SES, race and ethnicity often are associated with lifetime experiences of racism and discrimination, which in themselves can deny individuals access to control over their lives. Especially when opportunities for access to control are denied on the basis of ascribed characteristics such as race, rather than on the basis of ability, the repercussions for the sense of control are considerable (Varghese & Medinger, 1979).

Moving beyond mean differences in fatalism, there is evidence that the relationship between fatalism and well-being varies across ethnic groups. For example, there is evidence that we need to consider carefully the control–health relationship across diverse groups as well as across age cohorts. There are several studies comparing Latinos, African Americans, and European Americans on fatalism. For example, Neff and Hoppe (1993) report that low acculturated Latinos and African Americans demonstrated higher fatalism than Anglos, but also report that the combination of high fatalism and high religiosity was related to lowest levels of depression in the least acculturated Latino and African American males.

Sastry and Ross (1998), in a study of Asians, Asian Americans, and European Americans, found that although Asians and Asian Americans showed lower levels of control, the relationship between control and well-being that we find among European Americans was not supported in the Asian and Asian American samples. Vega (1992) cites evidence that, although locus of control has been found to be related to suicidal ideation in adolescents, Latinos, who are often described as more external or fatalistic, have lower suicide rates. He questions whether we have oversimplified complex processes to one simple construct. Regarding variations within control beliefs, Ross and Sastry (1999) cite evidence that there are differences within external control beliefs in relation to mental health depending on whether the target is a powerful person (negative relationship) or God (no relationship). They suggest that "belief that outcomes are in the hands of God may provide some comfort, hope, and meaning, which counteract the external attribution" (p. 387). Additional evidence comes from a study of fatalism among institutionalized elderly, in which it was found that external LOC was actually protective in their situation of low control (Varghese & Medinger, 1979), suggesting that fatalism may be an adaptive response in some environments.

Bastida (1987) has been very critical of the construct of fatalism and the ways in which it has been used. The use of such terms that are value laden result from what she calls an "Anglo construction of reality." She cites qualitative research in which she found that people distinguished between those experiences that are controllable and those that are not (and found that these evaluations were not related to adjustment). She prefers to label these "fatalistic" beliefs "realism." She also has criticized the extrapolation from one context to another. She points out that "fatalism" comes from a belief in fate, identified in ethnographic work characterized by systematic observation. She is critical of those who use the term *fatalism* to describe a group with which the researchers have no familiarity and no understanding of the language or culture. Consistent with our earlier discussion, fatalism indeed may represent a realistic assessment based on historical experiences in the United States.

BRINGING TOGETHER CULTURE AND CONTROL: AN INTEGRATIVE MODEL OF CONTROL

Although there are many definitions and models of control, one that provides a useful framework for the consideration of cultural variations in sense of control is that described by Abeles (1990, 1991), who presents a model placing the beliefs about the self in the context of the environment. It is a model that succeeds in bringing together many of the concerns of this chapter. First, he speaks of sense of control as an "umbrella term," incorporating beliefs and expectations about the self and the environment, inclusive of such constructs as LOC, personal efficacy, and learned helplessness. He uses the concept of schema, defined as a subjective theory about how the world operates, to describe the ways in which cultural context might influence subjective experience of the environment and beliefs about the self in relationship to the environment. Thus, he maintains, cultural beliefs about self and environment can influence the person's subjective sense of control.

Drawing from Abeles' (1990, 1991) model, we propose that culture provides a basis or structure for the control schema or subjective theory about the way the world operates and the person's relationship to that world (see Figure 3.1). This culturally based control schema will influence the individual's subjective sense of control, a set of beliefs and expectations about the self in relation to the environment. Sense of control in this context addresses these three questions: (1) Who is in control? (2) How is control exercised? and (3) What are the targets of control? We now turn to consider how the answers to these questions may vary across diverse groups. A basic tenet of this model is that it does not make preconceived judgments about which type of control is better, but instead asks how the control beliefs fit the environment.

As we have emphasized, a contextual model of control first asks where the control is located. Based on the characteristics of a specific ethnic or cultural group, we need to know whether it is the individual or a collective or group that is seen as being responsible for control. This implies that an individualistic or collective self is the more prominent view and that control is seen as lying in the hands of the individual or in the group of which that individual is a member. There is also the possibility that control lies outside that person or group, in the hands of a powerful other. This powerful other can be not only a deity but also powerful individuals or groups. Control outside the individual may also represent the enactment of some predetermined fate or the whim of chance.

Second, we need to ask how control is exercised, that is, the means or mechanisms by which control is exerted. One distinction to be made is whether the predominant form of control is primarily behavioral or cognitive. It may be a type of primary control that is acted on indirectly by influencing others rather than directly (Kojima, 1984). Thus, in some instances, a sense of control may be achieved by identifying with powerful others or by relying on the actions of powerful others on one's behalf.

Finally, we propose that, in order to understand cultural, as well as age variations in control, we need to better understand the targets of control. It is possible that some variability may lie in the domains toward which control is or is not exercised. We can ask whether control is

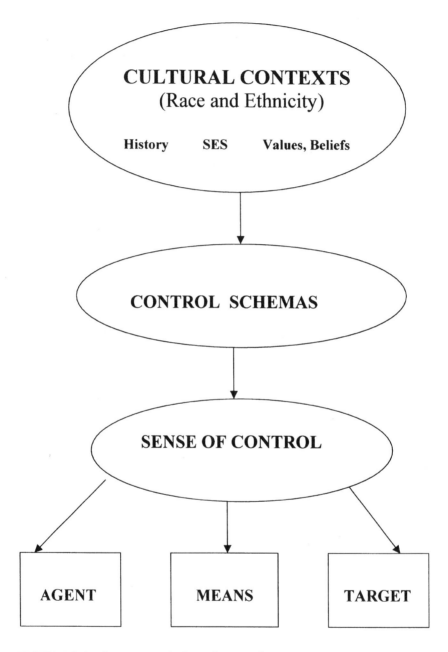

FIGURE 3.1   A contextual view of control.

directed toward the self and one's responses or toward the environment. By better understanding the specific targets of control, we may better understand the efficacy of different types of control. For example, as people age, there are more things over which they have less control (Pearlin & Skaff, 1996). The wise older person may be the one who can pick his or her battles. Both in diverse ethnic groups and among the elderly, we might ask whether control schemas are adaptive in the sense that they encompass what one can and cannot change. Subsequently, this may involve choosing one's targets of control accordingly and may represent a more adaptive control attitude than any one type of control for all occasions.

IMPLICATIONS FOR MEASUREMENT AND METHODOLOGY

When we administer a measure of sense of control to diverse cultural groups, we may obtain scores, but we do so with little understanding regarding the variation in frames of reference behind the answers people give (Rogler, 1999; Sastry & Ross, 1998). Critical to a consideration of variations in the meaning and manifestation of control in diverse groups is the issue of cultural sensitivity in measurement. There are three methodological issues (Vega, 1992) that stand out regarding cultural variations in sense of control: (1) Are the constructs relevant to the individuals being studies? (2) Are the constructs measured appropriately? and (3) Do they relate to other constructs in similar ways?

First, we must stop to question whether the constructs that we are so fond of are indeed universal, whether they have similar meaning across groups. Although issues of language and translation are important, what we must question is whether the construct of control "translates" across cultures (Rogler, 1999). Some constructs may be culture-specific, or emic (Triandis, 1997). However, even those that transfer across cultures, or etic constructs, may differ in salience and specific content (Pervin, 1999). This may mean broadening our constructs to take into account variations in context and meaning. Being willing to accommodate new meanings for constructs we previously have considered universal and invariant will take some flexibility. The model suggested may help in that process.

Second, we need to discern whether the measures used for these valued constructs are appropriate across diverse groups. This means that they possess content validity, appropriate to the group under study. Both the content of the questions used to elicit a construct and the format of the questionnaires and scales used may not be comparable across cultures (Rogler, 1999). If we want to study a construct across cultures, one goal is to develop emic (culturally appropriate) measures of etic (universal) constructs (Nopales-Springer & Stewart, 2001; Triandis, 1997). This would allow us to detect variability, as well as similarity, in content and meaning across cultures. This may require development of new measures or modification of old ones.

Finally, we need to question whether the control constructs that we use relate in the same way to other constructs across diverse groups (construct validity as well as criterion validity). For example, we may ask if one measure of control is related to other indicators of control and to outcomes in the same way across groups. This means examining whether the multiple measures of control are appropriate in meaning and measurement, then testing their relationship to outcomes.

AN EXAMPLE OF THE CONTEXT OF CONTROL

We move now to consider an empirical example of variability in sense of control across groups. The data come from a study of Latinos and European Americans with type 2 diabetes (Fisher et al., 2000). There are several ways in which ethnicity forms an important context for a discussion of control and health. First, in relationship to health, there are differences not only in prevalence and course of chronic diseases across ethnic groups but also in the lived experience of the disease (Angel & Thoits, 1987; Hunt, Valenzuela, & Pugh, 1998; Revenson, 1990). Diabetes is an especially serious problem among diverse ethnic and racial groups. In particular, it is estimated that, compared to European Americans in this country, Latinos have two to three times the rate of type 2 diabetes and are also more likely to develop complications (Carter, Pugh, & Monterrosa, 1996; Carter, Wiggins, Becker, Key, & Samet, 1993). Research that has attempted to impose the Health Belief Model, which includes self-efficacy beliefs, to understand diabetes in Latinos (specifically Mexican Americans) has found that this model was not useful in predicting outcomes (Hunt et al., 1998; Schwab, Meyer, & Merrell, 1994). In qualitative work, Hunt and colleagues (1998) found that Latinos were more likely to discuss control as a response to the perceived effectiveness of their treatments for diabetes, rather than as a precursor of outcomes.

In this study, we tested a commonly accepted model of control and health; that is, sense of control was expected to affect self-management behaviors, which in turn were expected to affect health outcomes (Skaff, Mullan, Fisher, & Chesla, in press). We operationalized control in two ways: a domain-specific measure of diabetes self-efficacy, or the degree to which persons with type 2 diabetes felt confident that they could do the things they needed to do to control their diabetes; and global mastery, their general sense of control over their lives. We examined these two levels of control in relation to both their self-management behaviors (diet and exercise) and their health outcomes (blood glucose levels [Hb_{A1C}] and general health).

In earlier work we found that there were no mean differences between Latinos and European Americans in self-efficacy, but European Americans scored higher on global mastery than Latinos. This difference disappeared, however, when we controlled for SES (Skaff, 1998). More recently, we used confirmatory factor analysis to test the comparability of the control measures across groups and found that the measures for both types of control were comparable across ethnic groups (Skaff et al., 2001). Using structural equation modeling, we also tested whether the relationships between control, self-care behaviors, and outcomes were similar across groups and found that the models differed between the two groups. Whereas self-efficacy was related to both diet and exercise for the European Americans, for Latinos it was global mastery that was related to these behaviors. For European-Americans, both diabetes self-efficacy and global mastery were related to self-reported health, independent of management behaviors. For Latinos, mastery, but not self-efficacy was related to self-reported health in the full model. Neither measures of control was related to Hb_{A1C} once management behaviors were in the equation.

Although these data do not allow us to disentangle the effects of SES and ethnicity on the relationships observed, the social class differences between the Latinos and European Americans in our sample suggest an interpretation that links access to resources and general life conditions to the relationships we observed. For the European Americans, who, in general, have higher incomes and education, as well as greater access to health care, their beliefs that they could do what was needed to manage their diabetes (self-efficacy) was related to their diet and exercise. Among Latinos, however, it was their sense of control over their lives in general (mastery) that was related to self-management behaviors. Hunt, Pugh, and Valenzuela (1997) suggest that self-management behaviors represent much more than a prescription for diabetes care among Latinos. They point out that those self-management behaviors take place in a broader context of resources, priorities, social responsibilities, and level of autonomy. When providing food and housing for one's family is a salient priority, caring for one's health may take on less significance. In other words, whereas the European Americans may be able to compartmentalize their self-management, for the Latinos, the larger context of their lives may be more salient. Thus, it is their sense of control over their lives in general that affects diet and exercise.

Surgenor, Horn, Hudson, Lunt, and Tennent (2000) make a useful distinction among beliefs about control, objective control conditions, and control experiences. Thus, although the Latinos reported equivalent levels of self-efficacy, it is the larger context of their lives that influences their management behaviors. Latinos with diabetes may feel capable of the behaviors to manage their disease (control beliefs), but when the actions to perform the behaviors must be exercised in a context full of barriers (objective control conditions), the experience of actual control may not match efficacy beliefs.

This analysis provides support for the possibility that even when we have comparable measures across groups, we also need to ask whether the same relationships prevail across diverse groups. This work suggests that we need to consider that culture can affect not only the meaning of control but also the consequences of sense of control.

FUTURE PERSPECTIVES

Before work can progress on cultural differences in sense of control, we must address more general questions regarding the cultural appropriateness of our research methodologies and the constructs we measure (Bastida, 1987; Betancourt & Lopez, 1993; Marin & Marin, 1991; Markus & Kitayama, 1991; Rogler, 1999). The challenge has been raised to consider the cultural insensitivity that is reflected in the unquestioned use of concepts and measures across cultures. Rogler (1999) points out that measures have been developed and standardized based on assumptions that apply to European Americans, but not necessarily to other cultural groups. Even when measures are translated to other languages, the translations are frequently literal, with the English version as the gold standard. He recommended a "culturally based skepticism" (p. 431) that would allow for reconsideration of the assumptions underlying our favorite constructs. One way to do this is to incorporate qualitative methods into our work to better understand the texture of meaning behind people's responses to our questions.

The constructs that have been used in the past may be too narrow to be useful in a diverse population. We propose that in order to examine control across diverse groups, we must do five things: (1) define control in a broader, more culturally relevant manner, using both qualitative and quantitative methods; (2) carefully examine the measures of control now in use to determine their cultural sensitivity; (3) develop more culturally sensitive measures that distinguish among the agents, means, and targets of control; (4) begin to identify the mediators that link race and ethnicity to sense of control; and (5) examine variability in the relationship between control beliefs and outcomes.

We have proposed a model for guiding consideration of cultural variations in meaning and measurement of control. The challenge lies in allowing constructs of control to expand to accommodate cultural variations in the agents of control, the means or mechanisms of control, and the targets of control. We must examine the culturally informed schemas that drive responses to measures of control and recognize the impact of context on control. We also need to be open to the possibility that culture can affect not only the meaning but also the consequences of sense of control. This, we believe, can have major implications for understanding the context of control–health relationships and, subsequently, for helping to explain racial/ethnic and economic disparities in health.

REFERENCES

Abeles, R. P. (1990). Schemas, sense of control, and aging. In J. Rodin, C. Schooler, & K. W. Schaie (Eds.), *Self-directedness: Cause and effects throughout the life course* (pp. 85–94). Hillsdale, NJ: Erlbaum.

Abeles, R. P. (1991). Sense of control, quality of life, and frail older people. In J. E. Birren & J. E. Lubbin (Eds.), *The concept and measurement of quality of life in the frail elderly* (pp. 297–314). San Diego: Academic Press.

Angel, R., & Thoits, P. (1987). The impact of culture on the cognitive structure of illness. *Culture, Medicine, and Psychiatry, 11,* 465–494.

Azuma, H. (1984). Secondary control as a heterogeneous category. *American Psychologist, 39,* 970–975.

Bastida, E. (1987). Issues of conceptual discourse in ethnic research and practice. In D. E. Gelfand & C. M. Barresi (Eds.), *Ethnic dimensions of aging* (pp. 51–63). New York: Springer.

Betancourt, H., & Lopez, S. R. (1993). The study of culture, ethnicity, and race in American psychology. *American Psychologist, 48,* 629–637.

Brandtstadter, J., & Rothermund, K. (1994). Self-perception of control in middle and later adulthood: Buffering losses by rescaling goals. *Psychology and Aging, 9,* 265–273.

Brown, T. N., Sellars, S. L., Brown, K. T., & Jackson, J. S. (1999). Race, ethnicity, and culture in the sociology of mental health. In C. S. Aneshensel & J. C. Phelan (Eds.), *Handbook of the sociology of mental health* (pp. 167–182). New York: Kluwer Academic/Plenum.

Carter, J. S., Pugh, J. A., & Monterrosa, A. (1996). Non-insulin dependent diabetes mellitus in minorities in the United States. *Annals of Internal Medicine, 125,* 221–232.

Carter, J. S., Wiggins, C. L., Becker, T. M., Key, C. R., & Samet, J. M. (1993). Diabetes mortality among New Mexico's American Indian, Hispanic and non-Hispanic white populations, 1958–1987. *Diabetes Care, 16,* 306–309.

Cohen, L. M. (1985). Controlarse and the problems of life among Latino immigrants. In W. A. Vega & M. R. Miranda (Eds.), *Stress and Hispanic mental health* (pp. 202–219). Rockville, MD: National Institute of Mental Health.

Davis, F. J. (1991). *Who is black?: One nation's definition.* University Park: Pennsylvania State University Press.

Fisher, L., Chesla, C., Skaff, M. M., Gillis, C., Kanter, R., Lutz, C. P., & Bartz, R. J. (2000). Disease management status: A typology of Latino and Euro-American patients with type 2 diabetes. *Behavioral Medicine, 26,* 53–66.

Fung, H. H., Abeles, R. P., & Carstensen, L. L. (1999). Psychological control in later life: Implications for life-span development. In J. Brandtstadter & R. M. Lerner (Eds.), *Action and self-development: Theory and research through the life-span* (pp. 345–372). Thousand Oaks, CA: Sage.

Hunt, L. M., Pugh, J. A., & Valenzuela, M. A. (1997). How patients adapt diabetes self-care recommendations in everyday life. *Journal of Family Practice, 46*(3), 207–215.

Hunt, L. M., Valenzuela, M. A., & Pugh, J. A. (1998). Porque me toco a mi?: Mexican American diabetes patients' causal stories and their relationship to treatment behaviors. *Social Science Medicine, 46,* 959–969.

Kohn, M. L., & Schooler, C. (1982). Job conditions and personality: A longitudinal assessment of their reciprocal effects. *American Journal of Sociology, 87,* 1257–1286.

Kojima, H. (1984). A significant stride toward the comparative study of control. *American Psychologist, 39,* 972–973.

Marin, G., & Marin, B. V. (1991). *Research with Hispanic populations.* Newbury Park, CA: Sage.

Markus, H. R., & Kitayama, S. (1991). Culture and the self: Implications for cognition, emotion, and motivation. *Psychological Review, 98,* 224–253.

Mirowsky, J., & Ross, C. E. (1984). Mexican culture and its emotional contradictions. *Journal of Health and Social Behavior, 25,* 2–13.

Mizell, C. A. (1999). African American men's personal sense of mastery: The consequences of the adolescent environment, self-concept, and adult achievement. *Journal of Black Psychology, 25,* 210–230.

Neff, J. A. (1993). Life stressors, drinking patterns, and depressive symptomatology: Ethnicity and stress-buffer effects of alcohol. *Addictive Behaviors, 18,* 373–387.

Neff, J. A., & Hoppe, S. K. (1993). Race/ethnicity, acculturation, and psychological distress: Fatalism and religiosity as cultural resources. *Journal of Community Psychology, 21,* 3–20.

Nopales-Springer, A., & Stewart, A. L. (2001). Use of health-related quality of life measures in older and ethnically diverse U.S. populations. *Journal of Mental Health and Aging, 71,* 173–179.

Oettingen, G., & Maier, H. (1999). Where political system meets culture: Effects on efficacy appraisal. In Y. T. Lee, C. R. McCauley, & J. G. Draguns (Eds.), *Personality and person perception across cultures* (pp. 163–190). Mahwah, NJ: Erlbaum.

Pearlin, L. I., & Schooler, C. (1978). The structure of coping. *Journal of Health and Social Behavior, 19,* 2–21.

Pearlin, L. I., & Skaff, M. M. (1996). Stress and the life course: A paradigmatic alliance. *The Gerontologist, 36,* 239–247.

Pervin, L. A. (1999). The cross-cultural challenge to personality. In Y.-T. Lee, C. R. McCauley, & J. G. Draguns (Eds.), *Personality and person perception across cultures* (pp. 23–41). Mahwah, NJ: Erlbaum.

Pill, R. M., & Stott, N. C. H. (1987). The stereotype of "working-class fatalism" and the challenge for primary care health promotion. *Health Education Research, 2,* 105–114.

Revenson, T. A. (1990). All other things are not equal: An ecological approach to personality and disease. In H. S. Friedman (Ed.), *Personality and disease* (pp. 65–94). New York: Wiley.

Rini, C. K., Dunkel-Schetter, C., Wadhwa, P. D., & Sandman, C. A. (1999). Psychological adaptation and birth outcomes: The role of personal resources, stress, and sociocultural context in pregnancy. *Health Psychology, 18,* 333–345.

Rodin, J. (1990). Control by any other name: Definitions, concepts, and processes. In J. Rodin, C. Schooler, & K. W. Schaie (Eds.), *Self-directedness: Cause and effects throughout the life course* (pp. 1–17). Hillsdale, NJ: Erlbaum.

Rogler, L. H. (1999). Methodological sources of cultural insensitivity in mental health research. *American Psychologist, 54,* 424–433.

Ross, C. E., & Mirowsky, J. (1989). Explaining the social patterns of depression: Control and problem solving—or support and talking? *Journal of Health and Social Behavior, 30,* 206–219.

Ross, C. E., Mirowsky, J., & Cockerham, W. C. (1983). Social class, Mexican culture, and fatalism: Their effects on psychological distress. *American Journal of Community Psychology, 11,* 383–399.

Ross, C. E., & Sastry, J. (1999). The sense of personal control: Social-structural causes and emotional consequences. In C. S. Aneshensel & J. C. Phelan (Eds.), *Handbook of the sociology of mental health* (pp. 369–394). New York: Kluwer Academic/Plenum.

Sastry, J., & Ross, C. E. (1998). Asian ethnicity and the sense of personal control. *Social Psychology Quarterly, 61,* 101–120.

Schooler, C. (1990). Individualism and the historical and social-structural determinants of people's concerns over self-directedness and efficacy. In J. Rodin, C. Schooler, & K. W. Schaie (Eds.), *Self-directedness: Causes and effects throughout the life course* (pp. 19–49). Hillsdale, NJ: Erlbaum.

Schulz, R., & Heckhausen, J. (1999). Aging, culture, and control: Setting a new research agenda. *Journal of Gerontology: Psychological Sciences, 54B,* P139–P145.

Schwab, T., Meyer, J., & Merrell, R. (1994). Measuring attitudes and health beliefs among Mexican Americans with diabetes. *The Diabetes Educator, 20,* 221–227.

Skaff, M. M. (1998, November). *Levels of control and health: Family and ethnic contexts.* Paper presented at the Gerontological Society of America, Philadelphia.

Skaff, M. M., Mullan, J. T., Fisher, L., & Chesla, C. (in press). Control, behavior, and health: A biopsychosocial view of type 2 diabetes.

Skinner, E. A. (1996). A guide to constructs of control. *Journal of Personality and Social Psychology, 71*(3), 549–570.

Surgenor, L. J., Horn, J., Hudson, S. M., Lunt, H., & Tennent, J. (2000). Metabolic control and psychological sense of control in women with diabetes mellitus: Alternative considerations of the relationship. *Journal of Psychosomatic Research, 49,* 267–273.

Triandis, H. C. (1995). The self and social behavior in differing cultural contexts. In N. R. Goldberger & J. B. Veroff (Eds.), *The culture and psychology reader* (pp. 326–365). New York: New York University Press.

Triandis, H. C. (1997). Cross-cultural perspectives on personality. In R. Hogan, J. Johnson, & S. Briggs (Eds.), *Handbook of personality psychology* (pp. 439–464). San Diego: Academic Press.

Varghese, R., & Medinger, F. (1979). Fatalism in response to stress among the minority aged. In D. E. Gelfand & A. J. Kutzik (Eds.), *Ethnicity and aging: Theory, research, and policy* (pp. 96–116). New York: Springer.

Vega, W. A. (1992). Theoretical and pragmatic implications of cultural diversity for community research. *American Journal of Community Psychology, 20,* 375–391.

Weisz, J. R. (1990). Development of control-related beliefs, goals, and styles in childhood and adolescence: A clinical perspective. In J. Rodin, C. Schooler, & K. W. Schaie (Eds.), *Self-directedness: Causes and effects throughout the life course* (pp. 103–145). Hillsdale, NJ: Erlbaum.

Weisz, J. R., Rothbaum, F. M., & Blackburn, T. C. (1984). Standing out and standing in: The psychology of control in American and Japan. *American Psychologist, 39,* 955–969.

Wheaton, B. (1983). Stress, personal coping resources, and psychiatric symptoms. *Journal of Health and Social Behavior, 24,* 208–229.

Commentary

Sense of Control and Aging: Racial and Cultural Factors

Kyriakos S. Markides

America's population is experiencing rapid rates of increasing racial and ethnic diversity much of it fueled by rapid rates of immigration from all parts of the world. This increasing diversity of the population is taking place not just in the United States but also in most western countries, including Canada, Australia, and Western Europe.

In the United States, preliminary data from the 2000 Census indicate that Hispanics now number over 35 million and are about equal to the African American population. Although most Hispanics are still of Mexican origin, there have been rapid increases of Hispanics from other origins, especially from various Central American origins. Even more diverse are the rapidly growing Asian origin populations now numbering over 10 million.

By 2050 about half of the Unites States population will be ethnic minorities, using current definitions. Definitions of majority-minority status and ethnicity are likely to change with rapidly shrinking proportions of non-Hispanic Whites and rising rates of intermarriage. Indeed, a higher proportion than expected picked more than one racial or ethnic group identity on the 2000 Census form, the first time that option was available.

Although most of the growing diverse groups of Americans are relatively young demographically, they are experiencing rapid rates of aging. Subsequently, an increasing proportion of the nation's elderly will be African Americans, Hispanic Americans, Asian Americans, and Native Americans, the four major ethnic groups currently considered minorities.

With these changes in mind, Skaff and Gardiner (this volume) call for more attention by the literature on sense of control to the social and cultural context in which it takes place, especially factors related to age and ethnicity/minority status. Indeed, all social and behavioral sciences, and the scientific establishment in general, must pay attention to the increasing diversity of the population of the United States, as well as the population of other western countries. I welcome this call to seriously look at ethnic and cultural factors as they might influence people's sense of control, other psychological factors, social factors, and how we age. We need research and better theory to help us understand the aging process.

As we look to the future, we must answer questions about the changing meaning of ethnic and cultural factors. Will the 100 million projected Hispanics in the United States by 2050 be culturally and socially "Hispanic" as we know them today? Will the increased ethnic diversity be translated into cultural diversity as we know it today? Will the cultures of sending countries in Latin America, Asia, and Africa also be changing as a result of globalization and economic development? For example, will these countries continue to be characterized as having "collectivistic" cultural orientations?

PSYCHOLOGY, CONTROL, AND CULTURE

Skaff and Gardiner propose that there is a need to bring the largely separate literatures on control and culture together so that psychological theories of control can be broadened. The authors say that what they "are proposing may be seen as heretical by some traditional scholars who believe that there are universal traits that stand . . . across times and cultures." When I first began seriously looking at the literature on ethnicity (especially with respect to aging) over 25 years ago, I recall reading a paper by an older and wiser scholar who at that time predicted that we were unlikely to discover that ethnicity and culture have significant influences on psychological variables. Rather, influences would be found in social factors and social relations. Clearly, Skaff and Gardiner think otherwise.

When looking at the psychological literature on aging, it becomes quickly apparent that ethnicity is not a major concern. For example, the *Handbook of the Psychology of Aging* (Birren & Schaie, 1996) has only one reference to race/ethnicity, specifically to religious support available to African Americans and Hispanic elderly by the church (McFadden, 1996). At the same time, the *Handbook of Aging and the Social Sciences* (Binstock & George, 1995) devotes a whole chapter to race/ethnicity and aging (Markides & Black, 1995). That literature has focused primarily on socioeconomic status (SES), financial resources, family relations and social supports, psychological well-being, and health and mental health. The latter has received growing attention in recent years partly because of the National Institutes of Health policy on including minorities in funded research on health and partly because of major initiatives to fund research on certain ethnic minority groups.

Is sense of control culturally invariant? The answer depends on what is meant by control. In describing their life span theory of control, Schulz, Wrosch, and Heckhausen (this volume) focus on primary and secondary control and argue that striving for control is a cultural universal that is invariant across time and place. Although there may be cultural variations in how control striving is expressed, the primacy of primary control is a culturally invariant trait.

In a recent article, Shaw and Krause (2001) examined racial variations in personal control and aging. Their measure of control (primary control, as they note) consisted of three items ("When bad things happen, we are not supposed to know why. We are just supposed to accept them"; "People die when it is their time to die, and nothing can change that"; "If bad things happen, it is because they are meant to be") that can be characterized as measures of fatalistic attitudes or external locus of control. As they note, the literature suggests that there are clear race differences in feelings of control (e.g., Mirowsky, Ross, & Van Willigan, 1996) as well as a decline in feelings of control with advancing years (Schulz, Heckhausen, & O'Brien, 1994). Although there were no racial differences in the association between age and control, racial differences in feelings of control persisted across age groups, suggesting that African Americans are disadvantaged as they face the challenges of advancing age. Because racial differences in control persisted after socioeconomic and health status differences were statistically removed, it is possible that other factors associated with race, such as history of discrimination and certain unknown cultural differences, are responsible for their findings.

Examining unique histories of ethnic groups in terms of how they might influence their sense of control (and other outcomes) is thus of great importance. Skaff and Gardiner write about the importance of how unique histories of certain groups, such as enslavement of African Americans, genocide of Native Americans, confiscation of land from Mexican Americans, and importation and imprisonment of Asian Americans, might influence sense of control. The literature has typically resorted to such unique histories to explain, for example, poor socioeconomic conditions in certain groups. How sense of control today in these groups is influenced by these unique histories has not been directly examined with the literature remaining rather speculative.

MIGRATION EXPERIENCES

Skaff and Gardiner write of the importance of examining the impact of different immigration experiences on sense of control and related constructs. They point to a variety of factors that might influence feelings of control, such as differences between countries of origin and destination, SES differences, language, and acculturation. Migration is on the rise worldwide, some of it forced by war and other conflict. Much of it, however, is voluntary. Although most migration is internal, taking place within countries, there has been greater interest by researchers in international migration and how it affects immigrants' socioeconomic and health status. Migration to western societies is mostly voluntary in nature, and research has focused on both positive and negative consequences. There is virtually no literature on how immigration affects immigrants' sense of control.

The literature on the health consequences of international migration to western societies has focused almost exclusively on the health problems and health needs of immigrants. Despite this focus, there is growing evidence, to the surprise of many, that immigrants appear to be as healthy as, if not healthier than, natives. One important reason is a "healthy migrant" or "migration selection" effect, which has been used to explain the relatively good health of Mexican Americans in the United States, a socioeconomically disadvantaged population (Markides & Coreil, 1986). More recently, Hummer, Rogers, Nam, and LeClere (1999) documented consistently lower mortality rates among the foreign-born in all major ethnic groups (Blacks, Hispanics, and those of Asian origin). Similar results have been observed in Canada with respect to various measures of health status (Chen, Ng, & Wilkins, 1996), as well as in Australia (Donovan, d'Espaignet, Merton, & van Ommeren, 1992) and Western Europe (Junghans, 1998).

Besides the fact that healthy people tend to be more apt to immigrate, western countries require medical screenings of prospective immigrants. Furthermore, most people immigrate for employment and occupational reasons, which require relatively good health. Finally, people who immigrate tend to have a positive outlook on their future, which is consistent with good health. All the above are consistent with the notion that people migrate in order to exercise better control over their lives. Yet research on immigrants' sense of control has not been conducted. Extant literature, however, suggests that we should be careful in assuming that immigrants from certain cultures will typically have collectivistic worldviews and be characterized by secondary control (Markides, 2001).

There has also been some interest in how immigration might influence the aging process and intergenerational relations. It has been observed that people immigrating early in life seem to adjust reasonably well to their new environments. Older immigrants, who typically move to be with their children, fare worse because of linguistic and cultural barriers. With time, their children become acculturated and assimilated into the larger society, and intergenerational frictions often develop (Markides & Black, 1995). Does aging in a foreign culture reduce older immigrants' sense of control? Probably for those immigrating late in life who remain socially and culturally isolated from the mainstream and whose children become part of the mainstream. Clearly, empirical studies testing this and similar hypotheses are needed.

SOCIOECONOMIC STATUS, RACE/ETHNICITY, AND CONTROL

Skaff and Gardiner point out the significance of understanding how socioeconomic status and race/ethnicity interact to influence outcomes. This has always been a big issue in the field of aging. They say that sometimes it "is difficult to disentangle the effects of SES on sense of control from those of race and ethnicity." One way to deal with the problem is to oversample middle- and upper-class ethnic minority respondents (which is often done). Another way is to also oversample lower SES non-Hispanic Whites. This may lead to a better understanding of the meaning of SES in different ethnic contexts. Will poor Whites be "worse off" on a number of indicators than poor minority respondents? We do not know (see Rudkin & Markides, 2001).

The authors note that controlling for SES often makes ethnic differences disappear. However, they go on to say that it may not make sense to statistically remove what is an important reality in people's life. We can also say that if ethnic differences disappear when SES is controlled, it does not mean that ethnicity or minority status is not important, because both are the cause of SES differences (Markides & Black, 1995).

CONCEPTUAL APPROACHES TO THE STUDY OF CONTROL ACROSS GROUPS

Skaff and Gardiner speak of "the growing literature applying the primary-secondary control distinction in the study of aging," which suggests a shift from primary to secondary control, as people get older (Brandt-stadter & Rothermund, 1994; Schulz & Heckhausen, 1999; see also, Schulz, Wrosch, & Heckhausen, this volume). It was good to see this because it is one of the few references to aging in the chapter. Yet we may want to place this statement in historical/cultural context, because there were probably times when older people exercised more primary control. At the same time, we live at a time when older people in western countries are commanding an increasing share of economic resources. There is also evidence that older people are becoming healthier and less disabled. Yet, as the authors point out, socioeconomic disparities between ethnic groups remain large (see Chen, 1999).

The authors present a model of culture and sense of control. This approach to how culture and ethnicity influence control can be applied to the study of other general constructs, such as self-esteem and psychological well-being. Fatalism, which is related to the concept of external locus of control, is mentioned with reference to the literature on Hispanics. As the authors note, this is somewhat controversial because the literature often stereotypes certain groups. When socioeconomic differences are controlled, differences in fatalistic attitudes often disappear. Yet low SES is a reality in certain groups' lives and has consequences for behavior, especially with respect to health. As the authors note, fatalistic attitudes do not always have negative consequences, especially with respect to mental health.

There is also discussion of the individualistic/collectivistic perspective on sense of control and the need to know more about whether it is the individual or the group that is more responsible for control. This reminds one of anecdotal evidence about end of life decisions in Mexican American elderly, who often would leave all decision-making to their children. The chapter also comments on issues related to measurement to achieve cross-cultural equivalence, not just linguistic equivalence. This is important, of course, in all cross-cultural research.

The authors' study of diabetes and control is interesting. It was good to see that they achieved comparability across Hispanics and non-Hispanic Whites on measures of control. When they looked at outcomes, they found that self-efficacy was related to diet and exercise among non-Hispanic Whites, whereas global mastery was related to these behaviors among Latinos. They conclude that even when measures are comparable across cultures, relationships with outcomes may vary, which may support the existence of cultural differences in how psychological variables influence behavior. However, why these differences exist remains unclear.

CONCLUSION

Skaff and Gardiner's (this volume) call for attention to ethnic and cultural factors in the study of sense of control should be applauded. These factors have not been a major part of psychological theory and the psychology of aging. This call is likely to be met with skepticism by those who believe in the cultural and historical universality of certain psychological traits. The literature also needs to make aging a more central issue: The issue is whether sense of control and related concepts changes differentially in different ethnic/cultural contexts as people age. Of particular importance is how immigration is influenced by sense of control and how it differentially influences sense of control at different ages or stages of the life course.

REFERENCES

Binstock, R. H., & George, L. K. (Eds.). (1995). *Handbook of aging and the social sciences* (4th ed.). San Diego: Academic Press.

Birren, J. E., & Schaie, K. W. (Eds.). (1996). *Handbook of the psychology of aging* (4th ed.). San Diego: Academic Press.

Brandtstadter, J., & Rothermund, K. (1994). Self-perception of control in middle and late adulthood: Buffering losses by rescaling goals. *Psychology and Aging, 9,* 265–273.

Chen, J., Ng, E., & Wilkins, R. (1996). The health of Canada's immigrants in 1994–1995. *Health Reports, 7,* 33–45.

Chen, Y. P. (1999). Racial disparity in retirement income security: Directions for policy reform. In T. P. Miles (Ed.), *Full-color aging: Facts, goals, and recommendations for America's diverse elders* (pp. 21–30). Washington, DC: Gerontological Society of America.

Donovan, J., d'Espaignet, E., Merton, C., & van Ommeren, M. (Eds.). (1992). *Immigrants in Australia: A health profile.* Ethnic Health Series No. 1. Canberra: Australian Institute of Health and Welfare.

Hummer, R. A., Rogers, R. G., Nam, C. B., & LeClere, F. B. (1999). Race/ethnicity, nativity, and U.S. adult mortality. *Social Science Quarterly, 80,* 136–153.

Junghans, T. (1998). How unhealthy is migrating? *Tropical Medicine and International Health, 3,* 933–934.

Markides, K. S. (2001). Migration and health. In P. B. Baltes & N. J. Smelser (Eds.), *International Encyclopedia of the Social and Behavioral Sciences* (pp. 9799–9803). New York and Amsterdam: Elsevier.

Markides, K. S., & Black, S. A. (1995). Race, ethnicity, and aging: The impact of inequality. In R. H. Binstock & L. K. George (Eds.), *Handbook of aging and the social sciences* (4th ed., pp. 153–167). San Diego: Academic Press.

Markides, K. S., & Coreil, J. (1986). The health of Southwestern Hispanics: An epidemiologic paradox. *Public Health Reports, 101,* 253–265.

McFadden, S. H. (1996). Religion, spirituality, and aging. In J. E. Birren & K. W. Schaie (Eds.), *Handbook of the psychology of aging* (4th ed., pp. 150–161). San Diego: Academic Press.

Mirowsky, J., Ross, C. E., & Van Willigen, M. (1996). Instrumentalism in the land of opportunity: Socioeconomic causes and emotional consequences. *Social Psychology Quarterly, 59,* 322–337.

Rudkin, L., & Markides, K. S. (2001). Measuring socioeconomic status of elderly people in health studies with special focus on minority aging. *Journal of Mental Health and Aging, 7,* 53–66.

Schulz, R., & Heckhausen, J. (1999). Aging, culture, and control: Setting a new research agenda. *Journal of Gerontology: Psychological Sciences, 54B,* P135–P145.

Schulz, R., Heckhausen, J., & O'Brien, A. T. (1994). Control and the disablement process in the elderly. *Journal of Social Behavior and Personality, 9,* 139–152.

Shaw, B. A., & Krause, N. (2001). Exploring race variations in aging and personal control. *Journal of Gerontology: Social Sciences, 56B,* S119–S124.

Skaff, M. M., Mullan, J. T., Fisher, L., & Chesla, C. (in press). Control, behavior, and health: A biopsychosocial view of type 2 diabetes.

Commentary

A Cultural Contextual Model of Personal Control: Controlling Reality or the Reality of Control

Pamela Braboy Jackson and John J. Wilkins III

> What is real? How do you define real? If you're talking about what you feel, smell, taste, and see, then real is simply electrical signals interpreted by your brain.
>
> —Morpheus, in the movie *The Matrix* (1999)

Culture consists of the physical or material objects and values, attitudes, customs, beliefs, and habits shared by members of a group and transmitted to the next generation. A conceptualization of cultural context implies an embeddedness of these ideals within a certain objective reality of materially based elements, often referred to as cultural capital. Thus, the meaning of control is partially dependent on ascribed statuses as they interconnect with the resources available to a group to help cope with life circumstances. Our comments will be limited to the conceptualization of cultural context in Skaff and Gardiner's (this volume) contextual model of personal control rather than the three dimensions of agency, mechanisms, and targets of control. The reclassification of these concepts should move forward future research in the area of personal control.

We will focus on the distinction between the cultural belief that people have the ability to personally control what is real and the reality of personal control. In essence, Skaff and Gardiner (this volume) argue that there is a reality outside of culturally sanctioned beliefs about personal control. Their inspiration comes from Abeles' (1990) model of personal control. But where objective reality operates independently in Abeles' model of sense of control, objective reality interacts with personal and vicarious experience in Skaff and Gardiner's chapter. Although we are in agreement with Skaff and Gardiner that variation in personal control is often a realistic assessment of opportunity structures, we reach this conclusion by different pathways. We believe that historical time is the organizing principle around most of the experiences described by Skaff and Gardiner. In fact, the primary source of variation in personal control as discussed by these authors is the unstable pathway of historical time. But reality, like many social constructs, is layered. Historical time interacts with the two layers we will discuss: status characteristics and cultural capital.

The purpose of this commentary, then, is to present a conceptual framework that permits the explication of historical time as a fundamental regulatory mechanism in human development (Elder, 1979). The primary focus, however, is on race/ethnicity, because much of the premise on which a contextual model is introduced by Skaff and Gardiner centers on the changing racial/ethnic composition of the population of the United States. The generality of the model can be seen in its relevance to other status characteristics, especially gender and age.

The primary function of the model is to explain both stability and change in personal control. The discussion will use existing research to highlight certain features of the model. Although empirical research will be needed before a contextual model can be fully appreciated, the model captures the complexity of time and can therefore serve as a useful point of departure for research on personal development. The following discussion is highlighted in Figure 3.2.

REALITY LAYER 1: STATUS CHARACTERISTICS

Race/Ethnicity

Historical time speaks directly to the ethnic dimension of the cultural model proposed by Skaff and Gardiner. Here, reality is situated in the

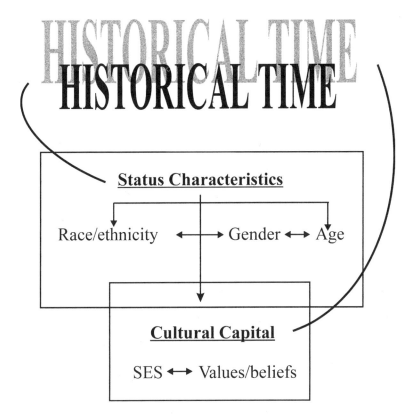

FIGURE 3.2   How historical time defines cultural context.

fact that the United States was colonized by Northern Europeans. In the process, Native Americans, African Americans, and Mexican Americans, in particular, lived the experience and carry the legacy of internal colonialism. The four components of colonialism that interact with perceive control are (1) control over a minority group's governance, (2) restriction of a racial minority's freedom of movement, (3) the colonial labor principle, and (4) the belief in the inferiority of a minority group's culture and social organization (Doob, 1996).

Historically, Whites have controlled the political process. The broadest American legislative effort to eliminate discrimination in politics was the 1965 Voting Rights Act. Nonetheless, the legacy of literacy tests, poll taxes, and grandfather clauses continues to resonate in the minds of many ethnic minorities. More recent accusations of intimidation by the police and voter fraud in Florida during the presidential race of 2000 did little to boost minority confidence in the political process. Similarly, Bee (1990) found that government officials still impose a great deal of control on Indian reservations that receive federal funding for business development. In other words, minorities continue to be politically disadvantaged and firmly believe that Whites are in control of the governance process.

The second element of internal colonialism is control over the movement of the group. This pattern is most evident in America's history of residential segregation. Following disfranchisement, Jim Crow measures were enacted in the late 19th and early 20th centuries to separate minorities and Whites in almost all areas of social life, including housing. More importantly, racial segregation was maintained by force and ideology. With the rise of vigilante groups such as the Ku Klux Klan, fear and humiliation were integral parts of everyday life for many Blacks. Today, ethnic minorities still report intimidation by majority group members, do not feel safe traveling to different parts of the United States, and are clearly not welcomed in certain U.S. cities.

The third element is the colonial labor principle, which dictates control over the type of work minorities can do. There is much evidence that early theories of eugenics promoted the view that Africans were good at hand work and Whites at mind work (Gould, 1981). Historically, Mexican immigrants have suffered under the colonial labor principle. Those individuals who were illegal aliens have especially been under employer control, forced to accept illegally low wages and vulnerable to layoffs during economic downturns (Hraba, 1994). In essence, minorities have been required to serve at the pleasure of those who owned or employed them.

The final component of colonialism is the belief that minorities should embrace the culture of the dominant group because minority culture, especially a minority's native language, is considered inferior. The plight of Spanish-speaking individuals, in particular, is a product of Anglo ethnocentrism, which ignores the value of any language other than English. When annexation of land territory occurs, the dominant power generally suppresses the language and culture of the minority. Through vicarious experiences of ancestors, these particular immigrants incorporate into their sense of control schema ideas about where they fit in the world.

Although a consideration of the inequities imposed on minorities implies that conflict theory is an appropriate paradigm for this piece, we believe the authors are arguing instead that a conflictual history has become part of minority culture. There is some evidence that there was a gradual and pervasive change in people's values. For example, freed African slaves following the Civil War thought they could achieve equal status, but ensuing conflicts and struggles reshaped their attitudes—a phenomenon often referred to as cultural drift. As such, a conflictual history may have become an integral component of the cognitive schema for historically disenfranchised ethnic minorities. There is a collective consensus of oppression among minority groups (Sigelman & Welch, 1991; Trimble & Richardson, 1982, 1983).

Other Status Characteristics

Like race/ethnicity, gender is a highly visible characteristic. However, it is the patriarchical power system that defines gender oppression. Gender roles vary across time and societies, but throughout recorded history women have commonly occupied a subordinate status. In fact, women were often included in early theories of eugenics and considered as biologically inferior to the Northern European male, as were Africans (Gould, 1981). In most western societies, men claim more power, prestige, and property than women (Healey, 1995, p. 25).

It was through the collective efforts of the women's liberation movement in the United States that many women gained the right to vote and were allowed to compete for high-paying jobs. It has only been in the last 40 years or so that women's lives have changed in terms of economic opportunities. Nonetheless, women are not equal partners with men in the economic, political, or social arena. For example, women earn approximately 70 cents for every dollar earned by men (U.S. Bureau of the Census, 1995), women continue to be underrepresented in political office (Clark, 1991), and much of the household responsibilities, including child care, fall on women (Ciscel, Sharp, & Heath, 2000; Stohs, 2000). Thus, women's standard of living is still tied to men's lives.

The link between age and historical time is much more complicated than race/ethnicity and gender, primarily because of the problem in distinguishing between age differences and age changes. Maddox (1979) referred to this issue as the age/period/cohort problem. Age is assessed through birth year. Period refers to the effects of a specific historical event on a group of people. Cohorts are groups of individuals born at roughly the same time.

Very briefly, much of the research on age and personal control considers age differences—comparing people of different chronological ages at the same measurement period. Thus, when older adults are found to report lower perceived control than younger adults, investigators interpret these findings as evidence of the aging process. An alternative explanation could be that the lower educational levels of the cohort of elderly in the study leads to diminished feelings of control. As Mirowsky (1995, p. 41) explains, "[T]he relative importance of education . . . suggests intergenerational improvements in lifetime living and working conditions. Older generations may have felt less in control of their own lives at all ages."

Period and cohort effects are related to historical circumstances. There may be particular cultural or historical conditions that shape each group. But age changes are often referred to as period effects. Longitudinal research is necessary to assess how one generation may be different from the next. These types of research designs highlight period effects while simultaneously eliminating cohort effects by studying the same people over time.

Nonetheless, the interaction between individual time and historical time results in birth cohort effects. As noted by Ryder (1965, p. 845), "[E]ach cohort has a distinctive composition and character reflecting the circumstances of its unique origination and history." Thus, for the purposes of a contextual model of personal control, a division by age groups over time would be a more telling story of the relationship between age and personal control than current designs that rely on information gathered at one point in time.

There are several issues the investigator must consider in exploring the context of personal control among the elderly. For example, there have been changing images of old age throughout history. In the 17th and 18th century in America, old age was treated with deference and respect because it was so rare. Thus, one might expect a relatively stable sense of personal control over the life course. However, some argue that the status and authority of the elderly have declined significantly as a result of modernization (Cowgill, 1986; Cowgill & Holmes, 1972). Modernization, especially through the introduction of health technology, has increased the number of older persons in the population. At the same time, social policies have altered our definitions of old age and placed certain features of society out of the control of older adults (e.g., full-time participation in the paid labor market). We should consider objective control in personal control models of the elderly simply because many events that accompany old age place limits on actual control (Rodin, 1990).

In essence, status characteristics generate the conditions that shape beliefs about personal control (Mirowsky, 1995). Not surprisingly, then, ethnic minorities, women, and older adults report a lower sense of personal control than Whites, men, and younger people, respectively (Hughes & Demo, 1989; Nolen-Hoeksema, Grayson, & Larson, 1999; Mirowsky, 1995). As demonstrated by the above discussion, these findings fit the historical reality of control. As suggested by the arrows between each status characteristic in Figure 3.2, elements within this dimension of the model may interact, such that women born following the women's liberation movement may have a stronger sense of personal control than women born before the movement; older ethnic minorities may feel less control than their younger peers; and minority females may be at a disadvantage in levels of control than White females. A sense of control generally reflects real resources and opportunities (Mirowsky & Ross, 1990). Although we suspect that real control influences perceived control, it is the temporal aspect of lives that is most important to consider in contextual models of control.

REALITY LAYER 2: CULTURAL CAPITAL

There is a reciprocal relationship between individual lives and the social structure in which people are embedded. The next level of our reality model, then, simply reflects certain features of the opportunity structure available within a society. It is social structure. Again, we take as our point of departure the model presented by Skaff and Gardiner. Instead of including SES and values/beliefs within the same layer of reality as history, we separate them to represent sources of cultural capital. Cultural capital can include educational credentials, knowledge, and the lifestyles of the people involved. Cultural capital can be viewed as personal resources available to individuals to help them cope with stress and organize information about the world.

In general, cultural capital cannot be fully understood exclusive of its interaction with external historical forces (Hareven, 1978). For example, there have been cultural changes in norms and beliefs across time pertaining to different social groups (e.g., ethnic minorities, women, and the elderly). Educational and economic opportunities have been allocated differently under different historical circumstances. Relatedly, images of the elderly in historical time were tied to the authority that older people exercised and the material and political resources they controlled.

Cultural capital is generally attained through socialization (values and beliefs). Although other types of capital are acquired well into adulthood (e.g., education, income, and occupation), social mobility studies continue to show the long-term effects of parental SES on adult well-being (e.g., Mizell, 1999). That is, even cultural capital is contingent on initial positions in the social structure.

Adopting a multilayered conceptual model whose components interact with historical time allows us to consider cross-cultural variation both within and outside a particular society. For example, newer voluntary immigrants to the United States and those older immigrants not affected by internal colonialism may not believe that their race/ethnicity is a relevant source of information about how the world works. They may, instead, rely on information about their cultural capital. Again, values and beliefs are one source of cultural capital that may help contextualize the sense of personal control schema. To the extent that there is consistency between the values and beliefs of the individual and the dominant host culture, the sense of control schema should fit the model set forth by the dominant culture (Liebkind & Jasinskaja, 2000). In the example by Skaff and Gardiner, John Wayne becomes the role model. We can expect individuals who do not measure up to John Wayne (believing that John Wayne is the man to be emulated) to report low levels of personal control. Similarly, highly educated individuals who immigrate to countries that value educational credentials should have a higher sense of control than their peers who enter the same society without such credentials. The relevance of cultural capital determines what is really possible to achieve—reality.

We may then ask, on what layer of reality are people more likely to rely? We believe the extent to which groups rely on information about status characteristics or cultural capital (or the interaction of these factors with historical time) depends on the salience of a particular identity. How do I see myself interacting with the environment? From what cognitive framework am I interpreting social interaction? What aspects of my emotional functioning do I value? These are questions raised by a cultural model of control. Other investigators have considered many of these issues as they relate to individual differences across cultures (see Oishi, 2000, for a review) and ethnic identity salience (see Larkey & Hecht, 1995; Thompson, 1999; Ting et al., 2000). In essence, a consideration of context attempts to account for differences in personal control without the yardstick of Anglo conformity.

CONCLUSION

So, then, what is real? Let us return to this philosophical question posed at the beginning of our discussion. According to many social scientists, race is nothing more than a social construct (Brown, 2001). Such categorization may help us simplify and organize external stimuli, but social constructs exist only in our minds. Our actions towards our environment are not restricted because of people's physical characteristics. We really can have family members and close friends who do not look like us. Can't we?

The premise of the film *The Matrix* was simply that many people operate under the illusion of control. Real control goes beyond what we can feel, smell, taste, and see. We live our lives and accept our personal circumstances even when we are not happy with our current existence. *The Matrix* has successfully blinded us from the truth. What is the truth? The truth is that we have limited our social relationships and activities to what others dictate can or cannot be realized. In other words, actual control is a reality; what we perceive as real is not actuality. Real control must be accessed beyond our current levels of thinking. We must free our minds. A cultural contextual model of personal control recommends a broader discussion of this issue among the scientific community, along with Hollywood. A cultural model of control urges us to change our definition of real because, ultimately, what we perceive as real is real in its consequences (Thomas, 1936).

REFERENCES

Abeles, R. (1990). Schemas, sense of control, and aging. In J. Rodin, C. Schooler, & K. W. Schaie (Eds.), *Self-directedness: Cause and effects throughout the life course* (pp. 85–93). Hillsdale, NJ: Erlbaum.

Bee, R. (1990). The predicament of the Native American leader: A second look. *Human Organization, 49,* 56–63.

Brown, P., Jr. (2001). Biology and the social construction of the race concept. In J. Ferrante & P. Browne, Jr. (Eds.), *The social construction of race and ethnicity in the United States* (pp. 144–150). Upper Saddle River, NJ: Prentice Hall.

Ciscel, D., Sharp, D., & Heath, J. (2000). Family work trends and practices: 1971–1991. *Journal of Family and Economic Issues, 21,* 23–36.

Clark, J. (1991). Getting there: Women in political office. *Annals of the American Academy of Political and Social Science, 514,* 63–76.

Cowgill, D. (1986). *Aging around the world.* Belmont, CA: Wadsworth.

Cowgill, D., & Holmes, L. (1972). *Aging and modernization.* New York: Appleton-Century-Crofts.

Doob, C. (1996). *Racism: An American cauldron.* New York: HarperCollins.

Elder, G. (1979). Historical changes in life patterns and personality. In P. B. Baltes & O. G. Brim, Jr. (Eds.), *Life-span development and behavior* (Vol. 2, pp. 117–159).

Gould, S. J. (1981). *The mismeasure of man.* New York: Norton.

Hareven, T. K. (1978). *Transitions: The family and the life course in historical perspective.* New York: Academic Press.

Healey, J. F. (1995). *Race, ethnicity, gender, and class.* Thousand Oaks, CA: Pine Forge Press.

Hraba, J. (1994). *American ethnicity.* Itasca, IL: Peacock.

Hughes, M., & Demo, D. H. (1989). Self-perceptions of Black Americans: Self-esteem and personal efficacy. *American Journal of Sociology, 95,* 132–159.

Larkey, L., & Hecht, M. (1995). A comparative study of African American and European American ethnic identity. *International Journal of Intercultural Relations, 19,* 483–504.

Liebkind, K., & Jasinskaja, L. I. (2000). Acculturation and psychological well-being among immigrant adolescents in Finland: A comparative study of adolescents from different cultural backgrounds. *Journal of Adolescent Research, 15,* 446–469.

Maddox, G. (1979). Sociology of later life. *Annual Review of Sociology, 5,* 113–135.

Mirowsky, J. (1995). Age and the sense of control. *Social Psychology Quarterly, 58,* 31–43.

Mirowsky, J., & Ross, C. (1990). Control or defense? Depression and the sense of control over good and bad outcomes. *Journal of Health and Social Behavior, 31,* 71–86.

Mizell, C. (1999). Life course influences on African American men's depression: Adolescent parental composition, self-concept, and adult earnings. *Journal of Black Studies, 29,* 467–490.

Nolen-Hoeksema, S., Grayson, S. C., & Larson, J. (1999). Explaining the gender difference in depressive symptoms. *Journal of Personality and Social Psychology, 77,* 1061–1072.

Oishi, S. (2000). Goals as cornerstones of subjective well-being: Linking individuals and cultures. In E. Diener & E. Suh (Eds.), *Culture and subjective well-being* (pp. 87–112). Cambridge, MA: MIT Press.

Rodin, J. (1990). Control by any other name: Definitions, concepts, and processes. In J. Rodin, C. Schooler, & K. W. Schaie (Eds.), *Self-directedness: Cause and effects throughout the life course* (pp. 1–17). Hillsdale, NJ: Erlbaum.

Ryder, N. B. (1965). The cohort as a concept in the study of social change. *American Sociological Review, 30,* 843–861.

Sigelman, L., & Welch, S. (1991). *Black Americans' views of racial inequality.* New York: Cambridge University Press.

Stohs, J. (2000). Multicultural women's experience of household labor, conflicts, and equity. *Sex Roles, 42,* 339–361.

Thomas, W. I. (1936). *Primitive behavior.* New York: McGraw-Hill.

Thompson, V. L. (1999). Variables affecting racial identity salience among African Americans. *Journal of Social Psychology, 139,* 748–761.

Ting, T. S., Yee-Jung, K., Shapiro, R. B., Garcia, W., Wright, T., & Oetzel, J. (2000). Ethnic/cultural identity salience and conflict styles in four U.S. ethnic groups. *International Journal of Intercultural Relations, 24,* 47–81.

Trimble, J., & Richardson, S. (1982). Locus of control measures among American Indians: Cluster structure analytic characteristics. *Journal of Cross-Cultural Psychology, 13,* 228–238.

Trimble, J., & Richardson, S. (1983). Perceived personal and societal forms of locus of control measures among American Indians. *White Cloud Journal, 3,* 3–14.

U.S. Bureau of the Census. (1995). *Current population reports* (Series P60). Washington, DC: Government Printing Office.

CHAPTER 4

Social Structure, Stress, and Personal Control

William R. Avison and John Cairney

O ver the past two decades, researchers in several disciplines have been interested in understanding how socially induced stress manifests itself in psychological distress, in symptoms of psychiatric disorder, or in other health problems. The prototypical models of the stress process that were developed to address these issues (e.g., Billings & Moos, 1982; Cronkite & Moos, 1984; Finney, Moos, Cronkite, & Gamble, 1983; Lazarus & Folkman, 1984; Lazarus, Kanner, & Folkman, 1980; Pearlin, Lieberman, Menaghan, & Mullan, 1981) had as their primary focus the nature of the association of sources of stress with their manifestations. All of them also postulated the existence of at least three critical groups of mediators—social supports, psychosocial resources, and coping resources—that alter the effects of stressors on illness or dysfunction. The result of this early work was the development of a stress process model that rapidly became one of the dominant paradigms in social scientific research on health and illness.

One of the most important developments in research on the stress process has been the specification of the ways in which various personal resources, social supports, and coping strategies affect the relationship between stressful experience and its distressful manifestations. These so-called mediators and moderators of the stress–distress relationship have been the subjects of a vast investigative effort on the part of social scientists. One of the most prominent of these factors is mastery or sense of personal control.[1]

In this chapter, we address four issues. First, we briefly describe the manner in which mastery has been located conceptually within the stress process model. Second, following Wheaton's (1985) instructive formulation, we provide some empirical examples of the stress-buffering or moderating effects of personal control on the stress–distress relationship and also describe examples of stress mediation. Third, we consider the pivotal importance of mastery for our understanding of social variations in mental health outcomes. Finally, we discuss the ways in which the stress process paradigm can assist us in examining the social malleability of mastery.

PERSONAL CONTROL IN THE CONTEXT OF THE STRESS PROCESS

The Stress Process Paradigm

Although there is some variation in the specific content of different stress models, the depiction of the process in Figure 4.1 captures the main components. Models of the stress process begin with the proposition that social and psychological sources of stress influence health outcomes. Indeed, there have been hundreds of empirical reports of the association between stressors and health outcomes, variously measured (see Aneshensel, 1992; McLean & Link, 1994; Monroe, 1992; Monroe & McQuaid, 1994; Turner, Wheaton, & Lloyd, 1995; Wheaton, 1994, for comprehensive reviews of this literature). Early work in this area focused primarily on stressful life events as the major sources of stressors; however, more recent investigations have examined other dimensions of stressful experience such as chronic stressors, adversities in early life, life traumas, and daily hassles. Regardless of the type of stressor studied, there is consensus among researchers that these sources of stress are interrelated. For example, Pearlin and colleagues (1981) suggested that stressful life events might affect mental health by generating new chronic strains or by changing the meaning of existing strains. Similar conclusions were reached by Brown and Harris (1978) and Paykel (1978). Wheaton (1990) presented a particularly compelling exposition of the ways in which preexisting chronic stressors condition

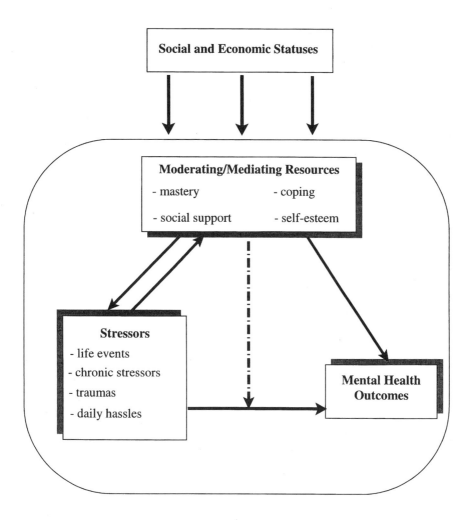

FIGURE 4.1 The stress process.

the effects of subsequent life events on distress. More recently, Pearlin, Aneshensel, and LeBlanc (1997) developed the concept of stress proliferation to describe how stressors in one area of an individual's life may generate additional stress in another area.

Another central postulate of all stress process formulations is the existence of factors that alter in some manner the impact of stressors on the expression of symptoms of illness or dysfunction. These factors either intervene between stress and illness or have interactive or buffering effects that moderate the impact of stressors on distress and disorder. In Pearlin's (1999) terms, "[M]oderating resources are conceived as having the capacity to hinder, prevent, or cushion the development of the stress process and its outcomes" (p. 405). In this context, social resources or social supports, coping resources or psychosocial resources, and coping responses or behaviors are three critical groups of mediating factors. Several important reviews of the literature on social support have been published (e.g., Cohen & Syme, 1985; Cohen & Wills, 1985; Sarason, Pierce, & Sarason, 1990; Turner & Turner, 1999). These reviews have provided incontrovertible evidence on the important role played by social support in the stress process. Moreover, they have demonstrated that the study of social support must take into account the multidimensional nature of the construct, including considerations of the structure of social networks, the functions of social support, and an awareness of the distinctions between perceived and actual support.

Individuals' psychosocial resources constitute a second important domain of mediators and moderators in stress process formulations. Research has demonstrated that self-efficacy and self-esteem are especially important psychosocial resources that affect the ways in which stressors manifest themselves as distress or disorder. Under the rubric of self-efficacy, numerous studies have demonstrated that personal constructs such as locus of control, mastery, helplessness, and fatalism have significant effects on individuals' mental health (Mirowsky & Ross, 1990; Ross & Sastry, 1999; Turner & Roszell, 1994). Similarly, there is substantial research documenting the benefits of self-esteem to mental health (Avison, 1995; Avison & McAlpine, 1992; Rosenberg, Schooler, & Schoenbach, 1989; Thoits, 1999; Turner, Lloyd, & Roszell, 1999; Turner & Roszell, 1994).

Third, variations in coping abilities and differences in the use of specific coping strategies are also central elements of stress process models. Early work on coping behaviors by Lazarus (1966), Pearlin and Schooler (1978), and Antonovsky (1979) stimulated considerable interest among stress researchers. Subsequent research has provided significant insights into the ways in which situational contexts and cognitive appraisals influence the choice of coping responses by individuals who experience stressful circumstances (Eckenrode, 1991; Menaghan, 1983; Moos, 1986). This large body of research attests to the complexity involved in understanding how individuals cope with socially induced stressors.

There is another important feature of the stress process model that resonates with a sociological perspective on the study of mental health. Most recent formulations explicitly specify the ways in which social contexts and other antecedents may condition the entire stress process. Pearlin (1989) argued persuasively that stress research has not consistently attended to the social structures that mold or condition the stress process. He maintained that the structure of social life, as reflected in statuses and social roles, has important implications for the kinds of stressors experienced by people, the kinds of mediators that are available to them, and the ways in which stressors manifest themselves. A distinctively sociological contribution to the stress process paradigm has been the emphasis placed on understanding how individuals' position in the social structure has important implications for exposure to stressors. Indeed, some would argue that the stress process model provides a useful tool for exploring the fundamental problem in the sociology of mental health: explaining the observed relationships between various social statuses and roles and measures of mental health and illness.

The result of this work has been the development of a stress process model that is widely used in the study of illness outcomes. Although various authors have modified it, variations in the stress process model typically involve the measures that are used to index the various constructs. In Figure 4.1, the solid lines symbolize causal paths that link the major constructs with one another. As can be seen, the model not only incorporates the possibility that resources mediate the effects of stressors on mental health outcomes but also predicts that resource variables may directly influence individuals' exposure to stress. The dotted line from resources that intersects the line representing the stress–outcomes relationship is meant to symbolize the moderating or buffering effect of resources. In this depiction, all of these relationships among stressors, resources, and outcomes are influenced in complex ways by social structural factors such as social and economic statuses, demographic markers, and social roles.

Mediators and Moderators in the Context of the Stress Process

Given the vast body of theory and empirical research on the role of personal resource variables in the stress process, it is disconcerting that there remains some conceptual vagueness about the mediating and moderating roles of constructs such as mastery, social support, and self-esteem. Part of this difficulty seems to emerge from researchers' realizations that these resources may have multiple functions in the stress paradigm.

This was most clearly articulated several years ago by Wheaton (1985), who set forth various models of stress buffering and stress mediation. In that article, he clearly described various potential roles that personal or coping resources such as mastery or social support might play in the stress process. He also specified quantitative methods for testing these various effects. In our view, this provides a clear theoretical and method-ological distinction between stress mediation and stress buffering.

Essentially, Wheaton argued that there are two potential models that represent the stress-buffering functions of resources such as personal control. These are presented in Figure 4.2. The first is perhaps the best known model in which mastery moderates the impact of stress on distress; that is, the impact of stress on distress declines as levels of control increase. Empirically, this can be assessed by testing for the statistical interaction of personal control and stress on distress. For most stress process researchers, this is the classic *interactive buffering effect* of mastery.

Wheaton also argued that there is another type of buffering effect that is frequently ignored in research. In this model, mastery is an intervening variable between stress and distress. Exposure to stressors results in an increase in personal control that, in turn, results in a decline in distress. Presumably, stressful experiences mobilize resources that reduce distress. Conceptually, this seems more likely to occur in the case of mobilizing social support or energizing one's coping efforts; however, as we will see, there may be examples of the *additive stress buffering* effects of mastery as well.

Figure 4.3 presents three other models that depict personal resources either as mediators or as deterrent effects. The first model portrays mastery as a factor that intervenes between exposure to stressors and ensuing distress. In this instance, increased exposure to stressors is associated with an erosion of the sense of personal control that manifests itself in increased psychological distress. This is the classic example of a personal resource operating as a *mediator variable.*

The second diagram portrays mastery as a variable that reduces indi-viduals' exposure to stressors. In this model, personal control affects distress only indirectly by reducing stressful experience. Wheaton refers to this as a *stress deterrence* model.

In the last diagram, mastery and stress each have independent effects on distress. In this case, the impact of personal control on distress is

The Interactive Stress Buffering Effect of Mastery:

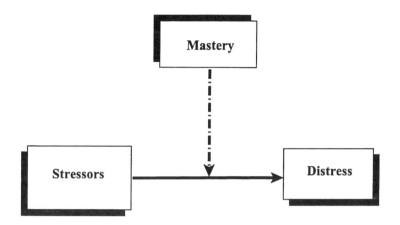

The Additive Stress Buffering Effect of Mastery:

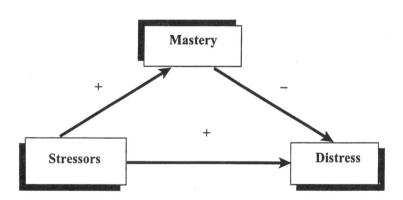

FIGURE 4.2   Models of stress buffering.

The Mediating Effect of Mastery:

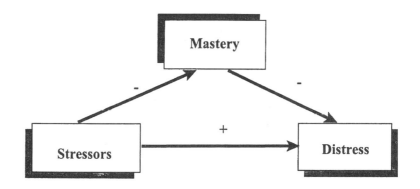

The Stress Deterrent Effect of Mastery:

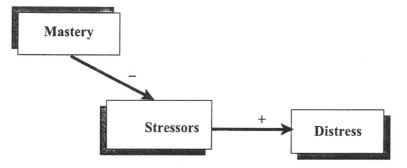

The Distress Deterrent Effect of Mastery:

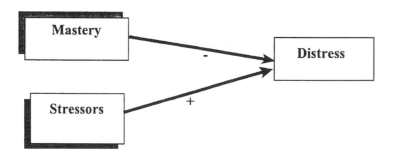

FIGURE 4.3   Models of stress mediation and deterrence.

unrelated to the level of stress exposure. As Wheaton (1985) noted, the effect of mastery on distress may counteract the effect of stress on distress. He suggested that this is an example of a *distress deterrence* model in which mastery may operate as a "generalized health-maintenance resource" (p. 359).

There are several advantages to thinking about the role of mastery in the stress process in terms of the models that Wheaton described. First, these different models alert us to the many ways in which mastery may influence the stress process. Second, the existence of multiple models opens up the possibility that mastery and other personal resources operate along multiple pathways or channels. Third, by attending to the distinctions among buffering, mediating, and deterrent models, we can better understand the influential role that personal control plays in affecting individuals' mental health.

Moreover, Wheaton's formulation is consistent with a point made by Pearlin (1999) in his reappraisal of the stress process:

> [T]here is nothing inherent about coping, social support, or mastery that destines them to be treated as moderating resources. Casting them as moderators is a conceptual strategy, not an empirical imperative. Indeed, the three resources could as plausibly be regarded as mediating conditions, where the effects of the other components of the stress process on outcomes are channeled through the resources. Their treatment as mediators assumes that resources are not immutable but can be diminished (or replenished) by the social and economic statuses surrounding the stress process and by the ensuing stressors. (pp. 405–406)

This is an important point because it draws attention to the multiple ways in which personal resources such as mastery may influence the stress process. In the next section, we provide examples of the mediating and buffering roles that personal control may play in the stress process.

EVIDENCE OF MEDIATING AND BUFFERING EFFECTS OF MASTERY

Given the substantial literature on the role of mastery in the stress process, there are numerous examples of mediating and buffering effects that we could cite. One of the earliest demonstrations of the mediating effect of mastery can be found in the original explication of the stress process by Pearlin and colleagues (1981). The authors showed how mastery is an important mediator of the relationship between economic strains that arise out of job disruption and psychological distress.

In this chapter, we have chosen to present examples of buffering and mediating effects that come mainly from our own studies. Over the last several years, we have conducted a program of research that has focused on the impact of various types of socioeconomic disadvantage on family mental health. In addressing this broad topic, we have been influenced greatly by the stress process model. One of the central themes of this research program has been to trace the effects that personal resources such as mastery have on the stress–distress relationship. In this context, we have conducted a number of community surveys. One of these, the Single-Parent Family Study (SPFS), is a longitudinal case-comparison study of 518 single-parent mothers and 502 married mothers and their children. Another survey, the Unemployment Study (US), is a longitudinal study of 900 nuclear families of which approximately one half had experienced a significant period of job loss. Both studies were conducted in London, Ontario, Canada.

Mediating and Interactive Buffering Effects among Single and Married Mothers

In the SPFS, we defined single mothers as separated, divorced, widowed, or never-married women with at least one child under age 17. This sample includes mothers who may have been legally married but were separated and not cohabiting as well as those living in extended families (usually with their own parents or adult siblings). The married mothers include women who lived with their husband or cohabiting partner and at least one child under age 17. Descriptions of the sampling strategy and measures employed in this study have been described elsewhere (Ali & Avison, 1997; Avison, 1995; Davies, Avison, & McAlpine, 1997).

In the analyses that follow, we explore how three different chronic stressors (financial strain, caregiving strain, and work–home role conflict) are significantly associated with increases in psychological distress and how two personal resources, mastery and self-esteem, both mediate and moderate these effects. Our analyses begin with an assessment of the ways in which structural factors and the three dimensions of chronic strain are associated with mastery. Table 4.1 presents the results of multiple regression analyses. Married mothers' mastery scores average 1.85 units higher than do those of single-parent mothers. Although better-educated women have significantly higher levels of mastery, this does not explain away the difference associated with family structure. Somewhat surprisingly, employment status has no significant effect on mastery. In the final regression equation, each of the three measures of chronic strain has a significant negative impact on mastery. Moreover, the inclusion of these stressors explains away the difference due to household status. Of these three types of chronic strain, the measure of problems in the caregiving role has the most important effect. It is also noteworthy that the impact of education on mastery persists even with controls for chronic strains.

Table 4.2 presents the results of regression analyses of the impact of selected structural variables, chronic strains, and psychosocial resources on psychological distress (as measured by the Center for Epidemiologic Studies–Depression Scale; CES-D). This series of regression analyses allows us to determine whether mastery mediates the effects of chronic strains on psychological distress. In Model 1, the significant impact of family structure persists after controlling for women's education, age, and employment status. On average, single mothers score 4.87 units higher on psychological distress than do married mothers. In the second equation, each of three dimensions of chronic stressors (financial strain, caregiving strain, and work–home strain) has a significant positive effect on psychological distress.

Two other observations are noteworthy. First, employment has a significant effect on distress once the effects of chronic strains are controlled. No doubt, this occurs because employed mothers report higher levels of caregiving strain and are exposed to work–home strain. Second, although controls for caregiving strain, work–home strain, and work strain substantially account for the difference in CES-D scores between single and married mothers, the effect of family structure on distress still persists.

In the final equation, the inclusion of mastery and self-esteem explains away the impact of employment status. These psychosocial resource variables also appear to mediate the effects of chronic strains, especially work–home strain, on psychological distress. Although the effects of financial strain and caregiver strain remain statistically significant, their association with distress is reduced considerably. Thus, we find clear evidence that a sense of personal control is an important

TABLE 4.1 Regression of Mastery on Structural Variables and Strains

Variable	I		II		III		IV	
	b	*B*	*b*	*B*	*b*	*B*	*b*	*B*
Family structure[a]	1.85**	.17	1.46**	.14	1.44**	.13	-.33	-.03
Age			-.00	-.00	-.01	-.01	-.06	-.07
Education			.34**	.18	.33**	.17	.27**	.14
Employment status[b]					.31	.03	.80	.07
Financial strain							-.12**	-.16
Caregiving strain							-.41**	-.36
Work–home strain[c]							-.23**	-.11
Constant	23.88		19.98		20.09		33.46	
R^2		.03**		.06**		.06**		.27**

b = unstandardized regression coefficient; *B* = standardized regression coefficient

[a]0 = single-parent family; 1 = two-parent family

[b]0 = not working; 1 = working

[c]Measured as deviations from the mean of employed women.

*p = .01

**p = .005

138

TABLE 4.2 Regression of CES-D Scores on Structural Variables, Strains, and Psychosocial Resources

Variable	I		II		III	
	b	B	b	B	b	B
Family structure[a]	-4.87**	-.23	-1.83*	-.08	-1.60	-.07
Age	-.11	-.07	-.03	-.02	-.05	-.03
Education	-.48**	-.12	-.38**	-.10	-.16	-.04
Employment status[b]	-1.60	-.07	-2.59**	-.11	-1.16	-.05
Financial strain			.15**	.10	.09*	.06
Caregiving strain			.78**	.35	.31**	.14
Work–home strain[c]			.46**	.11	.23	.06
Mastery					-.37**	-.19
Self-esteem					-.51**	-.34
Constant	28.90		5.61		41.96	
R^2		.10**		.28**		.43**

b = unstandardized regression coefficient; B = standardized regression coefficient

[a]0 = single-parent family; 1 = two-parent family
[b]0 = not working; 1 = working
[c]Measured as deviations from the mean of employed women.

*p = .01
**p = .005

mediator of the stress–distress relationship among single and married mothers.

We next computed interactive buffering effects of mastery for each type of chronic strain on psychological distress. For each combination of chronic strain and personal control, we calculated multiplicative interaction terms that were each added to the final regression equation displayed in Table 4.2. For the combined sample of mothers, there are statistically significant moderating effects of mastery for each of the three types of strain. In each case, our results indicate that the impact of chronic strain on distress declines as the level of personal control increases. When interactions were computed separately for single-parent and married mothers, no statistically significant differences were observed in the magnitudes of these buffering effects. That is, the buffering effects of mastery are of similar proportions for both groups of mothers. Similarly, there were no significant differences between working and nonworking mothers in the moderating effects of these psychosocial resources. Finally, we computed third-order interactions (household structure by employment status by psychosocial resource by chronic strain) to determine whether buffering effects might be specific to some combination of family structure and work. Once again, there were no significant interactions. Thus, in the absence of any significant pattern of differences in buffering effects, it seems that the moderating influences of mastery on chronic strains are not conditioned to any important degree by family structure or employment status.

Mediating Effects of Mastery among Families Experiencing Job Loss

A second test of potential mediating and interactive buffering effects of mastery comes from our investigation of job loss and the mental health of families. In the Unemployment Study, we generated a sample of 897 married couples with at least one child living at home. Following procedures suggested by Kessler, House, and Turner (1987), the sample was selected to overweight the proportion of currently unemployed (CU) and previously unemployed (PU) and to generate a sufficiently large sample of stably employed (SE) respondents. CU refers to involuntary loss of a steady job where the worker was employed more than 25 hours per week; unemployment must have been for a minimum of 4 weeks prior to the screening survey interview. PU refers to involuntary unemployment of at least 4 weeks at some time in the 4 years prior to the screening survey (roughly the duration of the economic recession at the time) where the individual had returned to a steady 25+ hours per week job. SE refers to steady employment in a 25+ hours per week job with no unemployment exceeding 4 weeks over the last 4 years. Thus, when we speak of unemployment in this study, we are focusing specifically on unemployment due to involuntary job loss. Individuals who left jobs or who were unemployed of their own volition were not included. De facto, we also excluded first-time job seekers who were unable to secure employment. Our approach throughout the analyses of the effects of unemployment is to contrast the stably employed with the currently and previously unemployed to avoid biases by selection out of employment.

The final sample consisted of 897 families. In terms of individual employment status, of the women in our study, 532 were SE, 97 were CU, 90 were PE, and 178 were categorized as "other." This group consisted largely of women who described themselves as housewives. A very small number of these women were students, physically disabled, or retired. Among men, 560 were stably employed, 136 were currently unemployed, and 177 were previous unemployed. Only 24 were categorized as "other."

We used the short form of the University of Michigan version of the Composite International Diagnostic Interview (CIDI) (Kessler, Andrews, Mroczek, Ustun, & Wittchen, 1998) to obtain diagnostic information on major depression, dysthymia, generalized anxiety disorder, panic disorder, and substance abuse. In the results reported here, we constructed a dummy dependent variable indicating whether each respondent had reported at least one episode of any of these disorders (as defined by the third edition, revised, of 1987 *Diagnostic and Statistical Manual*) in the 12 months preceding the interview.

Table 4.3 presents the results of analyses of the mediating and interactive buffering effects of mastery and self-esteem on the impact of job loss on mental health problems in the 12 months preceding interviews. In the first panel of Table 4.3, we present the results of logistic regression analyses computed separately for women and men. We regressed the presence of a DSM-III-R diagnosis on a dummy variable indicating whether the respondent had experienced unemployment over the last 4 years and on a dummy variable indicating whether the respondent's spouse had experienced job loss. Age, age-squared (to adjust for the potential nonlinear relationship between age and diagnostic outcome), and education are controlled in these analyses. Among women in our

TABLE 4.3 Effects of Unemployment, Mastery, and Self-Esteem on the 12-Month Prevalence of Mental Disorders

Predictors	Main Effects			Moderating Effects	
	Females b		Males b	Females b	Males b
Baseline					
Respondent unemployed	.51**		.57**		
Spouse unemployed	.46*	&	.23	NA	
Mastery					
Respondent unemployed	.30		.42	.01	-.10*
Spouse unemployed	.39		.28	.04	.09
Mastery	-.14***	&	-.09***		
Self-esteem					
Respondent unemployed	.21		.49*	.00	-.07*
Spouse unemployed	.51*	&	.29	.01	.02
Self-esteem	-.11***	&	-.06***		

*p = .05
**p = .01
***p = .001
& Gender difference significant at p = .05
b = unstandardized parameter estimate. Analyses include controls for age, age-squared, and education.

study, both their own and their spouse's unemployment are significant risk factors for a diagnosable mental disorder. Among men, only their own job loss predicts the experience of a mental health problem. Men are apparently unaffected by their wife's job loss.

In the remaining panels, the results of regression analyses that examine the impact of mastery and self-esteem are summarized. We see that mastery has a significant inverse effect on women's likelihood of having a disorder. Also, there is clear evidence that mastery mediates the impact of both women's own unemployment and their husband's job loss. A similar pattern is observed among men for the effects of their job loss on disorder.

Tests for interactions reveal only one significant modifying effect of mastery. Surprisingly, among men, the inverse association between mastery and diagnosis appears to hold only among the employed. Among unemployed men, mastery and diagnosis are unrelated. Thus, although there is evidence of a stress–mastery interaction, the nature of this conditional effect is not consistent with the interactive buffering effect described by Wheaton (1985).

For women, self-esteem has a significant negative association with disorder. Although self-esteem mediates the influence of women's own job loss on their mental health, it has no such effect with regard to their husband's unemployment. Despite the observation that self-esteem also has a significant direct effect on diagnosis for men, it does not explain away the impact of their unemployment experience on their mental health. As we observed with mastery, self-esteem appears to be negatively associated with disorder but only among employed men.

Throughout these analyses, we have included a measure of self-esteem to demonstrate that the effects of mastery and self-esteem differ from each other. Although these two constructs differ conceptually, there is a tendency in stress process research to think of these personal resources as factors that operate more or less identically within the paradigm. The results presented thus far suggest that there are subtle but important differences in the ways in which self-efficacy and self-esteem mediate or moderate the stress–distress relationship.

We believe this is an issue that warrants further research. It may be that some stressful experiences are particularly erosive of self-esteem, whereas others may be more likely to challenge individuals' sense of mastery. Moreover, the extent to which this occurs may be conditional on the social contexts of individuals' lives.

Evidence of the Additive Stress-Buffering Effect of Mastery

As we noted earlier, the possibility that exposure to stressors increases psychosocial resources that, in turn, result in reduced levels of psychological distress seems more likely for factors such as social support than for mastery. One can easily think of situations in which the experience of a stressor such as the death of a loved one might mobilize one's social support network and thereby reduce distress. Similar examples are more difficult to find when the psychosocial resource variable is mastery.

In previous work on stressful life events and crisis resolution (Turner & Avison, 1992), we have suggested that not all stressful experiences erode individuals' sense of control. Theoretically, some stressful experiences, especially those that are successfully resolved, should constitute opportunities for growth and personal development. In operational terms, one would expect successfully resolved life events to be positively associated with mastery, which, in turn, is negatively associated with psychological distress.

Turner and Avison (1992) presented results that are somewhat consistent with this model of additive stress buffering. They found that the number of unresolved stressful life events is negatively associated with mastery. By contrast, the number of successfully resolved events is unrelated to mastery. In fact, the regression coefficient for this effect is actually positive but not statistically reliable. These results suggest that the existence of an additive stress-buffering effect of mastery is at least tenable. Holahan and Moos (1990, 1994) addressed this possibility and reported that individuals who overcame high levels of stressors also reported significant increases in personal resources. This idea of personal growth in the face of crisis is an example of the additive stress-buffering model that may be useful for understanding how individuals in exceedingly high-stress circumstances survive psychologically.

THE FUNDAMENTAL IMPORTANCE
OF PERSONAL CONTROL

These examples of how personal control may function as a mediator or moderator of the stress–distress relationship provide only a partial examination of this construct's central importance in the stress process. Mastery also appears to play a critical role in accounting for the links between social statuses and mental health. Recently, Turner and Lloyd

(1999) provided an excellent overview of the social correlates of both psychological distress and major depressive disorder. In that article, they provided indisputable evidence that gender, age, marital status, and socioeconomic status (SES) are all significantly associated with mental health outcomes. They then estimated the mediating effects of several constructs that have been central to the stress process paradigm.

Turner and Lloyd (1999) made several telling observations about mastery's mediating influence. They reported that mastery plays a significant role in explaining gender and SES differences in both psychological distress and depressive disorder. It also appears to operate as a suppressor variable in terms of the difference in psychological distress between married and never-married individuals. If married individuals had levels of personal control that were as high as those of the never married, this difference in distress scores would actually increase. Estimates of the mediating effects of mastery relative to other constructs (stress exposure, self-esteem, social support, emotional reliance, and assertion of autonomy) reveal a most important finding. Sense of personal control is by far the most influential mediator of both the class–distress and class–depressive disorder relationships. Finally, Turner and Lloyd found no evidence of any interactive stress-buffering effects of mastery on either distress or depressive disorder.

The implications of these findings are far reaching. Turner and Lloyd's results suggest to us that mediators such as mastery do not operate in a pervasive fashion. That is, the observation that mastery may account for differences in mental health predominantly associated with gender and SES as opposed to other social factors implies that there is specificity to the mediation process in the stress paradigm. When we consider Turner and Lloyd's findings and our results that document mastery's mediation of the impact of both family structure and unemployment, this suggests that personal control's influence in the stress process is especially potent where variations of power differentials or social capital are at issue. Indeed, the perception of control over one's successes or failures in life seems intricately entangled with one's experience of power and opportunity. So, for example, individuals from middle- and upper-class positions are more likely to have jobs where they are in control of their circumstances and where they may have influence over others. The empowering features of middle- and upper-class occupations are in sharp contrast to the experiences of those in manual or semi-skilled jobs or, indeed, to the experience of those who have lost jobs.

Similarly, our interviews with single and married mothers reveal that a distinctive feature of single parenthood is the perception that there are constant work–home role conflicts that limit one's options in life. Moreover, single mothers' financial and caregiving difficulties restrict their opportunities to participate in social and leisure activities or even to consider certain kinds of jobs (Ali & Avison, 1997; Avison, 1995). These experiences ultimately lead to the erosion of their sense of mastery and to ensuing distress or depression.

Turner, Lloyd, and Roszell (1999) argued that findings of this kind "suggest that location in the social system effectively defines patterned differences in social experience generally, and in environmental responsiveness in particular, that are relevant to the acquisition and maintenance of mastery. . . . These resources, in turn, largely mediate the connection between SES and risk for depression" (p. 666).

If a sense of personal control is indeed a major conduit through which experiences of inequality and differential power are mediated, this suggests to us that stress process researchers need to integrate contemporary sociological theories on stratification, social capital, and power into their paradigms. By explicitly considering these constructs within the stress process, we will develop a better understanding of the ways in which social experiences manifest themselves in symptoms of distress and depression.

THE SOCIAL MALLEABILITY OF MASTERY

To this point, we have focused almost exclusively on the role of personal control as a mediator or moderator of the stress–distress relationship. The examples that we have presented have emphasized the roles that mastery plays in affecting individuals' psychological distress or depression. Relatively less research in the stress process paradigm has examined the extent to which the sense of personal control itself is socially modifiable.

In this regard, Turner and Roszell (1994) argued that the psychosocial resources that may be most important for individuals' mental health are those that are linked to individuals' positions in the social structure. This point of view represents a classic sociological perspective on stress and mental health. Turner and Roszell reminded us of the importance of social status in the stress process. Not only do differences in social position expose individuals to greater or lesser numbers of stressful experiences, these differences may also condition the development of psychosocial resources that enable individuals to cope with such stressors. This is a distinctive contribution of the sociological perspective to the stress process (Pearlin, 1989). Moreover, to ignore the ways in which social status influences the experience of stressors and their mediators is to assume that human experience is considerably more homogeneous than may be the case (Avison & Gotlib, 1994).

A brief and admittedly selective review of the literature on correlates of personal control clearly reveals that individuals' location in the social structure is an important determinant of this psychosocial resource. At the same time, however, there remain a number of unanswered questions about the social malleability of mastery.

Age and Mastery

Although evidence of both declining and increasing levels of mastery with age exist in the literature (Rodin & Timko, 1992), more recent studies conclude that levels of personal control decline with age. Three studies on this issue are particularly noteworthy (Mirowsky, 1995; Schieman & Turner, 1998; Wolinsky & Stump, 1996). Each confirms that mastery declines after the age of 50. There are, however, some discrepancies in these works concerning the rate of decline in mastery after this age. Two of the studies (Mirowsky, 1995; Schieman & Turner, 1998) report a significant drop in mastery after age 50. Wolinsky and Stump (1996), however, find that the decline in mastery is monotonic. It is important to note, however, that none of these studies is able to account for age-related differences in mastery by controlling for measures of health and role status. Thus, the negative relationship between age and mastery persists even after controlling for health and role-based transitions such as retirement and widowhood—events thought to be responsible for declining levels of mastery with age.

Socioeconomic Circumstances and Personal Control

Individuals from more advantaged socioeconomic positions tend to feel they have greater personal control over their lives and are less likely to believe in fate or the influence of powerful others in determining their own actions than individuals who occupy less advantaged positions in the social structure (Gurin & Brim, 1984; Lachman & Weaver, 1998; Levinson, 1981). The objective conditions that accompany socioeconomic positions shape personal beliefs about the self and one's ability to act in the social world. We know, for example, that unemployment constitutes a direct challenge to one's sense of self-efficacy that results in feelings of depression (Avison, 2001; Caplan, Vinokur, Price, & van Ryn, 1989) and that those in the workforce have higher levels of mastery than those who are not working (Ali & Avison, 1997).

Furthermore, among those who are employed, there are important variations in personal control. Kohn and Schooler (1982, 1983), for example, furthered our understanding of how social structure influences individual psychologies by describing the mechanisms through which the workplace contributes to the formation of self-identity. Most notably, their research shows that workers whose jobs are high in self-direction and substantive complexity tend to value individual freedom and possess a greater sense of control than workers from jobs where these characteristics are absent. Their work supports the hypothesis that a sense of personal mastery is shaped by SES because jobs high in self-direction and complexity tend to be associated with advantaged social position.

Where Kohn and his colleagues emphasized occupation as a measure of social status that influences mastery, Mirowsky (1995) focused on the role that educational attainment plays in fostering a sense of control or mastery among individuals. Through the education process, individuals learn to solve increasingly complex and subtle problems, which, in turn, builds self-confidence and assurance. Individuals begin to see themselves as having more control over their lives as they accumulate successes within the education system. Formal education reinforces the need to face problems proactively and persist until a solution is obtained. It also enhances communication and analytic skills, all of which enlarge one's ability to solve problems and thus increase the sense of personal mastery. Moreover, education is often the minimum necessary requirement to those better paying jobs that tend to reinforce a sense of mastery. For example, occupations that have the desirable qualities of self-direction and control identified by Kohn and Schooler (1982, 1983) are generally more accessible to those with high levels of formal education. Education, then, provides a means to secure more advantaged social positions, which, in turn, enhances the perception of personal control.

Each of these perspectives, though focusing on different aspects of stratification, share a common theme: Advantaged social positions lead to the perception that one has control over one's life. Conversely, those from disadvantaged positions experience circumstances that are less conducive to feelings of personal control.

Toward an Interactive Model of Socioeconomic Status, Age, and Mastery

In the face of this evidence concerning both age and SES variations in personal control, we find it surprising that little interest has focused on the possibility of an interactive rather than additive relationship among these constructs. Theory and research in the sociology of aging predict that as individuals age, their sense of control over their lives will change. Theory and research in social stratification suggest that such change will be influenced by individuals' position in the social structure. For example, if it is true that with age comes ill health, which, in turn, leads to lower perceived control (Rodin, 1986), we may ask if this is the same for individuals regardless of socioeconomic position. Previous research has determined that social position is linked to health, so that those from lower socioeconomic positions suffer greater rates of morbidity and mortality (Link & Phelan, 1995; Williams, 1990). Recent work has also shown that when age and SES are considered together, illness and disability among individuals from higher social class groups is postponed until well into old age, whereas morbidity emerges much earlier in the lower social class groups (House et al., 1994). If illness is connected to both social position and mastery, then it seems reasonable to hypothesize that changes in either of these personal resources with age will be contingent on socioeconomic standing. Indeed, it seems unlikely that the models of personal growth or loss of mastery can be generalized to all individuals regardless of social structural position.

Although the literature on mastery in the sociology of aging tends to disregard position in the social structure, the literature concerning social structure and personality largely ignores the importance of age. For example, although social position is regarded as a fundamental determinant of mastery (Turner & Roszell, 1994), little attention is given to how age may influence the class–personal efficacy relationship. Age, like education, is also a system of social stratification (Riley, 1971, 1987). As Riley, Johnson, and Foner (1972) noted, age is both a process that occurs within the individual and an indicator of his or her location in a social system. This duality of age (its biologic and sociologic properties) implies that "aging," as a process, will interact with systems of inequality (based on education, income, or occupation) to predict out-comes such as health (House et al., 1994) and personal resources. There is good reason to hypothesize that the relationship between social class and mastery may vary with age, and we must not assume that the experi-ence of social inequality, reflected by indicators of social status, will be the same regardless of age. Whether considered from an aging or social structure perspective, differences in mastery in the population are likely to be the result of both age and social structural differences.

Gender, Family Structure, and Personal Control

In their brief review of the literature on the effects of gender and marital status on personal control, Turner and Lloyd (1999) concluded that married persons have higher levels of mastery than do the nonmar-ried, but they conceded that the evidence is by no means overwhelming. Similarly, they found the evidence in support of gender differences in mastery to be contradictory, although it appears that more recent, large-scale community surveys reveal that men have slightly higher levels of personal control. In our own work on family structure and women's mental health, we found that single mothers have significant lower levels of mastery than do married mothers (Ali & Avison, 1997; Avison, 1995).

There is a pattern here that Turner and Lloyd have also noted. If one accepts the view that the gendered nature of society locates many women in social positions where there is less opportunity, less power, and less social capital, it follows that the hypothesis of a gender differ-ence in mastery is tenable. Similarly, given the social disadvantages that are associated with single parenthood, it ought to be no surprise that married mothers report higher levels of mastery than do single mothers.

Stressors and Mastery

Both theory and research make a strong case for the idea that individu-als' stressful life experiences should play important roles in shaping their sense of personal control. As we have seen, the proposed mediating role of mastery in the stress process paradigm leads directly to this hypothesis. Pearlin and colleagues (1981) were among the first to docu-ment this relationship and to note how stressors appear to erode the sense of control that individuals experience. Other researchers have also documented the detrimental impact of life stress on mastery (Mir-owsky & Ross, 1986; Seeman, Seeman, & Budros, 1988).

Nevertheless, it is somewhat surprising that more research has not focused on the impact of stress on mastery. For example, although researchers have demonstrated that different dimensions of stress (life events, chronic stressors, and traumatic events) have independent effects on psychological distress, this line of inquiry has not been pursued widely in studies of the correlates of personal control. If social experience shapes individuals' sense of personal control, this appears to be a fruitful direction that might be taken.

A Preliminary Examination of Some Social Correlates of Personal Control

This review of the correlates of mastery provides us with a framework for conducting some preliminary analyses of the predictors of mastery. For these analyses, the sample has been selected from the National Population Health Survey (NPHS), conducted by Statistics Canada. The NPHS was a 1994 telephone survey of a national probability sample of Canadian residents across all 10 provinces. Persons living on native reserves and military bases, in institutions, and in some remote areas in Ontario and Quebec were excluded. Of the 18,342 possible respondents age 12 and older, 17,626 participated (a response rate of 96.1%). For these analyses, only those age 20 and older were selected, reducing the sample to 15,789.

The measure of mastery in the NPHS is a 7-item scale derived from the work of Pearlin and Schooler (1978). The measure is scored such that higher scores indicate a greater sense of mastery (7 to 28). SES is measured by two different variables in these analyses: education and household income. Education is coded into 8 categories, ranging from no formal schooling (1) through holding a high school diploma (4) to holding a graduate degree or a degree in medicine. Household income was coded into 11 intervals, from no income (0) through $30,000 to $39,999 (6) to $80,000 (10). Gender was coded 1 for females, 0 for males. Age was an ordinal variable coded in 5-year intervals from 20 to 24 to those age 80 and over. Marital status included 3 dummy variables for married (the reference category), previously married (including widowed, divorced, and separated), and never married. In these analyses, we also examined the impact of three separate dimensions of stressors. Chronic stressors refer to ongoing difficulties in an array of roles. Stressful life events are indexed by a count of negative experiences that occurred to respondents in the year prior to interview. Traumatic

TABLE 4.4   The Social Distribution of Mastery in the National Population Health Survey

Variable	N	Mean	S.D.
Gender			
Male	6,739	19.93	4.25
Female	7,429	19.34	4.44
Age			
20–29	2,685	20.03	4.05
30–39	3,666	19.96	4.19
40–49	2,903	19.74	4.55
50–59	1,959	19.15	4.60
60–69	1,552	19.21	4.37
70–79	1,052	18.92	4.42
80+	351	18.49	4.34
Marital Status			
Married	9,620	19.63	4.35
Previously married	2,024	19.80	4.31
Never married	2,521	18.78	4.52
Education			
Elementary	3,523	18.47	4.46
High school	5,812	19.67	4.25
Some college	2,650	19.99	4.15
University degree	2,165	20.94	4.25
Income			
Less than $10,000	733	18.10	4.67
$10,000–29,999	2,164	18.22	4.54
$30,000–39,999	3,871	19.35	4.37
$40,000+	6,777	20.39	4.11

S.D. = standard deviation.

events are reports of major adversities occurring to respondents in childhood or young adulthood.

Table 4.4 presents mean mastery scores for these various social categories. Across all 5 variables—gender, age, marital status, education, and income—we observe statistically significant variations in mastery scores ($p < .001$). However, given the very large sample size of the NPHS, it is important to note that even relatively small differences in mastery scores are significant. For example, although males have significantly higher scores than females, the difference is just over .13 of a standard deviation. More substantial differences can be seen across the age spectrum. These data suggest that the decline in personal control with age is largely monotonic. With regard to marital status, never-married respondents appear to score lower on mastery than do currently or previously married individuals. Steeper gradients of mastery scores are apparent for both education and income.

One interpretation of these patterns is that mastery is more strongly associated with variables that reflect systems of stratification. Indeed, the steepest gradients of mastery occur for variations by age, income, and education, whereas differences associated with either gender or marital status are less pronounced.

Consistent with our earlier argument that it is important to examine the age stratification of mastery, we constructed graphs representing the interaction of age and education on mastery scores and age and income on mastery. These are displayed in Figure 4.4. The top figure shows the relationship between age and mastery within three different education levels. The education levels include less than high school, high school, and postsecondary (college or university). These categories make conceptual sense in terms of meaningful categories for educational attainment; they also roughly correspond to meaningful standardized scores. For example, the score corresponding to less than high school education is approximately equal to −1 standard deviation below the mean. The value for the high school level is close to the mean for education, and the unstandardized score corresponding to postsecondary education is about equal to 1 standard deviation above the mean for education. The predicted values of mastery are plotted by 10-year age cohorts for each level of education, controlling for gender and marital status. The pattern is quite striking. The widest gap in mastery by education occurs in the youngest age cohort. This gap becomes successively smaller across age cohorts until those age 80 and over, where the differences in mastery are small relative to younger groups. In other words, educational differences in mastery converge with age.

The bottom figure shows the relationship between age and mastery within three different levels of household income. Income levels correspond, respectively, to household incomes of $17,499 (low), 44,999 (medium), and 69,999 (high). Again, these income levels reflect standardized scores in the range of −1 to +1 standard deviation units. The widest gap in mastery occurs among the youngest cohort. The lines representing income levels converge across successively older cohorts,

Mastery Scores by Age and Education Level:

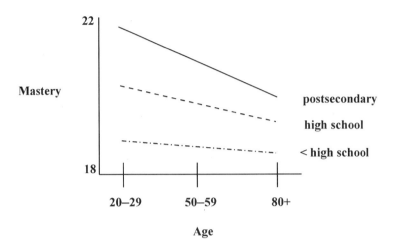

Mastery Scores by Age and Income Level:

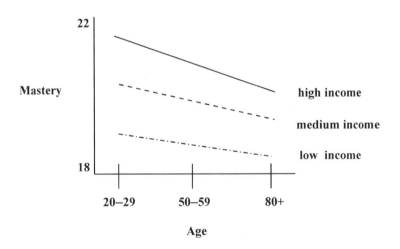

FIGURE 4.4   The age stratification of mastery.

reaching the most narrow point among those age 80 and over. Perhaps the most notable difference is the degree of convergence. In the age-by-income interaction model, there is evidence of convergence, but it is not as pronounced as the age-by-education model.

We next estimated the relative impact of these social factors on mastery. In Table 4.5, we began by regressing scores on mastery on gender, age, marital status (coded as two dummy variables), education, and income. The results of this regression analysis are summarized in Model I. Gender, age, education, and income each exert significant influences on mastery. Other analyses not displayed reveal that, as expected, education and income have more pronounced effects than gender or age.

In Models II to IV, we then added each dimension of stress to the regression equation to estimate the individual effects of chronic stressors, life events, and traumatic events on mastery as well as to examine these stressors' potential mediating effects. In Model II, chronic stressors have a substantial negative impact on mastery. The addition of this variable to the regression equation accounts for an additional 12% of the variance in mastery. We also observe that the gender difference in mastery is at least partially a function of higher levels of chronic strains among women. The only other mediating effect of chronic strain is the attenuation of the impact of education from .37 in Model I to .28 in Model II. In Model III, we can see that the measure of eventful stressors is a significant negative correlate of mastery, but its inclusion has virtually no mediational influence. A similar pattern occurs in Model IV for the inclusion of our measure of childhood and adolescent traumas. When all three dimensions of stress are simultaneously included in the regression equation, we can see that each has a significant, independent effect on mastery.

These results are not unlike those that we reported earlier in the chapter (Table 4.1) when we examined the impact of family structure and stressors on mastery among single and married mothers. Indeed, we found that three different dimensions of chronic stressors—financial difficulties, caregiving strain, and work–home role conflict—each had independent effects on mothers' sense of personal control. Moreover, these three kinds of stressors appeared to mediate completely the impact of family structure on mastery.

TABLE 4.5 Regression of Mastery on Structural Variables and Stressors in the National Population Health Survey

Variable	I b (B)	II b (B)	III b (B)	IV b (B)	V b (B)
Gender[a]	-.39** (-.14)	-.22* (-.02)	-.36** (-.04)	-.31** (-.04)	-.21** (-.02)
Age	-.01** (-.04)	-.03** (-.00)	-.02** (-.08)	-.02** (-.06)	-.04** (-.14)
Previously Married[b]	-.21 (-.02)	.17 (-.01)	-.15 (-.01)	-.13 (-.01)	.18 (-.02)
Never Married[b]	-.12 (-.01)	-.04 (-.00)	-.20 (-.02)	-.14 (-.01)	-.21 (-.01)
Education	.37** (.12)	.28* (.09)	.36** (.12)	.34** (.12)	.28** (.09)
Income	.02E-03** (.14)	.02E-03** (.11)	.02E-03** (.12)	.02E-03** (.13)	.02E-03** (.10)
Chronic Stressors		-.61** (-.36)			-.54** (-.33)
Life Events			-.80** (-.19)		-.27** (-.06)
Traumatic Events				-.52** (-.14)	-.09** (-.02)
Constant	17.82	21.25	19.10	18.76	21.54
R^2	.06**	.18**	.09**	.08**	.18**

b = unstandardized regression coefficient; B = standardized regression coefficient

[a] female = 1, male = 0

[b] reference category is married

*p < .01

**p < .001

SOME FINAL THOUGHTS ON THE SOCIAL MALLEABILITY OF PERSONAL CONTROL

These analyses raise several questions about the extent to which mastery is socially modifiable. Before addressing these issues, it is important to emphasize that the analyses we have presented are limited by their cross-sectional nature. This, of course, makes it difficult to specify the causal direction of the relationships between stressful experience and personal control. In all likelihood, the world is a dense causal web where reciprocal effects are operating.

Nevertheless, we believe that the patterns of associations that we have identified suggest that individuals' sense of personal control is a function of both proximal and distal social experiences. Indeed, the significant effects of both education and traumatic experiences in childhood and adolescence seem most plausibly to constitute formative experiences that may have influenced the development of mastery early in the life course.

The fact that the inclusion of chronic stressors and life events in the same regression model substantially reduces the impact of traumatic experience on mastery brings to mind the concept of chains of adversity experienced by some individuals. For example, Davies and colleagues (1997) observed that adversities in childhood and adolescence are associated with early onset of depression and subsequent hardships in adulthood. One interpretation of the results presented here is that traumatic events that occur early in the life course are formative experiences for the development of mastery in young people. The distal effect of traumatic experiences is mediated by the operant burden of stress. That is, individuals with a history of early traumatic experiences are more likely to encounter subsequent stressors as they move through the life course. These stressors, in turn, erode their sense of personal control. This interpretation appears to be consistent with studies of childhood adversities and their consequences for mental health in adulthood (Kessler & Magee, 1993, 1994; McLeod, 1991; Turner & Lloyd, 1995).

A somewhat different but complementary interpretation is that adversities in the early part of the life course are crucial for the development of mastery in childhood, adolescence, and early adulthood. Individuals who have experienced early adversities develop a fatalistic view of the world (one that reflects low personal control). In turn, low mastery contributes both to greater exposure to stressors, especially chronic stressors, and to greater distress, which may further erode mastery in adulthood.

These considerations suggest to us that it might be useful to think of mastery as a psychosocial characteristic that develops across the life course. In the earlier stages of life, socialization experiences, education, and exposure to adversities may each have profound effects on individuals' sense of personal control. Thereafter, more proximate factors—employment or the absence of it, income, and exposure to life events and chronic stressors, to name only a few—constitute the perceived successes and failures that modify people's sense of mastery further in the life course. Although the preliminary results that we have just presented are consistent with this conceptualization of the social malleability of mastery over the life course, considerably more research will be required to support this hypothetical process.

There is, however, one additional finding that is relevant to our consideration of the social malleability of personal control. Some might argue that the development of the individual's sense of personal control is mainly complete by early adulthood and that any variations thereafter are largely epiphenomenal. We have been able to assess this by examining intrapersonal changes in mastery scores over relatively short time periods in two samples. In the Single-Parent Family Study, mean mastery scores are 26.64 at time 1, with a standard deviation of 5.40. Eighteen months later, the mean was 26.69, with a standard deviation of 5.40. We then computed change scores, converted them to absolute values, and examined the distribution. Over 18 months, 24.1% of the women in this sample had changes in mastery that were more than the equivalent of 1 standard deviation below or above their initial scores. In Turner's study (Turner & Lloyd, 1999) of almost 1,400 adults age 18 to 55 in metropolitan Toronto, 31.8% experienced changes in mastery in excess of 1 standard deviation over a 12-month period.

In our view, this suggests that there is substantial intrapersonal change in personal control in adulthood. Changes of this magnitude cannot be attributed to measurement error or characterized as epiphenomenal. Moreover, short of accepting the argument that changes in mastery are the result of some kind of nonsocial, developmental trajectory, it seems reasonable to conclude that it should be possible to model the social or social psychological processes that contribute to its malleability.

CONCLUSION

All of these considerations attest to the importance of social structural and experiential factors in shaping mastery and to the pivotal role that mastery plays in the stress process. As both a mediator and a moderator of the stress–distress relationship, personal control constitutes one of the most important psychosocial resources that individuals possess. Moreover, it is clear that this construct is crucially important in understanding the connection between social statuses and illness. In particular, we believe mastery is a fundamentally important explanatory variable in understanding how systems of stratification produce variations in mental health.

If mastery plays such a central role in the stress process, it is crucial to know whether this resource is a socially malleable characteristic or a relatively stable, traitlike characteristic. Our preliminary investigation of this issue indicates that an individual's sense of control is in fact remarkably responsive to the social world.

Given the prominence of mastery as an explanatory variable in the sociology of mental health, it seems imperative that researchers turn their efforts toward a better understanding of its social and social psychological determinants. Such work is likely to achieve two important goals. It will further enhance the explanatory power of our theoretical models of social structure, stress, and illness. It also will provide much needed information about the kinds of preventive interventions that can enhance personal control and thus reduce the burden of illness.

ACKNOWLEDGMENT

This research was supported by funds from the National Health Research Development Program of Health Canada (6606-5020-63B and 6606-4262-64/2), the Social Sciences and Humanities Research Council of Canada, and by an Ontario Mental Health Foundation Senior Research Fellowship to William R. Avison. John Cairney was supported by a doctoral fellowship from the Social Sciences and Humanities Research Council of Canada.

NOTE

1. Throughout this chapter, we use the terms *mastery* and *sense of personal control* interchangeably. In doing so, we take the position argued by Turner and Roszell (1994) that terms such as *locus of control, fatalism, mastery, self-efficacy,* and *sense of powerlessness* are all labels for essentially the same construct. Ross and Sastry (1999) provide a concise discussion of the distinctions among these terms.

REFERENCES

Ali, J., & Avison, W. R. (1997). Employment transitions and psychological distress: The contrasting experiences of single and married mothers. *Journal of Health and Social Behavior, 38,* 345–362.

Aneshensel, C. S. (1992). Social stress: Theory and research. *Annual Review of Sociology, 18,* 15–38.

Antonovsky, A. (1979). *Health, stress, and coping.* San Francisco: Jossey-Bass.

Avison, W. R. (1995). Roles and resources: The effects of work and family context on women's psychosocial resources and psychological distress. In J. R. Greenley (Ed.), *Research in community and mental health* (Vol. 8, pp. 233–256). Greenwich, CT: JAI Press.

Avison, W. R. (2001). Unemployment and its consequences for mental health. In V. W. Marshall, W. Heinz, H. Krueger, & A. Verma (Eds.), *Restructuring work and the life course* (pp. 177–200). Toronto: University of Toronto Press.

Avison, W. R., & Gotlib, I. H. (1994). Introduction and overview. In W. R. Avison & I. H. Gotlib (Eds.), *Stress and mental health: Contemporary issues and prospects for the future* (pp. 3–12). New York: Plenum Press.

Avison, W. R., & McAlpine, D. D. (1992). Gender differences in symptoms of depression among adolescents. *Journal of Health and Social Behavior, 33,* 77–96.

Billings, A. C., & Moos, R. H. (1982). Stressful life events and symptoms: A longitudinal model. *Health Psychology, 1,* 99–117.

Brown, G. W., & Harris, T. (1978). *Social origins of depression: A study of psychiatric disorder in women.* New York: Free Press.

Caplan, R. D., Vinokur, A. D., Price, R. H., & van Ryn, M. (1989). Job seeking, reemployment, and mental health: A randomized field experiment in coping with job loss. *Journal of Applied Psychology, 74,* 759–769.

Cohen, S., & Syme, L. (1985). *Social support and health.* New York: Academic Press.

Cohen, S., & Wills, T. A. (1985). Stress, social support, and the buffering hypothesis. *Psychological Bulletin, 98,* 310–357.

Cronkite, R. C., & Moos, R. H. (1984). The role of predisposing and moderating factors in the stress-illness relationship. *Journal of Health and Social Behavior, 25,* 372–393.

Davies, L., Avison, W. R., & McAlpine, D. D. (1997). Significant life experiences and depression among single and married mothers. *Journal of Marriage and the Family, 59,* 294–308.

Diagnostic and Statistical Manual of Mental Disorders: DSM-III-R. (1987). Washington, DC: American Psychiatric Association.

Eckenrode, J. (Ed.). (1991). *The social context of coping*. New York: Plenum Press.

Finney, J. W., Moos, R. H., Cronkite, R. C., & Gamble, W. (1983). A conceptual model of the functioning of married persons with impaired partners: Spouses of alcoholics. *Journal of Marriage and the Family, 45*, 23–34.

Gurin, G., & Brim, O. G., Jr. (1984). Change in self in adulthood: The example of sense of control. In P. B. Baltes & O. G. Brim, Jr. (Eds.), *Lifespan development and behavior* (pp. 218–234). New York: Academic Press.

Holahan, C. J., & Moos, R. H. (1990). Life stressors, resistance factors, and psychological health: An extension of the stress-resistance paradigm. *Journal of Personality and Social Psychology, 58*, 909–917.

Holahan, C. J., & Moos, R. H. (1994). Life stressors and mental health. In W. R. Avison & I. H. Gotlib (Eds.), *Stress and mental health: Contemporary issues and prospects for the future* (pp. 213–238). New York: Plenum Press.

House, J. S., Lepkowski, J. M., Kinney, A. M., Mero, R. P., Kessler, R. C., & Herzog, A. R. (1994). The social stratification of aging and health. *Journal of Health and Social Behavior, 35*, 213–234.

Kessler, R. C., Andrews, G., Mroczek, D., Ustun, B., & Wittchen, H.-U. (1998). The World Health Organization composite international diagnostic interview short form (CIDI-SF). *International Journal of Methods in Psychiatric Research, 7*, 171–185.

Kessler, R. C., House, J. S., & Turner, J. B. (1987). Unemployment and health in a community sample. *Journal of Health and Social Behavior, 28*, 51–59.

Kessler, R. C., & Magee, W. J. (1993). Childhood adversities and adult depression: Basic patterns of association in a U.S. national survey. *Psychological Medicine, 23*, 679–690.

Kessler, R. C., & Magee, W. J. (1994). Childhood family violence and adult recurrent depression. *Journal of Health and Social Behavior, 35*, 13–27.

Kohn, M. L., & Schooler, C. (1982). Job conditions and personality: A longitudinal assessment of their reciprocal effects. *American Journal of Sociology, 87*, 1257–1286.

Kohn, M. L., & Schooler, C. (Eds.). (1983). *Work and personality: An inquiry into the impact of social stratification*. Norwood, NJ: Ablex.

Lachman, M. E., & Weaver, S. L. (1998). The sense of control as a moderator of social class differences in health and well-being. *Journal of Personality and Social Psychology, 74*, 763–773.

Lazarus, R. S. (1966). *Psychological stress and the coping process*. New York: McGraw-Hill.

Lazarus, R. S., & Folkman, S. (1984). *Stress, appraisal, and coping*. New York: Springer.

Lazarus, R. S., Kanner, A. D., & Folkman, S. (1980). Emotions: A cognitive-phenomenological analysis. In R. Plutchnik & H. Kellerman (Eds.), *Theories of emotion* (pp. 189–217). New York: Academic Press.

Levinson, H. (1981). Differentiating among internality, powerful others, and chance. In H. M. Lefcourt (Ed.), *Research with the locus of control construct: Assessment methods* (pp. 15–63). New York: Academic Press.

Link, B. G., & Phelan, J. C. (1995). Social conditions as fundamental causes of disease. *Journal of Health and Social Behavior*, (Special Issue), 80–94.

McLean, D., & Link, B. G. (1994). Unraveling complexity: Strategies to refine concepts, measures and research designs in the study of life events and mental health. In W. R. Avison & I. H. Gotlib (Eds.), *Stress and mental health: Contemporary issues and prospects for the future* (pp. 15–42). New York: Plenum Press.

McLeod, J. D. (1991). Childhood parental loss and adult depression. *Journal of Health and Social Behavior, 32,* 205–220.

Menaghan, E. G. (1983). Individual coping efforts: Moderators of the relationship between life stress and mental health outcomes. In H. B. Kaplan (Ed.), *Psychosocial stress: Trends in theory and research* (pp. 157–191). New York: Academic Press.

Mirowsky, J. (1995). Age and the sense of control. *Social Psychology Quarterly, 58,* 31–43.

Mirowsky, J., & Ross, C. E. (1986). Social patterns of distress. *Annual Review of Sociology, 12,* 23–45.

Mirowsky, J., & Ross, C. E. (1990). Control or defense? Depression and the sense of control over good and bad outcomes. *Journal of Health and Social Behavior, 31,* 71–86.

Monroe, S. M. (1992). Life events assessment: Current practices, emerging trends. *Clinical Psychology Review, 2,* 435–453.

Monroe, S. M., & McQuaid, J. R. (1994). Measuring life stress and assessing its impact on mental health. In W. R. Avison & I. H. Gotlib (Eds.), *Stress and mental health: Contemporary issues and prospects for the future* (pp. 43–73). New York: Plenum Press.

Moos, R. H. (1986). *Coping with life crises.* New York: Plenum Press.

Paykel, E. S. (1978). Contribution of life events to causation of psychiatric illness. *Psychological Medicine, 8,* 245–253.

Pearlin, L. I. (1989). The sociological study of stress. *Journal of Health and Social Behavior, 30,* 241–256.

Pearlin, L. I. (1999). The stress concept revisited: Reflections on concepts and their interrelationships. In C. S. Aneshensel & J. C. Phelan (Eds.), *Handbook of the sociology of mental health* (pp. 395–415). New York: Plenum Press.

Pearlin, L. I., Aneshensel, C. S., & LeBlanc, A. J. (1997). The forms and mechanisms of stress proliferation: The case of AIDS caregivers. *Journal of Health and Social Behavior, 38,* 223–236.

Pearlin, L. I., Lieberman, M. A., Menaghan, E. G., & Mullan, J. T. (1981). The stress process. *Journal of Health and Social Behavior, 22,* 337–356.

Pearlin, L. I., & Schooler, C. (1978). The structure of coping. *Journal of Health and Social Behavior, 19,* 2–21.

Riley, M. W. (1971). Social gerontology and the age stratification of society. *The Gerontologist, 11,* 79–87.

Riley, M. W. (1987). On the significance of age in sociology. *American Sociological Review, 52,* 1–14.

Riley, M. W., Johnson, M. E., & Foner, A. (1972). *Aging and society: 3. A sociology of age stratification.* New York: Russell Sage.

Rodin, J. (1986). Aging and health: Effects of the sense of control. *Science, 233,* 1271–1276.

Rodin, J., & Timko, C. (1992). Sense of control, aging and health. In M. G. Ory, R. P. Abeles, & P. D. Lipman (Eds.), *Aging, health and behavior* (pp. 207–236). Newbury Park, CA: Sage.

Rosenberg, M., Schooler, C., & Schoenbach, C. (1989). Self-esteem and adolescent problems: Modeling reciprocal effects. *American Sociological Review, 54,* 1004–1018.

Ross, C. E., & Sastry, J. (1999). The sense of personal control: Social-structural causes and emotional consequences. In C. S. Aneshensel & J. C. Phelan (Eds.), *Handbook of the sociology of mental health* (pp. 369–394). New York: Plenum Press.

Sarason, B. R., Pierce, G. R., & Sarason, I. G. (1990). Social support: The sense of acceptance and the role of relationships. In B. R. Sarason, I. G. Sarason, & G. R. Pierce (Eds.), *Social support: An interactional view* (pp. 97–128). New York: Wiley.

Schieman, S., & Turner, H. A. (1998). Age, disability, and the sense of mastery. *Journal of Health and Social Behavior, 39,* 169–186.

Seeman, M., Seeman, A. Z., & Budros, A. (1988). Powerless, work, and community: A longitudinal study of alienation and alcohol use. *Journal of Health and Social Behavior, 29,* 185–198.

Thoits, P. A. (1999). Self, identity, stress, and mental health. In C. S. Aneshensel & J. C. Phelan (Eds.), *Handbook of the sociology of mental health* (pp. 345–368). New York: Plenum Press.

Turner, R. J., & Avison, W. R. (1992). Innovations in the measurement of life stress: Crisis theory and the significance of event resolution. *Journal of Health and Social Behavior, 33,* 36–50.

Turner, R. J., & Lloyd, D. A. (1995). Lifetime traumas and mental health: The significance of cumulative adversity. *Journal of Health and Social Behavior, 36,* 360–376.

Turner, R. J., & Lloyd, D. A. (1999). The stress process and the social distribution of depression. *Journal of Health and Social Behavior, 40,* 374–404.

Turner, R. J., Lloyd, D. A., & Roszell, P. (1999). Personal resources and the social distribution of depression. *American Journal of Community Psychology, 27,* 643–672.

Turner, R. J., & Roszell, P. (1994). Psychosocial resources and the stress process. In W. R. Avison & I. H. Gotlib (Eds.), *Stress and mental health: Contemporary issues and prospects for the future* (pp. 179–210). New York: Plenum Press.

Turner, R. J., & Turner, J. B. (1999). Social integration and support. In C. S. Aneshensel & J. C. Phelan (Eds.), *Handbook of the sociology of mental health* (pp. 301–319). New York: Plenum Press.

Turner, R. J., Wheaton, B., & Lloyd, D. A. (1995). The epidemiology of social stress. *American Sociological Review, 60,* 104–125.

Wheaton, B. (1985). Models for the stress-buffering functions of coping resources. *Journal of Health and Social Behavior, 26,* 352–365.

Wheaton, B. (1990). Life transitions, role histories, and mental health. *American Sociological Review, 55,* 209–223.

Wheaton, B. (1994). Sampling the stress universe. In W. R. Avison & I. H. Gotlib (Eds.), *Stress and mental health: Contemporary issues and prospects for the future* (pp. 77–114). New York: Plenum Press.

Williams, D. R. (1990). Socioeconomic differentials in health: A review and redirection. *Social Psychology Quarterly, 53,* 81–99.

Wolinsky, F. D., & Stump, T. E. (1996). Age and the sense of control among older adults. *Journals of Gerontology (Psychological Sciences and Social Sciences), 51,* S217–S220.

Commentary

Personal Control: Mediation, Measurement, and Malleability

Richard H. Price

Avison and Cairney (this volume) offer a fine summary of the role of personal control in understanding the antecedents, mechanisms, and outcomes of stressful life experiences as pioneered in the work of Pearlin (1989). For a number of years, Avison and his colleagues have conducted programmatic work that embeds their exploration of the stress process in the lives of vulnerable populations. Their work, which implicates the critical role of personal and social resources in well-being, helps us understand differences in vulnerability for populations located in social contexts of disadvantage. In their chapter, Avison and Cairney take us a little bit further. They distinguish between the moderating effects of social and personal resources and the different mediational roles that these resources can play in articulating the processes that link stresses to distress and disorder. They also connect these critical issues of cause and consequence to questions of social stratification, then reflect on the malleability of the psychological sense of personal control. This is a rich and provocative beginning that invites us to carry the conversation forward.

I want to comment on three issues where we have had a fair amount of experience at the Michigan Prevention Research Center at the Institute for Social Research. The first has to do with the causal role that personal control may play in the stress process. I am particularly interested in a phenomenon that Bill Avison has called "the chain of adversity." Beyond that, I want to comment on the issues of measurement and meaning of personal control. This is far from a closed issue, and I want to suggest that additional theoretical development and construct validity work on the construct of personal control could serve us well. Finally, I want to comment on the issue of mallcability of personal control, where I think there are numerous theoretical and research opportunities that can be exploited.

EXTENDING THE BOUNDARIES OF THE STRESS PARADIGM

Drawing on an earlier seminal review by Wheaton (1985), Avison and Cairney (this volume) describe the potential roles of personal control as moderators of the strength of relationship between stressors and strains and as mechanisms mediating the process by which stressors lead to disorder. They argue that personal control may serve a number of different roles in the stress process. For example, under some circumstances, stressors may actually mobilize one's sense of personal control, whereas in other cases, stressors may erode the sense of control, leading to poor health and mental health outcomes. They also suggest that personal control can have direct effects on stressors or work jointly with stressors to either exacerbate or attenuate the impact of stressors on disorder. Of course, a major theoretical challenge is to specify the circumstances that lead to mobilization on the one hand, or erosion on the other.

All of the conceptual models described by Avison and Cairney imply that disorder is the end point in the stress process. Put simply, the conceptual task of stress models has been to explain how and why exposure to stressors leads to disorder, and, of course, by the same token help explain why often apparently severe stressors do not seem to lead to enduring disorder at all. Indeed, one of the great strengths of the stress paradigm has been that it simplified our understanding of stress, clipping off the phenomenon at the edges, nearly always leaving disorder as the end point. But loss of the sense of personal control could be a consequence of disorder rather than a cause. That is, the causal direction of personal control and disorder may be, under some circumstances, reversed. It is plausible that depression, for example, may actually lead to erosion in the sense of mastery, which, in turn, may impair functional status and exacerbate somatic complaints. Similar ideas have been suggested by Barnett and Gotlieb (1988) and are much more commonly invoked in clinical research. In a similar vein, Kessler and Price (1993) hypothesized that links between primary and secondary disorders, mental and physical disorders often thought to be comorbid, are actually part of such causal sequences. This expansion of the stress paradigm opens new hypotheses regarding the role of personal control in the genesis of disorder and disability. For example, the stress process can be specified in more complex mediational models that depict an entire "chain of adversity," to use a term I first heard used by Bill Avison, in describing the cascade of stressors in the lives of vulnerable individuals facing stressful life events. That chain of adversity can produce disorder that, in itself, influences later functioning or motivation.

Although we may wish to extend the stress paradigm, we also must acknowledge the likely complexity of the causal texture of the phenomenon. As Avison and Cairney observe, "In all likelihood the world is a dense causal web where reciprocal effects are probably operating" (p. 31). It is entirely possible that the causal arrow is pointed, not just in the opposite direction, but in both directions. Disorder is sometimes a powerful influence on eroded personal control, and in other cases, personal control ameliorates the effects of stress on strain. By examining more complex mediational chains, not only can we increase our capacity to specify complex events as they unfold over time, we can also better describe the specific texture of particular life events for particular populations.

MEASUREMENT AND MEANING OF PERSONAL CONTROL

Avison and Cairney make a bold assertion. They say, "Throughout this chapter, we use the terms *mastery* and *sense of personal control* interchangeably. In doing so, we take the position argued by Turner and Roszell (1994) that concepts such as *locus of control, fatalism, mastery, self-efficacy,* and *sense of powerlessness* are all labels for essentially the same construct."

This is both a bold theoretical assertion and a brave empirical claim. Consider for a moment the unmarried mothers whom Avison and his colleagues studied. When unmarried, unemployed mothers reported lower scores on mastery, how are we to interpret their reports? Are they veridical perceptions of their present circumstances? Or do reports of mastery and sense of control reflect some sort of individual difference that is a determinant of life circumstances? Is their report of low levels of mastery a result of the cascades of adverse life events that they have encountered? Or are low levels of mastery an indication of a global cognitive response of learned helplessness, or perhaps even a symptom of depression itself? These are challenging questions, but I wonder whether declaring these various terms and measures as equivalent is the best strategy for getting answers.

I believe that understanding the measurement and meaning of mastery, personal control, and related constructs calls for a serious program of construct validity studies. We need, as Cronbach and Meehl (1995) suggested in their classic article, to create a "nomological network" of control constructs that specifies the relationships among them and resolves claims of substantive equivalence predictive power. If we had such a set of construct validity data for multiple outcomes, it would provide a much more solid footing for both the conceptual framework and the empirical measurement of personal control. Here are a couple of important issues that are both matters of theoretical meaning and measurement.

First, there is the question of the specificity of referents in measures of personal control. We know that personal control measured in a more global way (asking in general about one's overall sense of control or mastery) may respond quite differently to environmental changes than measures framed in more situation-specific ways. For example, scales that measure something as specific as "job search self-efficacy" may respond quite differently to intervention attempts than more global measures of mastery or personal control.

Second, there is the question of attributions of control to one's own abilities and skills or to the environment. Recent reviews of the literature suggest that many measures of personal control are admixtures of judgments about one's own ability and judgments about the controllability of various environmental contingencies (Skinner, 1995, 1996). These should be distinguished both conceptually and empirically. It is quite plausible that different populations interpret controllability of the same stressor quite differently, depending on their judgments of their own abilities or the intractability of any environmental contingencies they face. Lumping both aspects of control together will obscure this crucial distinction. A systematic program of construct validity research would go some distance toward resolving these questions. These are, at bottom, theoretical questions about the measurement and meaning of the construct of control that require clarification if concepts such as mastery, sense of personal control, internal control, efficacy, and helplessness are to become part of a more coherent theoretical and empirical picture (Ginexi, Howe, & Caplan, 2000).

IS PERSONAL CONTROL MALLEABLE?

The question of whether or not personal control is malleable is a very broad one and needs some additional specification. What aspects of personal control might be malleable? If we believe that the distinction between judgments of one's own abilities and perceptions of the controllability of events is a useful one, that is clearly one way of unpacking the question. Are particular kinds of experiences optimal for shaping one's sense of personal control for either better or worse? If personal control is indeed malleable, what outcomes may be influenced? Does an enhanced sense of mastery influence health and mental health outcomes or occupational or educational outcomes? Over what time course might these changes take place? Are short-term changes possible, and if so, do they endure?

Related to these questions is a second set of choices having to do with research tactics and strategies used in trying to understand the nature and scope of malleability. Passive observational studies to answer questions about malleability are of real but limited value. Although intriguing leads can be identified from data of this kind, I am not sure that we can find out much more. I am nearly as skeptical about what many people call "natural experiments." In most cases, sample selection problems that are hard to clearly identify make studies of "natural experiments" seem more useful than they ultimately turn out to be. Of course, laboratory experiments, the favorite tool of many experimental social psychologists, can produce dramatic short-term outcomes, but often the outcome measures are lacking in external validity.

Theory-driven field experiments may hold some promise in helping us to answer questions about the malleability and consequences of self-control. For example, the Michigan Prevention Research Center has developed a program to help workers experiencing involuntary job loss to more effectively seek reemployment and cope with the multiple challenges and stresses of unemployment and job search (Caplan, Vinokur, & Price, 1997; Vinokur, Price, & Schul, 1995). The randomized field experiments we have conducted are designed to examine the impact of the program on unemployed workers and may be regarded as experimental tests of hypotheses regarding the causal role of employment status on mental health and the malleability of protective factors for mental health, such as sense of personal control.

The impact of the JOBS program on mental health and other outcomes has been studied in replicated randomized field trials involving unemployed workers and their partners (Caplan, Vinokur, Price, & van Ryn, 1989; Vinokur et al., 1995). The program returns unemployed workers to new jobs more quickly, produces reemployment in jobs that pay more (Vinokur, van Ryn, Gramlich, & Price, 1991), and reduces mental health problems associated with prolonged unemployment (Vinokur, Price, & Schul, 1995). A long-term follow-up study (Vinokur, Schul, Vuori, & Price, 2000) indicates that the program prevents the occurrence of major depressive episodes up to 2 years later. In addition, the program has been shown to inoculate workers against the adverse effects of a second job loss (Vinokur & Schul, 1997). In comparison to control group counterparts, program participants who regained employment, then suffered a second job loss did not experience the same discouragement and increased depressive symptoms that afflicted control group participants who had the same labor market experience. It appears that the program psychologically inoculates participants against subsequent job loss setbacks because they gain an enhanced sense of mastery over the challenges of job search (Vinokur & Schul, 1997). Furthermore, in a 2-year follow-up, Vinokur and colleagues (2000) showed that intervention participants with lower mastery scores at baseline showed poorer mental health and role functioning 2 years later, but, at the same time, showed greater gains in mental health and role functioning as a result of exposure to the intervention than did control group participants with higher baseline levels of mastery.

These results suggest that field experiments can tell us not only about the malleability of the sense of control but also reveal how intentional efforts to improve the sense of mastery or control may benefit the health and well-being of individuals experiencing life adversities. A wide variety of negative life events may be amenable to field experimentation using theory-driven interventions that can simultaneously illuminate risk mechanisms and increase coping resources, such as the sense of personal control.

CONCLUSION

Despite the numerous scientific publications, our fundamental understanding of the psychological sense of control in the stress process is moving ahead very slowly. It may be that the general conceptual paradigm used to frame our empirical questions about stress and coping, as robust and useful as it has been, has largely exhausted the empirical possibilities. Or it may be that the meaning of fundamental constructs such as personal control and mastery is not sufficiently specified and that additional "unpacking" of the construct is needed. Or it may be that the empirical methods used so far are capable of yielding only a limited range of answers and that a shift of methodological tactics is needed. I believe we need to move ahead on all three fronts.

First, we need to expand the stress paradigm rather than abandon it. We could fruitfully begin by taking Avison's idea of "chains of adversity" seriously. This means that we need to expand the paradigm and consider more dynamic longitudinal models of the causes and consequences of acute and chronic health and mental health conditions where disorders can also be seen as independent variables influencing other disabilities and psychological states. Unpacking the theoretical meaning of personal control presents us with a second opportunity for progress. Until we begin to distinguish the various psychological components that underlie global judgments of personal control, we will be using very blunt measurement instruments that are unlikely to yield much new insight. In particular, we need to understand how individuals make causal attributions about their own abilities and about the environment in making judgments about their sense of control or mastery. Finally, we may need to break old and comfortable methodological habits of limiting ourselves to observational studies in our study of stress and personal control. Theoretically driven experimental attempts to influence one's sense of control may hold some real promise in understanding the malleability of control and may also suggest ways to enhance people's mastery and sense of efficacy.

ACKNOWLEDGMENT

This research was supported by funds from the National Institute of Mental Health supporting the Michigan Prevention Research Center (P30MH38330) and the Joyce Foundation (3299/23323).

REFERENCES

Barnett, P. A., & Gotlieb, I. H. (1988). Psychosocial functioning and depression: Distinguishing among antecedents, concomitants, and consequences. *Psychological Bulletin, 104,* 97–126.

Caplan, R. D., Vinokur, A. D., & Price, R. H. (1997). From job loss to reemployment: Field experiments in prevention-focused coping. In G. W. Albee & T. P. Gullotta (Eds.), *Primary prevention works: Issues in children's and families' lives* (Vol. 16, pp. 341–379). Thousand Oaks, CA: Sage Publications.

Caplan, R. D., Vinokur, A. D., Price, R. H., & van Ryn, M. (1989). Job seeking, reemployment, and mental health: A randomized field experiment in coping with job loss. *Journal of Applied Psychology, 74*(5), 759–769.

Cronbach, L. J., & Meehl, P. E. (1995). Construct validity in psychological tests. *Psychological Bulletin, 52,* 281–302.

Ginexi, E. M., Howe, G. W., & Caplan, R. D. (2000). Depression and control beliefs in relation to reemployment: What are the directions of effect? *Journal of Occupational Health Psychology, 5*(3), 323–336.

Kessler, R. C., & Price, R. H. (1993). Primary prevention of secondary disorders: A proposal and agenda. *American Journal of Community Psychology, 21*(5), 607–634.

Pearlin, L. I. (1989). The sociological study of stress. *Journal of Health and Social Behavior, 30,* 241–256.

Turner, R. J., & Roszell, P. (1994). Psychosocial resources and the stress process. In W. R. Avison & I. H. Gotlieb (Eds.), *Stress and mental health: Contemporary issues and prospects for the future* (pp. 179–210). New York: Plenum Press.

Skinner, E. A. (1995). *Perceived control, motivation, and coping.* Thousand Oaks, CA: Sage.

Skinner, E. A. (1996). A guide to constructs of control. *Journal of Personality and Social Psychology, 71,* 549–570.

Vinokur, A. D., & Schul, Y. (1997). Mastery and inoculation against setbacks as active ingredients in the JOBS intervention for the unemployed. *Journal of Consulting and Clinical Psychology, 65*(5), 867–877.

Vinokur, A. D., Price, R. H., & Schul, Y. (1995). Impact of the JOBS intervention on unemployed workers varying in risk for depression. *American Journal of Community Psychology, 23,* 39–74.

Vinokur, A. D., Schul, Y., Vuori, J., & Price, R. H. (2000). Two years after a job loss: Long-term impact of the JOBS program on reemployment and mental health. *Journal of Occupational Health Psychology, 5*(1), 32–47.

Vinokur, A. D., van Ryn, M., Gramlich, E. M., & Price, R. H. (1991). Long-term follow-up and benefit-cost analysis of the Jobs Program: A preventive intervention for the unemployed. *Journal of Applied Psychology, 76*(2), 213–219.

Wheaton, B. (1985). Models for the stress-buffering functions of coping resources. *Journal of Health and Social Behavior, 26,* 352–365.

Commentary

Social Aspects of Stress: Networks, Choices, and Values

Jane D. McLeod

M y comments address three broad questions about the role of personal control in the stress process: (1) How does the concept of personal control help us understand the stress process? (2) How does the study of the stress process help us understand the concept of personal control? and (3) How do these intertwined research programs help us understand the nature of social life? These questions lead us to consider the assumptions that stress researchers make about the nature of human action and about the relative importance of social structure and human agency in its determination. Their answers challenge those assumptions and suggest new avenues of inquiry that would enhance the contributions of stress research to our understanding of individual psychology, as well as social life.

HOW DOES THE CONCEPT OF PERSONAL CONTROL HELP US UNDERSTAND THE STRESS PROCESS?

Stress researchers typically conceptualize personal control, or mastery, in general terms, as a global sense of control that contributes to well-being in similarly global ways. Among stress researchers, mastery is a concept that is often equated with locus of control, self-efficacy, fatalism, and related constructs, and that is intended to capture the general belief that one can "master, control, and shape one's own life" (Ross & Sastry, 1999).[1] Thus, mastery is a personal or intrapsychic resource, one dimension of the self-concept. It refers to a set of self-beliefs that we hold internally, that we carry with us, and that we can then apply to a broad set of problems and situations.

Conceptualized in this way, the concept of mastery both conforms to and reveals the individualistic bias of the stress paradigm. Building on a tradition of lab-based research on adaptive responses to stressful situations (Selye, 1956), stress researchers conceive of stressors as assaults from outside the individual that disrupt the bodily and psychological homeostasis internal to that individual.[2] Whereas stress researchers were relatively quick to recognize the centrality of appraisal and meaning in the experience of stress (Lazarus & Folkman, 1984), we have been somewhat remiss in acknowledging the fundamentally social nature of stress. By that, I mean that stress is experienced by individuals within a web of social relations and affiliations, and each stage in the stress process is influenced by that embeddedness (Thoits, 1995).

A Social Model of Stress

When thinking about how people experience stress, researchers tend to envision isolated individuals who encounter potentially stressful experiences, appraise and interpret those experiences, make decisions about how to respond to those experiences, then become either distressed or not, depending on the effectiveness of their responses. Despite the analytical appeal of that type of model, it oversimplifies what is in reality a much more complex process. Very few people experience stress in complete isolation from others (regardless of their perceptions of the availability of support). Other people become involved in our stress, both voluntarily and involuntarily. They have psychological reactions to our stress, and their reactions change what the stress means to us. We construct interpretations of potentially stressful experiences in interaction with them. Other people help us decide what to do, and they respond to what we do, which changes what we do next. Whereas the social support literature certainly recognizes that other people may offer advice or assistance (see Kessler & McLeod, 1985; Turner & Turner, 1999, for reviews), the processes of interpretation and decision making that potentially stressful experiences initiate occur whether or not other people are "supporting us." In fact, the processes of interpretation and decision making may be perceived as unsupportive if they require management of conflicting or unwanted interpretations and advice (Pearlin & McCall, 1990). In short, I am arguing for an interactionally based understanding of stress and mastery—an understanding that would move us away from models of stress that place the individual, rational actor at the center, and toward models that conceptualize stress as a network-based process (consistent with Pescosolido's [1992] reconceptualization of health services research).

How would thinking about the stress process in this way change our understanding of mastery's relevance? We can think this through with respect to two of the models that Avison and Cairney (this volume) present. One of those models assigns mastery the role of a stress deterrent: People use their feelings of mastery to modify their perceptions of stressful experiences so that those experiences no longer seem as threatening or to avoid stress by regulating their physical and social environments. Assuming that feelings of mastery actually translate into effective action (an assumption to which I will return), this model seems quite reasonable on its face and is consistent with broader theoretical claims about the centrality of perception in the stress process (Lazarus & Folkman, 1984) and about the capacity of individuals to shape their future lives (Elder, George, & Shanahan, 1996; George, 1999).

The mechanisms through which mastery may deter stress become more complicated when we think of stress as a social process. Mastery may modify our perceptions of potentially stressful experiences, but those perceptions are also subject to the influence of important others who may or may not share our views. We may succeed in promoting our interpretation over theirs, but mastery may not be the most important intrapsychic resource for achieving that goal. Mastery may have additional limits as a stress deterrent because we are often confronted with stressors that derive from our associations with other persons (Kessler & McLeod, 1984; Turner, Wheaton, & Lloyd, 1995). Although our personal levels of mastery may help us avoid environmental assaults, they do not necessarily keep us from becoming involved in the troubles of our friends and loved ones. (In fact, feelings of mastery may even lead us to extend ourselves into the lives of others because we believe that our efforts will prove helpful.) The stress deterrent potential of mastery is thereby constrained by the structure and content of the social networks of which we are a part.

We can apply similar logic to mastery's role as a buffer for the effects of stress on distress. The image that guides discussions of the buffering effect is that of an isolated individual whose intrapsychic resources, or lack thereof, influence coping responses. The presumption of research on buffering, not always precisely confirmed, is that people who are masterful are better than other people at soliciting social support when they need it and at choosing effective coping strategies. This presumed process becomes decidedly more complex when other people who have become invested in the stressful experience give and seek support themselves, and suggest and try their own coping strategies, some of which may undermine those that we favor. If we were to pose the question how does mastery become part of the complex interpersonal negotiations and struggles inherent in coping with stressful experiences? we would have trouble answering it because we tend not to locate stressful experiences within social collectives (see Caplan, 1981; Coyne, Wortman, & Lehman, 1988, for exceptions).

Mastery, Choice, and Action

Mastery's presumed link to choice, decision, and action has been one of its most compelling contributions to the literature on stress. As yet, however, we know very little about how mastery influences the choices that people make about how to respond to stress. People who feel masterful seem to persist in their coping efforts to a greater degree than people who do not feel masterful (Krause, 1999), but the presumption in much stress research is that mastery also predicts specific types of coping strategies or styles. As Thoits (1995) discussed so effectively, it is reasonable to speculate, for example, that people who have higher levels of mastery would choose more active coping strategies and that those active coping strategies would serve as particularly effective stress moderators. However, although persons with high levels of mastery are more likely than persons with low levels of mastery to report using problem-focused strategies and active coping styles (Mirowsky & Ross, 1989; Pearlin & Schooler, 1978), problem-focused strategies and active coping styles are not uniformly effective in ameliorating the effects of stressors on physical and mental health (Mattlin, Wethington, & Kessler, 1990; Menaghan, 1983). Furthermore, we do not really know why people with high levels of mastery choose more problem-focused strategies. Is it that they perceive themselves as more competent to solve problems? Is it that mastery influences perceptions of constraint so that people who feel more masterful also feel more free to choose problem-focused strategies without fear that their efforts will be blocked? Is it instead that persons with high levels of mastery have developed the skills that they need to enact active coping strategies? Our inability to answer these questions suggests that we still do not fully understand the concept of mastery itself (a point to which I will return) and that we have not adequately incorporated choice and decision making into models of stress.

The lack of attention to choice and decision making in stress research reflects a more general reluctance to acknowledge the possibility that stressors have personal, as well as structural, origins. Although there is movement in the field to think more seriously about how people contribute to the stress they experience (Pearlin, 1991; Thoits, 1995), most stress researchers remain tied to the traditional conceptualization of stressors as events and circumstances that happen to us. Researchers who do acknowledge the personal origins of stress treat them as confounders of the stress–distress relationship rather than as processes of central interest in their own right.[3] The reluctance of researchers to incorporate the personal origins of stress into our models reflects an underlying assumption that personal origins represent purely internal processes that can be understood without reference to the social environment. I contend, in contrast, that the personal origins of stress represent traces of past and present structural, interactional, and experiential constraints on human action—a conceptualization informed by the life course paradigm within sociology.

A central tenet of the life course paradigm is that "individuals construct their own life course through the choices and actions they take within the constraints and opportunities of history and social circumstance" (Elder, 1997, pp. 961–962). In essence, people make choices based on the options they are able to perceive, and those choices influence their future life paths. Perceived options, in turn, are influenced by structural arrangements, previous successes and failures, vicarious observation, the responses of valued others, and cultural norms and values—all of which are appropriately conceptualized as social in origin.[4] Broadening our notion of the "social" in social stress would enrich our understanding of origins of stressors and of their consequences. Moreover, acknowledging the role of choice throughout the life course would enhance rather than diminish our ability to see the true nature of social constraints on perceptions and actions.

As a concept that is intended to capture people's relationships with the world around them, mastery should play a central role in analyses of constraint, choice, and action. Mastery shapes our perceptions of possibility, as well as our predispositions to act or to accept. It reflects our previous experiences of success and failure in modifying the environment, and also contributes to our ability to modify that environment in the future. Like self-esteem (Rosenberg, 1981), mastery is both social product and social force that develops in transactional relationship with the social environment over the life course. It serves as an important link between social structure and individual action, the life course and human agency. Yet, as important as this link is, we know very little about its nature and strength.

In sum, I argue here for a social model of stress that takes seriously the negotiated character of stressful experiences and the interplay of choice and constraint in stress responses. Conceptualizing stress in this way promises new insights into the stress process that are visible in high relief when we consider the special case of older adults. Compared with those in the middle years, older adults more often live in situations where their decisions are subject to the scrutiny of others, a structural arrangement that is supported by cultural norms regarding aging and competency. As a result, older adults' interpretations of events and their coping efforts may be particularly subject to challenge. Age-related variations in the interpretation of events common among elders (e.g., retirement and hospitalization; Davies, Saunders, & Newton, 1987; Hughes, George, & Blazer, 1988) further complicate intergenerational negotiations about the meaning and appropriate responses to major life transitions. Moreover, whereas older adults bring a lifetime of experience to their coping efforts, structural arrangements, cultural norms, and the aging process itself heighten constraints and encourage dependency. Studies of the contributions and limitations of mastery in the face of structural and ideological constraints would offer more general insights into the social nature of stress.

HOW DOES THE STUDY OF THE STRESS PROCESS HELP US UNDERSTAND THE CONCEPT OF PERSONAL CONTROL?

I turn here to a more fundamental question about the origins of mastery's health-protective effects. What is it that mastery gives us? As I've suggested before, stress researchers have claimed that mastery matters because it influences what people perceive, what they feel capable of doing, and what they actually do, influences that operate at each stage of the stress process (i.e., stress deterrence, stress buffering, etc.). What remains unclear, however, is how each of these influences operates and which influence is most powerful. As a point of entry into this topic, in much the same way that people have asked whether the perception of support is enough to buffer the effects of stressful experiences or whether the things that other people actually do for us make a difference (Turner & Turner, 1999; Wethington & Kessler, 1986), we can ask whether the perception of control is enough or whether mastery has to manifest itself in externally observable change in order to influence stress. Or, to say it in a different way, is personal control akin to other positively biased perceptions that seem to promote well-being (Taylor, Kemeny, Reed, Bower, & Gruenewald, 2000), or does its effectiveness depend on its embeddedness in concrete reality?

Some research suggests that the answer to this last question is no or, in any case, that there is a threshold beyond which feelings of control overreach reality and become harmful to psychological health. For example, Wheaton (1985) observed a parabolic relationship between mastery and depression: Mastery is negatively related to depression up to a point, but further increases in mastery beyond that point increase feelings of depression. Similarly, Mirowsky and Ross (1990) found that mastery has "diminishing returns" when the perception of control becomes illusory rather than grounded in the concrete realities of life. They contend that it is the combination of motivation and realistic appraisal that really improves psychological well-being. Both of these findings imply that positively biased perceptions of mastery are harmful rather than beneficial, although they do not specifically address the question of whether perceptions of control have to manifest themselves in concrete thought or action to be effective.

At the same time, the work of Pearlin and Skaff (1996) on personal control among the elderly and their caregivers shows that people are motivated to maintain a sense of control by reconstructing reality. They do so by shifting values and priorities, by selectively attending to the parts of their lives over which they have control and ignoring the parts of their life that they do not, and by drawing on memories of past efficacious actions to support their personal theories of control. Perceptions of mastery that are maintained in the face of conflicting evidence may be illusory, to some extent, but they are also grounded in a perceived and constructed reality that shifts over time (see Jackson and Wilkins, this volume). Depending on how far people reach to construct a sense of mastery, that sense may in fact bear little relation to potential action but may nevertheless constitute a resource for coping with stress. The question of how mastery is created through experience and how it is implicated in processes of self-verification, self-enhancement, and identity formation merits more attention from stress researchers.

The Social Origins of Mastery

An alternative approach to the question of what mastery is involves study of its social origins. The research that Avison and Cairney present on the social malleability of mastery provides evidence for clea social patterning. Mastery increases with socioeconomic status, it is higher among persons who are or have been married, it is higher among men than women, although perhaps not by much, and it declines with age. Although the nature of Avison and Cairney's sample precludes an examination of race, prior research shows consistently that African Americans have lower levels of mastery than Whites in the United States (Hughes & Demo, 1989; Ross & Mirowsky, 1989). Together, these results support the general conclusion that occupancy of advantaged social positions engenders feelings of mastery.

What is it about those advantaged social positions that matters? Most sociological theories of the origins of mastery locate them in socially structured experiences of power and opportunity (Avison & Cairney, this volume; Mirowsky & Ross, 1989; Rosenfield, 1989). We learn that we have (or do not have) control as a result of observing our abilities (or inabilities) to achieve desired outcomes and to avoid those that are less desirable. Unexpected, uncontrollable stressors teach us that the world is unpredictable, random, and uncontrollable. Constant striving for goals that we cannot attain leaves us all too aware of our ineffectiveness in the face of powerful others. Ross and Mirowsky (1989) elaborated these claims in a theory of personal control, in which they traced low personal control to structural powerlessness, structural inconsistency (the disjuncture between means and ends), alienated labor, dependency, and role overload. According to their theory, these structural conditions decrease the chances for the effective assertion of control from which people learn to see themselves as efficacious. We can extend their theory to explain status variations in mastery: People in lower status positions are more likely than those in higher status positions to be structurally powerless, to lack the means to achieve desired ends, and so on, and they are therefore less likely to have opportunities for efficacious action. The greater exposure to stress that has been observed among lower status groups may originate from these same conditions and, inasmuch as stressors decrease control, becomes implicated in status variations in mastery (Avison & Cairney, this volume).

As we continue to do research that enhances the precision of these arguments, we need to think more concretely about how these processes of power and opportunity play out with respect to specific indicators of status, both individually and in combination, and about the role of values and psychological centrality in mastery within different domains of life.

With respect to the first point, the argument that mastery arises from powerlessness and constrained opportunities works well in the case of socioeconomic status. It is easy to see, for example, how occupations that permit self-directed work or that involve supervision over other people promote the belief that one has the ability to shape one's own life, and that occupations in which one is engaged in routine work or that involve being supervised closely by someone else would engender feelings of powerlessness, particularly at work (Kohn & Schooler, 1983). Money also buys a certain degree of control (Thoits, 1995), and education both teaches its students the benefits of taking an active stance toward life and gives students the skills they need to follow through (Mirowsky, 1995).

We can apply similar logic to explaining race and gender differences in mastery, but here the need for more nuance becomes clear. There is substantial variation in the paths that men and women choose and in their abilities to control their paths based on socioeconomic, employment, and marital status. Similarly, racial and ethnic variations in power and opportunity depend on gender and socioeconomic status. Furthermore, the nature of the power and opportunity to which Whites and men have access differs from that which comes solely from achieved statuses. Sociological theories of stratification have begun to grapple with the complexities of overlapping and interactive systems of stratification (e.g., Chafetz, 1997; Collins, 1990; Cotter, Hermsen, & Vanneman, 1999), but those theories have not yet filtered into stress research.

With respect to the second point, it also seems reasonable to propose that the relationship between various status indicators and mastery varies across different domains of life. Women who are raising children and not working for pay may feel a general lack of control over their lives, but they may also feel quite efficacious as parents. In fact, given the current social context, they may feel more efficacious if they have chosen not to work outside the home than if they are employed by necessity. Similarly, lacking control over one's job may diminish one's sense of personal control at work, but there may be other domains of one's life that remain untouched.

What this point brings me to is the importance of considering values and the psychological centrality of different life domains when studying the effects of stress on mastery. Extending the arguments of Thoits (1992) and Krause (1994), stressors may be more likely to affect mastery when they alter the chance of successful performance in valued social roles. Stressors that diminish one's ability to perform competently in arenas of life that are unimportant to one's sense of self are unlikely to diminish mastery to the same extent. Avison and Cairney (this volume) make a similar point in their discussion of job conditions and mastery among women. The effect of specific job conditions on women's mastery may depend on how central the breadwinner or worker role is to their identities.

These arguments suggest that social status variations in mastery may arise from structural differences in power and opportunity, but also from socially influenced values and identities. I might also emphasize the importance of considering selection processes as well. Even in the case of socioeconomic status, as Avison and Cairney imply, we have to remain open to the possibility that persistent individual differences in mastery at young ages affect later attainment. More generally, any social statuses that are achieved rather than ascribed are likely to reflect lifelong processes of action and reaction involving personal control. Rather than dismissing these effects as confounders, we should integrate them into our models of stress and mastery in order to facilitate an examination of stress and achievement over the life course (Shanahan, Hofer, & Miech, this volume).

We also can think these processes through with reference to Avison and Cairney's finding of an age difference in the relationship between education and mastery. Why would it be that education matters less to mastery for older cohorts than for younger cohorts? It could be that there is some type of selection process operating in which mastery predicts survival differentially depending on levels of education. Alternatively, formal education may become less important to one's ability to perform valued social roles competently as one becomes older. Or there may have been fewer differences in opportunities for efficacious action based on education earlier in the 20th century than there are now, given changes in the nature of labor markets in western industrialized countries. The plausibility of each of these alternatives supports the potential relevance of selection, opportunity, and values to status variations in mastery.

HOW DO THESE INTERTWINED RESEARCH PROGRAMS HELP US UNDERSTAND THE NATURE OF SOCIAL LIFE?

My comments to this point already allude to the potential contributions of research on stress and mastery to more general models of social life. For example, studies of how mastery becomes implicated in interpersonal negotiations regarding stressful experiences would inform more general questions about how social support is invoked and how social networks identify, assign value to, and draw on the intrapsychic resources of their members to solve problems—a naturalistic analogue to experimentally based expectations states theory. To take another example, studies building on the concept of mastery to develop models of decision and action in the stress process would contribute to more general discussions of structure and agency within sociology (e.g., Sewell, 1992; Shanahan, 2000).

Perhaps most compellingly, research on stress and mastery offers a conceptual framework for articulating the implications of stratification for the psychological lives of individuals (Aneshensel, 1992; Pearlin, 1989). In the best tradition of social structure and personality research (House, 1981), it vividly illustrates how social structured inequalities create untenable life circumstances, impinge on freedom and choice, and deprive some persons of well-being while others thrive. Thus, it contributes to the broader agenda of research concerned with the nature and implications of the inequitable distribution of resources in society.

In the specific area of aging and life course studies, research on stress and mastery has the potential to link individualistic models of aging with the critical models favored by political economists. Critical models emphasize state processes that reinforce domination and marginalization of the aged through policies that create contradictions between the needs of aging individuals and the existing social structure (see Estes, Wallace, & Linkins, 2000, for a review). These contradictions are experienced at the individual level as stress, loss of control, and physical and psychological distress. Processes of individual adaptation over the life course—as emphasized by activity theory, continuity theory, and theories of successful aging—are constrained by societal imperatives (e.g., the need to retire) and social programs (e.g., Medicare) that systematically disempower older adults. Sensitive studies of how mastery and stress evolve over the life course, particularly at older ages, have the potential to reveal the structural underpinnings of personal struggles to grow old with grace and dignity.

More generally, a careful review of research on mastery shows that the patterns of relation between stratification and mastery have remained stable over several decades of research despite substantial changes in the nature of stratification in the United States during that time. What this suggests is that variations in mastery are inherent to stratified societies. People with power value the powerlessness of others and use the means available to them to reinforce it (whether or not they are conscious of doing so). In complement, people without power learn the futility of their efforts and thereby lose incentive to seek it (Wilson, 1991). As Avison and Cairney note, personal control is a fundamental component of the mechanisms linking stratification, stress, and mental health. Our efforts to understand the social nature of and responses to stress will be necessarily incomplete until we integrate a more complex model of stratification into our research. Similarly, we will never understand the true nature of stratification in the United States unless we further elaborate the mechanisms by which structures of disadvantage translate into diminished self-concepts, personal troubles, and psychological distress.

ACKNOWLEDGMENT

The writing of this chapter was supported by NIMH Training Grant T32 MH14588. Many thanks to Kathryn Lively, Leonard Pearlin, and Steven Zarit for their comments on an earlier draft.

NOTES

1.   There is room in stress research for more debate about the utility of global versus domain-specific conceptualizations of mastery and for discussion of its relation to self-efficacy and related concepts. See Chapter 1 and the preceding commentary by Price in this volume.

2. The engineering model of stress (Smith, 1987) has become more popular in recent years. According to that model, stressors are forces external to the individual that become stressful when they exceed the capacity of the individual to resist. Although this model avoid Selye's (1956) assumption that stressors influence health through physiological responses, it nevertheless shares the assumptions of externality of the stressor and individuality of response (see Wheaton, 1999, for a more thorough discussion).

3. For example, Dohrenwend, Link, Kern, Shrout, and Markowitz (1987) and Brown (1974) recognize that stressful circumstances can be caused by the individual. They attempt to eliminate such circumstances from their analyses in order to derive "clean" estimates of the effects of stress on mental health. Consistent with Thoits (1995), I would argue that eliminating these types of stressors from the analysis removes most of what happens to people from the purview of stress research.

4. This list of influences on perceived options parallels Bandura's (1986) list of the determinants of self-efficacy.

REFERENCES

Aneshensel, C. S. (1992). Social stress: Theory and research. *Annual Review of Sociology, 18,* 15–38.

Bandura, A. (1986). *Social foundations of thought and action: A social cognitive theory.* Englewood Cliffs, NJ: Prentice Hall.

Brown, G. W. (1974). Meaning, measurement, and stress of life events. In B. S. Dohrenwend & B. P. Dohrenwend (Eds.), *Stressful life events: Their nature and effects* (pp. 217–245). New York: Wiley.

Caplan, G. (1981). Mastery of stress: Psychosocial aspects. *American Journal of Psychiatry, 138,* 413–420.

Chafetz, J. (1997). Feminist theory and sociology: Underutilized contributions for mainstream theory. *Annual Review of Sociology, 23,* 97–120.

Collins, P. H. (1990). *Black feminist thought: Knowledge, consciousness, and the politics of empowerment.* Boston: Unwin Hyman.

Cotter, D. A., Hermsen, J. M., & Vanneman, R. (1999). Systems of gender, race, and class inequality: Multilevel analyses. *Social Forces, 78,* 433–460.

Coyne, J. C., Wortman, C. B., & Lehman, D. R. (1988). The other side of support: Emotional overinvolvement and miscarried helping. In B. H. Gottlieb (Ed.), *Marshaling social support: Formats, processes, and effects* (pp. 305–330). Newbury Park, CA: Sage.

Davies, A. D. M., Saunders, C., & Newton, T. J. (1987). Age differences in the rating of life-stress events: Does contextual detail make a difference? *British Journal of Clinical Psychology, 26,* 299–303.

Dohrenwend, B. P., Link, B. G., Kern, R., Shrout, P. E., & Markowitz, J. (1987). Measuring life events: The problem of variability within event categories. In B. Cooper (Ed.), *Psychiatric epidemiology: Progress and prospects* (pp. 103–119). London: Croom Helm.

Elder, G. H., Jr. (1997). The life course and human development. In R. M. Lerner (Ed.), *Handbook of child psychology: 1. Theoretical models of human development* (pp. 939–991). New York: Wiley.

Elder, G. H., Jr., George, L. K., & Shanahan, M. J. (1996). Psychosocial stress over the life course. In H. B. Kaplan (Ed.), *Psychosocial stress: Perspectives on structure, theory, life course, and methods* (pp. 247–292). San Diego: Academic Press.

Estes, C. W., Wallace, S., & Linkins, K. W. (2000). Political economy of aging and health. In C. E. Bird, P. Conrad, & A. M. Fremont (Eds.), *Handbook of medical sociology* (5th ed., pp. 129–142). Upper Saddle River, NJ: Prentice Hall.

George, L. K. (1999). Life-course perspectives on mental health. In C. S. Aneshensel & J. C. Phelan (Eds.), *Handbook of the sociology of mental health* (pp. 565–583). New York: Kluwer Academic/Plenum.

House, J. S. (1981). Social structure and personality. In M. Rosenberg & R. Turner (Eds.), *Sociological perspectives on social psychology* (pp. 525–561). New York: Basic Books.

Hughes, D. C., George, L. K., & Blazer, D. G. (1988). Age differences in life event qualities: Multivariate controlled analyses. *Journal of Community Psychology, 16,* 161–174.

Hughes, M., & Demo, D. H. (1989). Self perceptions of black Americans: Self-esteem and personal efficacy. *American Journal of Sociology, 95,* 132–159.

Kessler, R. C., & McLeod, J. D. (1984). Sex differences in vulnerability to undesirable life events. *American Sociological Review, 49,* 620–631.

Kessler, R. C., & McLeod, J. D. (1985). Social support and mental health in community samples. In S. Cohen & S. L. Syme (Eds.), *Social support and health* (pp. 219–240). New York: Academic.

Kohn, M. L., & Schooler, C. (1983). *Work and personality: An inquiry into the impact of social stratification.* Norwood, NJ: Ablex.

Krause, N. (1994). Stressors in salient social roles and well-being in later life. *Journals of Gerontology, 49,* 137–148.

Krause, N. (1999). Mental disorder in late life: Exploring the influence of stress and socioeconomic status. In C. S. Aneshensel & J. C. Phelan

(Eds.), *Handbook of the sociology of mental health* (pp. 183–208). New York: Kluwer Academic/Plenum.

Lazarus, R. S., & Folkman, S. (1984). *Stress, appraisal, and coping.* New York: Springer.

Mattlin, J. A., Wethington, E., & Kessler, R. C. (1990). Situational determinants of coping and coping effectiveness. *Journal of Health and Social Behavior, 31,* 162–172.

Menaghan, E. G. (1983). Individual coping efforts: Moderators of the relationship between life stress and mental health outcomes. In H. B. Kaplan (Ed.), *Psychosocial stress: Trends in theory and research* (pp. 157–191). New York: Academic.

Mirowsky, J. (1995). Age and the sense of control. *Social Psychology Quarterly, 58,* 31–43.

Mirowsky, J., & Ross, C. E. (1989). *Social causes of psychological distress.* New York: Aldine de Gruyter.

Mirowsky, J., & Ross, C. E. (1990). The consolation prize theory of alienation. *American Journal of Sociology, 95,* 1505–1535.

Pearlin, L. I. (1989). The sociological study of stress. *Journal of Health and Social Behavior, 30,* 241–256.

Pearlin, L. I. (1991). The study of coping: An overview of problems and directions. In J. Eckenrode (Ed.), *The social context of coping* (pp. 261–276). New York: Plenum.

Pearlin, L. I., & McCall, M. E. (1990). Occupational stress and marital support: A description of microprocesses. In J. Eckenrode & S. Gore (Eds.), *Crossing the boundaries: The transmission of stress between work and family* (pp. 39–60). New York: Plenum Press.

Pearlin, L. I., & Schooler, C. (1978). The structure of coping. *Journal of Health and Social Behavior, 19,* 2–21.

Pearlin, L. I., & Skaff, M. M. (1996). Stress and the life course: A paradigmatic alliance. *The Gerontologist, 36,* 239–247.

Pescosolido, B. A. (1992). Beyond rational choice: The social dynamics of how people seek help. *American Journal of Sociology, 97,* 1096–1138.

Rosenberg, M. (1981). The self-concept: Social product and social force. In M. Rosenberg & R. H. Turner (Eds.), *Social psychology: Sociological perspectives* (pp. 593–624). New York: Basic Books.

Rosenfield, S. (1989). The effects of women's employment: Personal control and sex differences in mental health. *Journal of Health and Social Behavior, 30,* 77–91.

Ross, C. E., & Mirowsky, J. (1989). Explaining the social patterns of depression: Control and problem-solving—or support and talking. *Journal of Health and Social Behavior, 30,* 206–219.

Ross, C. E., & Sastry, J. (1999). The sense of personal control: Social-structural causes and emotional consequences. In C. S. Aneshensel & J. C. Phelan (Eds.), *Handbook of the sociology of mental health* (pp. 369–394). New York: Kluwer Academic/Plenum.

Selye, H. (1956). *The stress of life*. New York: McGraw-Hill.

Sewell, W. H. (1992). A theory of structure-duality, agency, and transformation. *American Journal of Sociology, 98,* 1–29.

Shanahan, M. J. (2000). Pathways to adulthood in changing societies: Variability and mechanisms in life course perspective. *Annual Review of Sociology, 26,* 667–692.

Smith, W. K. (1987). The stress analogy. *Schizophrenia Bulletin, 13,* 215–220.

Taylor, S. E., Kemeny, M. E., Reed, G. M., Bower, J. E., & Gruenewald, T. L. (2000). Psychological resources, positive illusions, and health. *American Psychologist, 55,* 99–109.

Thoits, P. A. (1992). Identity structures and psychological well-being: Gender and marital status comparisons. *Social Psychology Quarterly, 55,* 236–256.

Thoits, P. A. (1995). Stress, coping, and social support processes: Where are we? What next? *Journal of Health and Social Behavior (Special Issue),* 53–79.

Turner, R. J., & Turner, J. B. (1999). Social integration and support. In C. S. Aneshensel & J. C. Phelan (Eds.), *Handbook of the sociology of mental health* (pp. 301–320). New York: Kluwer Academic/Plenum.

Turner, R. J., Wheaton, B., & Lloyd, D. (1995). The epidemiology of social stress. *American Sociological Review, 60,* 104–125.

Wethington, E., & Kessler, R. C. (1986). Perceived support, received support, and adjustment to stressful life events. *Journal of Health and Social Behavior, 27,* 78–90.

Wheaton, B. (1985). Personal resources and mental health: Can there be too much of a good thing? In J. R. Greenley (Ed.), *Research in community and mental health* (pp. 139–184). Greenwich, CT: JAI Press.

Wheaton, B. (1999). Social stress. In C. S. Aneshensel & J. C. Phelan (Eds.), *Handbook of the sociology of mental health* (pp. 277–300). New York: Kluwer Academic/Plenum.

Wilson, W. J. (1991). Studying inner-city social dislocations: The challenge of public agenda research. *American Sociological Review, 56,* 1–14.

CHAPTER 5

Planful Competence, the Life Course, and Aging: Retrospect and Prospect

Michael J. Shanahan, Scott M. Hofer, and Richard A. Miech

Planful competence refers to individual differences in people's ability to choose roles that are well suited to their interests and talents, and to pursue these roles effectively and with perseverance. As such, planful competence describes goal-directed behaviors that are specific to the life course, often covering many decades. Prior research suggests that planfulness during adolescence shapes educational and occupational trajectories, family life, and later life review, although these relationships are conditioned in significant ways by historical change. We extend these insights to the study of aging through hypotheses that interrelate planfulness in adolescence and achievements and well-being through adulthood. Despite the promise of prior work in this area, deficiencies are noted and directions for future research are proposed that focus on the highly interactive nature of planfulness.

From a life course perspective, personal agency in old age reflects decades of experiences that are powerfully shaped by one's place in society and by planning and personal effort. Yet how can these manifold and diverse experiences be conceptualized and studied in an empirical framework? From its inception, the life course paradigm recognized the theoretical importance of personal agency in shaping the biography, although two distinct approaches can be identified.

First, the founders of the life course paradigm emphasized the reactive, group-based responses of people to social change. Thomas and Thomas (1932) viewed social change as a source of crisis that defined social situations and elicited "adaptive strivings and processes of adjustment" within the family and other significant social groups (p. 177; see also Volkart, 1951). According to Thomas (1909), this homeostatic process of crisis-attention-control is integral to the life course: "The incidents of birth, death, adolescence, and marriage, while not unanticipated, are always foci of attention and occasions for control" (p. 13). Similarly, in his path-setting *Children of the Great Depression,* Glen Elder (1974/1999) revealed how the timing of historical events in the life course powerfully shapes the meaning of social change: Younger and older children responded differently to familial stressors, and these different responses in turn had long-lasting implications for values, motivations, and indicators of social adjustment.

Second, other life course theorists emphasized the active role that individuals play in identifying and pursuing their futures. Charlotte Bühler promoted the developmental study of agency with her conceptual model of "the goal-directed life" (Bühler & Massarik, 1968). According to this perspective, the life course must be analyzed as "integrated strivings" to fulfill the personal goals and aspirations of a self-consciously chosen life project (for a review of related constructs, see Emmons, 1997). More recently, in *American Lives,* John Clausen (1993) proposed that planful competence represents a multidimensional trait that describes individual differences in people's capacity to make plans and pursue them effectively. People with high levels of planfulness tend to make plans that suit their talents and interests and to follow through with these plans with perseverance and sociability.

The future study of agency in the life course, however, must bridge these two approaches by focusing on how interactions between individual differences and situational characteristics shape the major contours of life histories. People make plans about education, career, and family life, but they are also confronted with opportunities and limitations that are unique to their place in history and to their social location. This insight has been illustrated in preliminary fashion by research on birth cohort differences in the expression of planful competence (Shanahan & Elder, 2002; Shanahan, Elder, & Miech, 1997). These studies reveal that planful competence influences one's socioeconomic achievements and marital life, but these relationships are significantly conditioned by historical circumstance. For men whose lives were severely disrupted by the Great Depression and World War II, even high levels of planfulness are of little consequence; for men born just several years later, high levels of planfulness are associated with, for example, higher levels of socioeconomic attainments and greater marital stability. Evidence also suggests that planfulness during adolescence is positively correlated with favorable life review in old age.

In this chapter, we review the evidence on planful competence and propose avenues for future research. We begin by locating planful competence within the broader framework of life course studies and by reviewing the empirical evidence that suggests links among planfulness, social change, and the life course. We then propose hypotheses that interrelate planfulness during adolescence with development in adulthood and successful aging. Finally, we review limitations to prior studies and identify a series of objectives for future research. Some of these objectives involve the measurement of planful competence, and others focus on the interactive nature of planfulness.

A BRIEF HISTORY OF PLANFUL COMPETENCE

The Emergence of the Life Course Paradigm

In concept, the life course refers to a sequence of age-graded events and social roles that are embedded in social structure and historical change. The life course also defines a paradigm that guides research in terms of the identification and formulation of problems, the selection of variables, and rationales for research design and data analysis. As Elder (1998) explains, the life course emerged as a response to three challenges that were confronting investigators in the behavioral sciences: (1) to replace child-based, growth-oriented accounts of development with concepts that apply to aging across the life course, (2) to consider how human lives are socially organized over time, and (3) to relate lives to an ever-changing society. In responding to these challenges, life course theory has uniquely forged a unique conceptual bridge between developmental/aging processes and ongoing changes in society.

The first challenge led to the formulation of life span concepts of development, especially within the expanding field of life span developmental psychology (Baltes, Lindenberger, & Staudinger, 1998). The second challenge was addressed by way of "role theoretical perspectives" on human lives. Into the 1960s, role and relationship theories provided a way of thinking about socialization, generational succession, and social networks. Yet role theory did not specify the timing of role entries or exits or the duration of time-in-role. Also, generational membership failed to locate people with needed precision in historical time and thus according to social change. The third challenge was addressed by theory and research on age and time. Of special relevance to this chapter, life course theorists developed an appreciation of historical variations in people's experiences and lives. Ryder (1965) proposed the term *cohort* as a concept for studying the life course in relation to social change. Cohort refers to the age at which people enter a social system; thus, a birth cohort locates people in history according to their year of birth.

These conceptual streams (life span concepts of development, social relations/life cycle, and age and historical time) came together in the now-celebrated study of children who were born in the early 1920s, grew up in the Great Depression, then entered the military service in World War II (Elder, 1974/1999). The project examined the effects of drastic income loss in the Great Depression on the life experience of the Oakland, California, cohort members (born 1920–1921) with that of a younger Berkeley, California, cohort, born in the late 1920s. For example, the younger boys were more adversely affected by family hardship when compared to the older boys, although such differences faded in the adult years through the impact of military service, family support, and higher education.

The Great Depression studies, along with the subsequent research that they inspired, have led to the emergence of a set of core principles of life course studies that were originally formulated to explain the variable effects of transitions on aging (for a complete discussion, see Elder, 1998). Most basic is the premise that behavior cannot be fully understood by focusing on the specific life stage in question, defined by age or social role. Thus, behavioral adaptations in old age are not influenced by current circumstances alone, but by developmental trajectories that extend back to childhood and by anticipations of the future.

The *principle of lifelong processes* states that human development and aging are lifelong ontogenetic processes.

Another source of variability in human lives is historical change. Beyond studies of the Great Depression, research has examined, for example, the impact of World War II on men's lives (e.g., Sampson & Laub, 1996) and the life course influence of Freedom Summer in the American civil rights movement (McAdam, 1988). Accordingly, the *principle of lives in time and place* asserts that the life course of individuals is embedded in and shaped by the historical times and places that they experience over their lifetime. Historical change may be expressed in different ways, however, in different ecological settings. This variation is vividly illustrated by the differential effects of World War II. For American men of disadvantage, mobilization into the war at a young age frequently led to educational and occupational advancement (Sampson & Laub, 1996). Life stage provides another source of historical variation in life outcome, as expressed by the *principle of timing*. The impact of a succession of life transitions or events on human development and aging is contingent on when they occur in a person's life.

Planful Competence and Individual Differences in Agency

Though structured by social institutions and relationships, the life course is also constructed by the choices that people make. The *principle of human agency* asserts that people construct their own life course through their choices and purposeful action, which take place within the constraints and opportunities of history and social circumstances. The brief history of agency in the life course illustrates the general trend in life course studies from static role theory to dynamic, contextualized accounts of lives. Contemporary studies of agency trace to socialization and role theory perspectives on competence (Smith, 1968). Thus, Inkeles (1966) defined competence as the ability to attain and perform roles (e.g., student, father, and physician). Foote and Cottrell (1955) emphasized the interpersonal dimension of competence, referring to the diverse individual differences that relate a planning orientation to the control of situations and their outcomes (e.g., intelligence and empathy).

Although these and related formulations defined competence in terms of selecting appropriate roles and performing these roles well, they were nonetheless static views that failed to consider the inherently dynamic nature of lives. In an effort to integrate notions of role competence with the life course, Clausen (1991) proposed *planful competence:* the thoughtful, assertive, and self-controlled processes that underlie choices about involvements in social institutions and interpersonal relationships as these choices reflect the pursuit of life goals. That is, if the life course is viewed as a set of age-graded roles that are socially embedded, then aging reflects in part individual differences in how people select these roles, pursue them through purposeful action, and perform them in social settings. Thus, planfulness represents interindividual differences that explain in part why some people chose occupational goals or spouses that are well suited to their abilities, interests, and personal profile, while others did not.

Clausen maintained that planful competence encompassed three principle dimensions: intellectual investment (also referred to as cognitive commitment), self-confidence (or security and interpersonal ease), and dependability (or effectiveness). How were these dimensions defined in their original formulation? Intellectual investment refers to self-reflexivity, the ability to recognize one's strengths and weaknesses and select settings that promote a person–context fit. Intellectual investment also is found in the flexibility of one's thinking, including valuing one's independence, facing uncertainty with relative ease, and maintaining a sense of organization under stress. People who are intellectually flexible are open to life's contingencies and capable of reevaluating and revising life plans. Thus, with its emphasis on cognitive skills, intellectual investment reflects not only the ability to plan one's future with a high degree of self-reflexivity but also self-monitoring and the openness to revise one's plans as needed.

Self-confidence encompasses feelings of security with one's self, especially in social settings. Clausen (1993) contrasts self-confident adolescents with those who feel victimized. The former have self-trust, feeling at ease in interpersonal interactions and viewing themselves as capable of dealing with circumstances. Thus, it is not high self-confidence per se that is important, but rather the capacity to self-regulate one's emotions in social situations: Because of a positive self-system, youth are more apt to be outgoing, to exhibit positive emotions, and to inhibit self-defeating impulses when dealing with others. Thus, the self-confidence dimension focuses on the regulation of emotion to promote effectiveness in social interactions.

Finally, dependability refers to one's self-control and effectiveness in social settings. Effective adolescents demonstrate perseverance, ambition, and responsibility. Thus, dependability represents a motivational component that is focused on carrying through with plans.

Viewed from the perspective of contemporary scholarship in self-regulation and motivation, the dimensions of planfulness are diverse, a topic to which we will return in the concluding section of this chapter. Yet as a construct intended to describe cross-situational dispositions across the life course, planfulness is strategic for its "level of analysis." As Karoly (1993) explains, research that examines deliberate action invariably focuses on a specified time frame. Microgenetic accounts typically focus on short-term plans that are pursued in highly structured settings, most typically the laboratory. For example, children may be asked to solve the Tower of Hanoi puzzle or to plan a birthday party (e.g., Scholnick & Freidman, 1993); similarly, adults may be asked to react to vignettes that present a problem (e.g., see Blanchard-Fields & Chen, 1996). These fine-grained analyses typically investigate the detailed psychological processes that characterize a planning sequence or problem solving, as well as how these processes change over time.

In contrast, midlevel analyses focus on behaviors that occur over longer periods of time, including strategies used to accomplish self-chosen tasks. For example, Cantor and her colleagues investigated the strategies that college students use to achieve their goals and the implications of these strategies for the self (Cantor & Fleeson, 1991; Cantor, Norem, Niedenthal, Langston, & Brower, 1987). Indeed, the "conative revolution" in motivational psychology—reflecting interest in self-chosen tasks and the strategic actions that ensue—refers to midlevel approaches to deliberate action (Little, 1999). For example, Cantor and her colleagues (1987) assessed strategies used to address such goals as managing one's time more wisely or becoming a better student over a 2-year period.

Planful competence, however, refers to a "pansynoptic level" that provides an overview of deliberate behavior over many years, if not decades. Older children and adolescents make plans with respect to educational, occupational, and marital roles, and these plans are pursued and modified over many years. Planful competence, with its emphasis on cross-situational, relatively enduring traits, represents a multidimensional construct with which to assess individual differences in the ability to negotiate such long-term processes.

Moving beyond static notions of competence based on role theory, Clausen (1991) offered an age-sensitive model that links adolescence with later adulthood: Planful competence at about age 15 is a critical resource with which one defines a trajectory into adulthood. As demographers have observed (e.g., Rindfuss, Swicegood, & Rosenfeld, 1987), the transition to adulthood represents a demographically dense period during which many fundamental decisions about the life course are made. School, work, and family roles are selected, and these frequently have important implications for the subsequent life course (Mortimer & Johnson, 1998).

Clausen (1991, 1993) argued that individual differences in planful competence during adolescence have pervasive influences on adult development indirectly by shaping the transition to adulthood. According to this reasoning, more planful adolescents make better choices (i.e., choices that more accurately fit their interests, values, and talents with opportunities afforded by the social context) than less planful adolescents, and these better choices establish relationships and institutional commitments that endure into adulthood and provide the context for achievement and satisfaction. As Clausen observed, "[T]hose who have the attributes [of planfulness] in adolescence will have better prepared themselves for adult roles and will have selected, and been selected for, opportunities that give them a head start" (1991, p. 809).

Empirical Studies of Planful Competence in the Life Course

The Bay Area Studies

Drawing on a Q-sort measurement strategy (see Appendix A), Clausen (1991, 1993) demonstrated in a series of articles that planful competence during adolescence had important implications for a wide range of outcomes in adulthood. The model posited that individual differences in planful competence in senior high school predicted educational attainment and career and marital stability. This was a significant theoretical argument given that, for many decades, sociologists held that parental socioeconomic status was the most important predictor of a son's educational attainment, while virtually ignoring the role of competence in school achievements.

In this context, Clausen's finding that planful competence predicted years of education was especially noteworthy. Controlling parental socioeconomic status and the student's level of intelligence, planfulness was a significant, positive predictor of attained grade level. In fact, the standardized effect was a relatively large .54 for boys. When the dimensions of planfulness were entered separately into the equation, intellectual investment and dependability proved the most important predictors, with standardized effects exceeding .30 in magnitude. Similarly, controlling parental socioeconomic status, intelligence, and educational attainment, planful competence predicted occupational status in later adulthood, at ages 53 to 62. The magnitude of this effect was also impressive ($b = .60$, $p < .01$).

These results provide initial evidence that planful competence is a critical psychological resource for one's status achievements and life course. Both school and work are highly structured contexts in which people must pursue their goals. Among boys from families of the same socioeconomic status and with the same levels of intelligence (hence, we may infer, boys with similar educational and occupational ambitions in life), planful competence distinguished youth who would receive more education and attain more prestigious jobs. (For women, planfulness was of little consequence, perhaps reflecting the stereotypes and discrimination that women of those former cohorts faced.)

Beyond educational and occupational attainment, Clausen (1991, 1993) also showed that planfulness was related to marital careers and personality stability. Thus, people who are more planfully competent in senior high school go through fewer marriages than less planfully competent students: Among men and women in the top third of the planfulness distribution, more than 90% were married only once, as contrasted with about 50% being married more than once in the bottom third. Divorce itself was weakly related to planfulness, but dependability proved especially important for women. Women who could be described as capable, effective, and likely to finish a task were also significantly less likely to experience divorce. Planfully competent women were also more likely to report marital satisfaction in later life ($r = .35$, $p < .01$) than less planfully competent women. Originally, Clausen suggested that marital life would be better among planful adolescents because they make good choices (of spouses) and are capable in their interpersonal relationships. The prominent role of dependability in these results, however, suggests that enduring marriages reflected the efforts of women who were prepared to deal with the contingencies of life and persevere with tasks despite hardships.

The Terman Studies

If Clausen moved the sociological study of competence beyond static role conceptions, he nevertheless neglected the role of context. Given the large cohort differences that Elder (1974/1999) observed with these same data, Clausen's research was strangely silent on how the effects of planful competence might be moderated by historical experiences. That is, does agency always influence the life course, or are its effects moderated by changes in social systems brought on by historical events? To examine this possibility, Shanahan and colleagues (1997) drew on the longest running longitudinal data set in the United States, the Terman Sample of Gifted Children, and distinguished between men born between 1904 and 1910 (the "older cohort," $n = 448$) and those born between 1911 and 1917 (the "younger cohort," $n = 408$). The older cohort of men experienced the Great Depression of the 1930s as they were entering the labor market. Many of these men experienced disruptions in their early family life and career with entry into military service in their mid-30s. In contrast, the younger cohort experienced the Great Depression during their adolescent years and often entered the labor market and began their families during the economic abundance of the postwar period.

How do these differences in historical settings moderate the connection between planfulness during adolescence and later adulthood? Table 5.1 presents results from a structural equation model in which planful competence predicts educational attainment and occupational prestige for the two cohorts separately (see Appendix A for details of measurement). The results show that planful competence at age 14 has a highly significant, positive effect on educational attainment at age 30 for the younger cohort only ($b = .48$, $p < .001$). In fact, the effect of adolescent planfulness on educational attainment at age 30 is significantly greater for the younger cohort members when compared with the effect observed among men from the older cohort. Indeed, the explained variance of educational attainment in the younger cohort (.33) is notably larger than that found in the older cohort (.06). Education generally links family of origin to occupational status, and this mediational process was observed for status attainment among the Terman men at age 30. An examination of the indirect effects (not shown) reveals that planful competence has a significant, indirect effect on occupational status at age 30 in the young cohort only.

These results illustrate that planful competence interacts with historical setting to influence pathways through life. Adolescent planful competence is significantly related to education in the younger birth cohort at age 30; those with less planfulness have lower levels of educational attainment because less planful men are likely to choose work over

TABLE 5.1 Planfulness During Adolescence and Achievements in Early Adulthood, Terman Sample of Gifted Children (Men Only)

	Education, Age 30		Occupational Status, Age 30	
	Young	Old	Young	Old
Planfulness, age 14	.48***	.08	−.15	.14
	.10	.08	1.11	.77
Family SES	.48***	.37***	.38	1.08
	.12	.10	1.27	.91
Intelligence	.00	.01	.12	−.08
	.01	.01	.13	.12
Education	—	—	7.55***	7.65***
	—	—	.93	.56
R-Squared	.33	.06	.44	.44

Chi-square = 31.13_{31}, $p = .46$; unstandardized results reported
SES = socioeconomic status
***$p < .001$

further schooling. This contrasts with the pattern observed among men in the older cohort, in which educational attainment is high, regardless of planfulness. These men were typically in college when the Great Depression hit, and many of them prolonged their education because there were no jobs. In fact, other analyses reveal that adolescent planful competence was more strongly related to degree completion among the younger birth cohort members only. In contrast, men in the older cohort completed their degrees and continued their educations regardless of planful competence because historical circumstance provided no alternative in the form of employment.

The Terman data also provided a rough measure of "biographical agency in early adulthood" based on items assessed in 1940, when the older cohort was roughly 32 and the younger cohort was roughly 27 years of age (see Shanahan & Elder, 2002). The measure is comprised of self-ratings for self-confidence, persistence, and whether the respondent's "life is completely integrated toward a definite goal," as reflected in personal time use. The items for this measure therefore do not substantially overlap with items for the adolescent planfulness measure. Furthermore, the measure of biographical agency in early adulthood is not tapping the cognitively committed dimension. Therefore, this construct is not covering the full conceptual domain of planful competence, although self-confidence, persistence, and purposefulness are important facets of that construct.

With these limitations in mind, the variable "biographical agency in early adulthood" was entered into the model of educational attainment. Results reveal that agency in early adulthood significantly predicts education, but only for the older cohort ($b = .37$, $p < .01$ for the older cohort; $b = .08$, $p > .10$ for the younger cohort). For men whose lives were severely disrupted by economic downturn and war, it was agency in early adulthood that predicted their final educational attainment, not planfulness during adolescence. These men returned from war to restart careers, and those men with high levels of planfulness often returned to school for further education before reentering the labor market. Men from the younger cohort had effectively finished their educations before the war and initiated careers in the postwar period. Thus, planful competence is significantly related to educational attainments, but it is planfulness during adolescence for the younger cohort, and agency in early adulthood for the older cohort.

In a series of additional analyses, the relationships between planfulness and measures of occupational achievement (income gain between 1940 and 1959 and status fluctuations) and family life (divorce status) in adulthood were examined. Are these same patterns of complex interactions between planfulness and history observed in other domains of life? The planfulness and agency measures predict education, which, in turn, predicts income gain and status fluctuations. The results point to an interesting conclusion: Agency in early adulthood increased income gain and decreased status fluctuations, but only for the older cohort. Men from the older cohort who were more agentic in early adulthood tended to experience greater income gains in the postwar years, but also to experience fewer occupational setbacks than men in the younger cohort. The results suggest that, for these indicators of attainment, the younger cohort experienced their remarkable successes in the labor market because they started their careers after the war, in a time of unparalleled economic expansion. That is, planfulness did not distinguish their careers because men with even low levels of planfulness tended to do well in the labor market. On the other hand, after the war, men from the older cohort were restarting their careers, and it was a sense of agency in early adulthood that promoted renewed occupational trajectories.

Shanahan and Elder (2002) also examined links between planfulness and family life, focusing on divorce. The results indicate that planfulness in adolescence leads to a decreased likelihood of divorce, but only among men in the younger cohort ($b = .01$, $p > .10$ for the older cohort; $b = -.06$, $p < .01$ for the younger cohort). For many men in the older cohort, World War II proved to be a very disruptive event for their marital lives, leading to divorce irrespective of planfulness. In contrast, men in the younger cohort often postponed marriage and parenthood until after the war; in this circumstance, consistent with Clausen's (1991, 1993) research, planful men made better choices with respect to family formation. These coefficients differ significantly in magnitude between the two groups.

When viewed in their totality, these results suggest that the effects of planful competence in the life course are highly contingent on historical circumstance. For men in the older cohort, planful competence in adolescence did not predict later socioeconomic achievements or indicators of family life; for these men, agency in early adulthood predicted their occupational achievements as they restarted their careers after the war. It was not a resource that made divorce less likely, however. For men in the younger cohort, planfulness in adolescence predicted their educational attainment and likelihood of divorce, but not their occupational achievements, which tended to be high regardless of their planfulness because of the booming postwar economy. Thus, the results show not only that agency interacts in complex ways with historical change to shape the biography, but also suggest that agency can be a salient factor at different times in the life course. Clausen's hypothesis that planfulness during adolescence is critical to adulthood is not always true, as observed in the unique effects of agency at roughly age 30 among members of the older cohort.

PLANFUL COMPETENCE AND AGING

Dramatic differences in health and well-being are often observed among the elderly. Although these differences reflect a wide range of proximal factors (as suggested by other contributions to this volume), they also reflect a lifetime of experiences, particularly those surrounding one's education, occupational prestige, and income. In turn, these achievements reflect complex combinations of social context and agency as they unfold through historical time and through the life of each person.

Our interactive model of agency and social structures suggests two hypotheses about the planfulness and the elderly. First, *planfulness in adolescence or in early adulthood may predict indicators of well-being and adjustment in old age by way of life course achievements.* When participants in the Bay Area studies were in their 60s, they were asked to graph their level of life satisfaction from early childhood to the present (Clausen, 1993). Clearly, this is speculative measure. Nevertheless, women with high planfulness in adolescence plotted higher levels of satisfaction across the life course. Self-confidence in adolescence was particularly salient to life satisfaction through the 50s and into the early 60s ($r = .39$, $p <$ .01). Men high in adolescent planfulness reported high mean levels of satisfaction through their 20s, 30s, and 40s, but not 50s or early 60s. In the Terman sample, biographical agency in early adulthood (late 20s, early 30s) was positively and significantly related to a measure of global life satisfaction in the late 60s. Thus, planfulness in adolescence and young adulthood may promote positive life reviews in later adulthood, a relationship likely mediated by achievements in school and work and in the family.

Second, *planfulness among the elderly may serve as a critical psychological resource in maintaining well-being.* Many of the normative life transitions associated with the elderly—retirement, leaving one's home, coping with the loss of a spouse—require good interpersonal skills, a sense of effectiveness, and reflexivity. Moreover, these same psychological resources may promote the day-to-day conditions that encourage well-being, including the maintenance of dense and interconnected networks of social supports, ready access to good medical services, and opportunities for engagement in the community and in productive activities. Although planfulness may have traitlike properties, over the course of several decades its dimensions will undoubtedly change in level for most people, as suggested by the age-related changes observed in many facts of problem solving (Blanchard-Fields & Chen, 1996). Thus, controlling planfulness in adolescence, one's unique level of planfulness in later life may facilitate adjusting to the new roles of old age, including, for example, retiree, (great-)grandparent, and widow.

In turn, these two expectations may be interrelated in that a lifetime of positive experiences may enhance levels of adult planfulness, whereas a lifetime of negative experiences may lead to decrements in adult levels. Accordingly, a positive cycle occurs as early planful behaviors are rewarded by successes, thereby encouraging further planful behavior. In later life, these people view themselves as capable and agentic, with high levels of planfulness to face the exigencies of old age. In contrast, a negative cycle occurs when early experiences foster a sense of learned helplessness, suggesting that traits such as effectiveness, reflexivity, and interpersonal ease are of little utility in one's life. These experiences dampen planful competence, which, in turn, may lead to further negative experiences. These people face old age with low levels of planfulness, reflecting many decades of experiences that reinforce the belief that competence is of little consequence.

DIRECTIONS FOR FUTURE RESEARCH

Although the results of previous studies are encouraging and suggestive, extant research has necessarily relied on data archives that are limited in important respects. Indeed, empirical study has proceeded with Campbell and Stanley's (1966) caveats for quasi-experimental research in mind: The best possible designs, measures, and statistics have been used, and limitations have been clearly identified (see Elder, Pavalko, & Clipp, 1993, for a discussion of using archival data sets). At the same time, new efforts are needed that build on previous findings that address these limitations. These new efforts should focus on measurement and the interactive nature of planfulness.

Measurement

Data sets that encompass large segments of the life course have not expressly measured planfulness (see Appendix A for details). Thus, future efforts should focus on developing a measure of planfulness that is consistent with contemporary psychometric efforts in the study of motivation, personality, and self-regulation. Such a measure would tap relatively traitlike features of personality that reflect self-reflexivity (including conscientiousness and openness to new experience) and interpersonal ease (including a lack of neuroticism and extroversion), but also motivational constructs. A major challenge will be developing all three dimensions of planfulness, acknowledging that emotion, cognition, and motivation jointly contribute to deliberate action (Karoly, 1993).

Once a psychometrically sound measure has been developed, the resulting data should be analyzed according to both variable- and person-oriented strategies. Previous efforts to operationalize planful competence have relied on a variable-centered approach. Accordingly, measures of planfulness have been based on the degree of covariation among the items across individuals. As Caspi (1998) observed, however, "the appropriate unit of analysis may be the person, not the variable" (p. 320). A person-centered approach would focus on how the dimensions of planfulness are organized within persons. Indeed, Clausen's (1991) theory suggests that a person-centered strategy is more appropriate. People with high levels of self-reflexivity, interpersonal ease, and perseverance are the most planfully competent people. People with high levels of two dimensions, however, are missing a critical set of skills that facilitate deliberate action across the life course. That is, it is not the covariation among the dimensions across persons or the relative rankings that matter; rather, planfully competent people will have high levels of all three dimensions, which will act synergistically to promote deliberate action.

Person–Context Interactions

Karoly (1993) recognized "operational boundaries" to self-regulation, which refer to limits placed on one's ability to engage in deliberate action. That is, many factors moderate the effects of personal characteristics such as self-efficacy and perseverance. Indeed, psychologists have long noted potential moderators of self-direction, including, for example, sensitivity to goal-relevant feedback, attributional habits under conditions of success or failure, and tolerance for boredom or role overload. (Conversely, high levels of these variables may facilitate the expression of self-direction.) Thus, one challenge to future research is the identification of psychological variables that moderate the effects of planful competence. A likely candidate is intelligence or, more precisely, "computational superstructures" such as perception encoding, memory storage and retrieval, and a declarative knowledge base (Karoly, 1993).

Far less attention has been paid, however, to how manifold aspects of context can serve as operational boundaries, that is, how person and context interact. Although our conceptual model emphasizes the interactive nature of person and context in describing agentic behavior, the empirical demonstration of this point has been limited to a historical period of extreme situations, namely, the Great Depression and World War II. When no jobs are available, men will remain in school and planfulness will not predict their educational achievement. When the younger men start their careers in a soaring economy, they will succeed irrespective of planfulness. In these extreme circumstances, the effect of an individual's planfulness was "turned off" by context. Yet most historical change, indeed, most social experience, is far less dramatic. A challenge for future research will be identifying and generic features of context that may act as operational boundaries, then studying how continuous fluctuations moderate the expression of planfulness across groups defined by age and cohort. Research on educational warehousing is suggestive: As the unemployment rate increases, enrollment rates in secondary schools increase. This was clearly true during the Great Depression (and was linked to planfulness), but it remains to be seen whether fluctuations in unemployment could moderate the expression of planfulness in less dramatic instances.

In addition to the renewed study of historical change, future attention should be directed to the study of social location as an operational boundary. There is some evidence that planfulness favors those people whose lives are already advantaged. As Brewster Smith (1968) observed, competence could differentiate the lives of the disadvantaged, or, in contrast, it could favor those who can best capitalize on it. In both the Berkeley and Terman data sets, few findings suggest that planfulness was a resource among women. Given discrimination and stereotypes, a gifted, driven woman from the Terman sample became a homemaker, but not by her own choice. It may be that planfulness favors people whose status suggests advantage, including, for these samples, white men from upper-class families.

CONCLUSION

Given the multifaceted nature of agentic behavior, no single approach to deliberate action will suffice in explaining why people succeed or fail in the pursuit of their goals. Planful competence was specifically proposed by John Clausen for the study of purposive action across the life course. Consequently, it may be related to microgenetic processes of agency (i.e., psychological and social processes occurring in episodes), but its primary focus is individual differences in people's ability to select and pursue major roles in the life course. Prior research goes a long way in suggesting the utility of planfulness in the study of lives; perhaps the most important lesson learned thus far is that agency and social structure interact in historically complex ways. Yet theoretical considerations suggest other interactions, which have yet to be studied.

These complexities include person-centered synergies among the dimensions of planfulness, other psychological properties that enhance the effects of planfulness, the role of less dramatic historical changes in moderating the expression of planfulness, and how planfulness interacts with social location to shape lives. The investigation of these nuances will clearly require collaborative efforts between students of life span psychology and life course sociology.

APPENDIX A

Assessing Planful Competence with the Bay Area and Terman Studies

To examine links between adolescence and adulthood, Clausen drew on existing longitudinal archives that spanned many decades of life: the Berkeley Growth Study, the Berkeley Guidance Study, and the Adolescent (Oakland) Growth Study. The Berkeley subjects were recruited at birth, with a combined sample size of 313 newborns. The Guidance Study drew on every third birth in Berkeley, California, between 1928 and 1929, most of them born at home; the Growth Study included infants born in local hospitals at the same time. The Adolescent Growth Study drew on 10- to 12-year-olds who were expected to attend Claremont High School in Oakland, California; the sample was commenced in 1931 and included 215 White, English-speaking youth. The three studies included follow-ups in adulthood, although they proceeded on unique paths until 1982, when the samples were merged. Data were last collected by mail in 1990 and drew 188 responses.

At the time of the first adult follow-up (approximately 30 or 37 years of age), the subjects' personalities were rated. Experts drew on the California Q-sort, 100 items that describe basic aspects of personality, intellect, interpersonal skills, and value orientations. Drawing on the complete case files, two or three experts rated each person in the sample for each of the 100 items; they followed this procedure three times, covering junior high school, senior high school, and early adulthood. Different expert raters were used for the three periods, ruling out "source variance" for any relationships observed across the three phases of late adolescence and early adulthood. The composite scores had an interrater reliability of .70 (for further details, see Block & Haan, 1971). A component analysis revealed six dimensions; Clausen (1993) considered three of these dimensions to be acceptable measures of planful competence: self-confidence, cognitively committed, and dependable (Milsap & Meredith, 1988).

Items corresponding to each dimension are shown in Appendix Table 5.2. The data were not collected to assess planfulness, however, and the resulting measure should be view with caution for both methodological and conceptual reasons. Methodologically, the sample size is relatively small, and the sample itself is not representative of a defined population, suggesting that replication would be especially necessary. Moreover, the Q-sort is an ipsative procedure that ranks characteristics within persons; it may not be entirely suited for the study of interindividual differences. The content validity of the measure is also questionable.

APPENDIX TABLE 5.2   Clausen's Measure of Planful Competence Based on the Bay Area Studies

Dimension 1. Self-Confidence (Interpersonal Ease, Secure)

Positive Items	Negative Items
—Satisfied with self	—Feels cheated, victimized
—Calm, relaxed in manner	—Fearful, vulnerable to threat
—Arouses liking and acceptance	—Self-defeating
—Straightforward, candid	—Has preoccupying thoughts
—Turned to for advice	—Disorganized under stress
—Gregarious	—Thin-skinned

Dimension 2. Cognitively Committed (Intellectually Invested)

Positive Items	Negative Items
—Values intellectual matters	—Uncomfortable with
—High intellectual capacity	uncertainty
—Introspective	—Conventional
—Values independence	—Basically submissive
—Has wide interests	—Disorganized under stress
—Thinks unconventionally	—Gives up when frustrated

Dimension 3. Dependable (Effective)

Positive Items	Negative Items
—Dependable and responsible	—Rebellious, nonconforming
—Productive, gets things done	—Undercontrolled
—Overcontrol of impulses	—Self-defeating
—Satisfied with self	—Pushes limits
—Calm, relaxed in manner	—Unpredictable and changeable
—Ambitious	

For example, it is unclear why "gives up when frustrated" would not be a negative item for dependability, as opposed to cognitively committed, or why "disorganized under stress" would not be a negative item for dependability as opposed to self-confidence or cognitively committed. Missing from self-confidence are strong negative items like hostility and anxiety, which are known to be salient factors that shape one's interpersonal relationships. It is also unclear why a cognitively committed person would have high ambitions or would be unconventional or would remain organized under stress. Finally, conceptual descriptions of dependability suggest resilience in the face of stress, as well as a sense of capability and preparedness. In short, the items and the mode of analysis were not designed with planfulness in mind, and the resulting measure may not be replicable or fully valid. The magnitude of these problems, however, is not known.

Reliance on the Terman data is also somewhat problematic. The Stanford-Terman longitudinal study (Terman, 1925) began data collection in the early 1920s under the direction of Lewis Terman, professor of psychology at Stanford University. The study used a purposive sampling procedure to identify 1,000 children in the California public school system (grades 3 to 12) with an intelligence quotient of 140 or more. Eventually, 856 boys were invited to participate in the study (women were also included in the sample, but those data have not been analyzed with respect to planful competence). Questionnaires were administered by mail on four occasions before the war (1922, 1928, 1936, and 1940), focusing on matters of family, education, and work. Military experience was the main subject of questionnaires administered by mail in 1945 and 1950. Since then, survey data have been collected in six waves, timed approximately 5 to 10 years apart, for a total of 12 waves of data spanning 69 years. Thus, the data offer a singular opportunity to interrelate adolescent experiences with later adulthood, but the sample is quite unique.

The Terman data provide rough approximations for each dimension of planful competence: For dependability, an item assessing perseverance was used; for self-confidence, a desire to excel; and for cognitively committed, conscientiousness and a desire to know (all items: 1 = low to 13 = high). Clearly, this is not an ideal measure of a construct as complex as planful competence, especially with respect to self-confidence. Parents assessed the child's planful competence in the 1922 questionnaire for the older cohort (mean age of the children = 14) and in the 1927–1928 questionnaire for the younger cohort (mean age

of the child = 15). The standardized factor loadings are .60 (perseverance), .68 (desire to excel), .46 (desire to know), and .60 (conscientiousness). In preliminary models, this measure of planfulness during
adolescence predicted educational attainment and, indirectly, occupational prestige in much the same way that Clausen's measure had.
This provided some evidence for construct validity. Nevertheless, the
construct is lacking in content validity because it does not cover the
full "conceptual space" suggested by planful competence.

REFERENCES

Baltes, P. M., Lindenberger, U., & Staudinger, U. M. (1998). Life-span
theory in developmental psychology. In R. M. Lerner (Ed.), *Handbook
of child psychology: 1. Theoretical models of human development* (5th ed., pp.
1029–1043). New York: Wiley.
Blanchard-Fields, F., & Chen, Y. (1996). Adaptive cognition and aging.
American Behavioral Scientist, 39, 231–248.
Block J., with N. Haan. (1971). *Lives through time.* Berkeley, CA: Bancroft.
Bühler, C., & Massarik, F. (Eds.). (1968). *The course of human life: A study
of goals in the humanistic perspective.* New York: Springer.
Campbell, D. T., & Stanley, J. C. (1966). *Experimental and quasi-experimental
designs for research.* Chicago: Rand McNally.
Cantor, N., & Fleeson, W. (1991). Life tasks and self-regulatory tasks. In
M. L. Maehr & P. R. Pintrich (Eds.), *Advances in achievement motivation*
(Vol. 7, pp. 327–369). Greenwich, CT: JAI.
Cantor, N., Norem, J. K., Niedenthal, P. M., Langston, C. A., & Brower, A.
M. (1987). Life tasks, self-concept ideals, and cognitive strategies in a
life transition. *Journal of Personality and Social Psychology, 53,* 1178–1191.
Caspi, A. (1998). Personality development across the life course. In R.
Lerner (Ed.), *Handbook of child psychology: Vol. 1. Theoretical models of
human development* (pp. 311–380). New York: Wiley.
Clausen, J. (1991). Adolescent competence and the shaping of the life
course. *American Journal of Sociology, 96,* 805–842.
Clausen, J. (1993). *American lives: Looking back at the children of the Great
Depression.* Berkeley: University of California Press.
Elder, G. H., Jr. (1974). *Children of the Great Depression: Social change in life
experience.* Chicago: University of Chicago Press. (Reissue, Boulder, CO:
Westview Press, 1999.)
Elder, G. H., Jr. (1998). The life course and human development. In R.
M. Lerner (Ed.), *Handbook of child psychology: Vol. 1. Theoretical models
of human development* (pp. 939–991). New York: Wiley.

Elder, G. H., Pavalko, E. K., & Clipp, E. C. (1993). *Working with archival data: Studying lives.* Newbury Park, CA: Sage.

Emmons, R. A. (1997). Motives and life goals. In R. Hogan, J. Johnson, & S. Briggs (Eds.), *Handbook of personality psychology* (pp. 485–512). San Diego: Academic Press.

Foote, N. M., & Cottrell, L. S., Jr. (1955). *Identity and interpersonal competence: A new direction in family research.* Chicago: University of Chicago Press.

Inkeles, A. (1966). Social structure and the socialization of competence. *Harvard Educational Review, 36,* 265–283.

Karoly, P. (1993). Mechanisms of self-regulation: A systems view. *Annual Review of Psychology, 44,* 23–52.

Little, B. R. (1999). Personality and motivation: Personal action and the conative revolution. In L. A. Pervin & O. P. John (Eds.), *Handbook of personality: Theory and research* (pp. 501–524). New York: Guilford.

McAdam, D. (1988). *Freedom summer.* New York: Oxford University Press.

Milsap, R., & Meredith, W. (1988). Component analysis in cross-sectional and longitudinal data. *Psychometrika, 53,* 123–134.

Mortimer, J. T., & Johnson, M. K. (1998). New perspectives on adolescent work and the transition to adulthood. In R. Jessor (Ed.), *New perspectives on adolescent risk behaviors* (pp. 425–496). New York: Cambridge University Press.

Rindfuss, R. R., Swicegood, G. G., & Rosenfeld, R. A. (1987). Disorder in the life course: How common and does it matter? *American Sociological Review, 52,* 785–801.

Ryder, N. B. (1965). The cohort as a concept in the study of social change. *American Sociological Review, 30,* 843–861.

Sampson, R. J., & Laub, J. H. (1996). Socioeconomic achievement in the life course of disadvantaged men: Military service as a turning point, circa 1940–1965. *American Sociological Review, 61*(3), 347–367.

Scholnick, E. K., & Friedman, S. L. (1993). Panning in context: Developmental and situational considerations. *International Journal of Behavioral Development, 16,* 145–167.

Shanahan, M. J., & Elder, G. H., Jr. (2002). History, agency, and the life course. In L. Crockett (Ed.), *Agency, motivation, and the life course* (pp. 145–186). Lincoln: University of Nebraska.

Shanahan, M. J., Elder, G. H., & Miech, R. A. (1997). History and agency in men's lives: Pathways to achievement in cohort perspective. *Sociology of Education, 70,* 54–67.

Smith, M. B. (1968). Competence and socialization. In J. A. Clausen (Ed.) *Socialization and society* (pp. 271–320). Boston: Little, Brown.

Terman, L. M. (1925). *Genetic studies of genius: 1. Mental and physical traits of a thousand gifted children.* Stanford, CA: Stanford University Press.

Thomas, W. I. (1909). *Source book for social origins.* Boston: Richard G. Badger.

Thomas, W. I., & Thomas, D. S. (1932). *The child in America.* New York: Knopf.

Volkart, E. H. (1951). Introduction: Social behavior and the defined situation. In E. H. Volkhart (Ed.), *Social behavior and personality: Contributions of W. I. Thomas to theory and social research* (pp. 1–32). New York: Social Science Research Council.

Commentary

Planful Competence Across the Life Span: An Issue of Construct Validity

Fredda Blanchard-Fields

T he chapter, "Planful Competence, the Life Course, and Aging: Retrospect and Prospect," by Michael Shanahan and Scott Hofer (this volume) focuses on an issue of major importance in the life span developmental literature: how representations of personal control change with age and influence adaptive functioning. From a psychological perspective, the majority of work in this area focuses on beliefs of personal control over cognitive abilities and how that influences behavior. By contrast, Shanahan and colleagues take a broader perspective of control in terms of planful competence and explore its relationship to historical time and well-being. Planful competence involves personal control through self-controlled processes that underlie choices in the pursuit of one's personal life goals. In addition, at the onset the authors argue that the developmental trajectory of planful competence is in the large part determined by historical context.

PLANFUL COMPETENCE AS A KEY CONSTRUCT

This contextual approach to the area of personal control admirably upholds the spirit and tradition of the many past conferences on social structure and aging from a life span perspective. In particular, the research discussed by Shanahan and colleagues is grounded in a macro-sociological level of analysis, yet it also represents a compelling attempt to meld psychological and sociological constructs and, in turn, makes an interesting contribution to the literature on personal control across the life span.

From a life span developmental perspective, the chapter contributes to our understanding of how broad generational and historical effects influence the developmental trajectory and impact of planful competence. In other words, findings indicate differential effects on the trajectory of planful competence in that early socialization influences later adulthood achievements as a function of the historical time in which one is raised. This highlights a concern of many life span developmental researchers: We need to move away from static conceptualizations of our psychological constructs and not simply give lip service to the profound effects of a changing historical context.

In addition, Shanahan and colleagues' examination of planful competence, a psychological construct, as a predictor variable contributes further to the sociological understanding of its influence across the life span. This line of research moves away from simply relying on status variables as predictors of well-being and achievement in adulthood. Status variables, for example, age, gender, and socioeconomic status (SES), are complex and are to an important extent mediated by other important psychological variables. Planful competence may indeed be one of the important constructs. Similarly, the authors note that whereas sociologists have typically held that parents' SES was the most important predictor of a son's educational attainment, the mediating role of competence in this relationship may matter even more.

CONSTRUCT VALIDITY OF PLANFUL COMPETENCE

Herein lie some of the tough issues that are unavoidable when research focuses on analyses of archival data. One of the critical issues to address in this research approach is construct validity. Given the construct at hand, planful competence, and coming from a history of examining such variables from a psychological/individual level of analysis, I was particularly interested in the construct validity of planful competence and how it relates to other relevant psychological constructs. The authors acknowledge this concern as well. I would like to now examine

TABLE 5.3 Construct Definitions of Planful Competence

	Self-Confidence	Dependability	Intellectual Investment
Clausen's concept	Sense of security Self-trust	Self-control Effectiveness	Self-reflexivity Flexibility in thinking
	Self-esteem	Perseverance, ambition	Values independence
	Capable	Initiative	Faces uncertainty
	Resilient	Self-regulation	Cognitive skills
California Q-sort	Satisfied with self	Dependable	Values intellectual
	Calm	Productive	Proactive
	Straightforward	Calm	Values independence
	Invulnerable	Ambitious	Unconventional
	Thick-skinned	Controlling	Faces uncertainty
NEO study	Low anxiety/ hostility	Competence	Orderly and dutiful
	Positive	Self-disciplined	Achievement-oriented
	Warm	Invulnerable	Deliberate
Terman data Adolescence	Desire to excel	Perseverance	Conscientious and desire to know
Early adult	Self-confidence	Persistence	Integrated goals

NEO = Neuroticism–Extroversion–Openness to Experience

both the conceptual definitions of planful competence and their empirically based counterparts.

As Shanahan and colleagues note, there are readily observable discrepancies across reported studies of planful competence. For example, Clausen (1991) maintains that planful competence involves three components: self-confidence, dependability, and intellectual investment. Table 5.3 illustrates different operational definitions of each of these components that have been used in various studies, including the primary study reported by Shanahan and colleagues. As observed in Table

5.3, there is considerable overlap in definitions. For example, whereas Clausen includes "being capable" as part of self-confidence, definitions of dependability include competence and effectiveness. How do these definitions differ? Similarly, "being invulnerable" is included in Clausen's concept of self-confidence and studies using the Neuroticism–Extroversion–Openness to Experience (NEO, 1992) inventory's concept of dependability. Finally, the desire to excel defines adolescent self-confidence in the Terman data, and achievement orientation defines intellectual investment in the NEO (Costa & Zonderman, 1991; Costa & McCrea, 1992). Each of the research definitions of the three components of planful competence includes a mixture of personality variables, beliefs and values, abilities, and control-related behavior (e.g., thick-skinned, valuing independence, cognitive skills, and self-regulation, respectively).

The variability in the operational definitions of planful competence across data sets gives rise to a number of concerns. The authors themselves state that the studies using the California Q-sort assessment of planful competence were "not designed with planfulness in mind." That seems to be a problem that plagues our understanding of this construct and is unfortunately an unavoidable artifact of archival data analysis. It is critically important to focus future data collection on specifically measuring planful competence. The issue is whether further analyses using archival data of this kind will be of help in clarifying this construct.

Again, it should be emphasized that it is rare to be able to examine the effects of constructs such as planful competence longitudinally, and in these cases we must rely on archival data. The authors should be commended in the care taken to caution us about this. So, from a psychological perspective, I would like to examine this issue in more depth and reveal what I think are areas in need of future research.

Beyond the interesting finding that planful competence in adolescence and early adulthood differentially predicts successful outcomes in later adulthood, one still needs to interpret further individual differences in planful competence. For example, is planful competence a preexisting cognitive style or dispositional trait leading to increased educational attainment, or is it an outcome of the broad process of socialization? Treating planful competence as a cognitive style or a personality construct without considering the other dimensions of individual differences that are associated with it may yield misleading conclusions. I would argue for a combination of experimental techniques and differential approaches to identify the mechanisms by which planful competence may or may not influence behavior.

However, before we can even experimentally assess the construct, the measurement of planful competence needs much development. Along these lines, Shanahan and his colleagues fully acknowledge that the construct of planful competence covers a wide range of conceptual ground. As Table 5.4 illustrates, if we simply examine the conceptual definition posited by Clausen, we can see that it incorporates a multitude of psychological constructs. For example, dependability or effectiveness incorporates such constructs as personal control (e.g., primary vs. secondary), self-regulation orientations, emotion regulation, and problem-focused orientations in problem solving, as well as dispositional characteristics of perseverance, ambition, and responsibility. Each of these constructs has witnessed a prolific amount of empirical study in its own right. For example, primary and secondary control, as well as self-regulatory orientations of assimilative persistence and accommodative flexibility, has been demonstrated to exhibit differential trajectories across the life span (Brandtstäder, 1999; Heckhausen & Schulz, 1995, 1999). On one hand, primary or proactive direct control over one's

TABLE 5.4 Psychological Constructs Incorporated in the Three Components of Planful Competence

Dependability
    Personal control (primary vs. secondary)
    Self-regulation orientation
    Emotion regulation
    Problem-focused orientations in problem solving
    Dispositional characteristics of perseverance, ambition, and responsibility

Self-Confidence
    Self-efficacy
    Self-attributions
    Self-esteem
    Self-concept

Intellectual Investment
    Cognitive skills
    Need for structure
    Tolerance for ambiguity
    Need for cognition
    Realistic thinking
    Attributional flexibility

environment and assimilative persistence (tenaciously pursuing one's goals) is emphasized in youth. On the other hand, secondary control (e.g., relying on others or identifying one's control in the hands of others) and accommodative flexibility (adjusting one's goals to self-regulatory loss) are more indicative of later adulthood.

Self-confidence incorporates such constructs as self-efficacy, self-attributions, self-esteem, and self-concept, which also have received a substantial amount of empirical investigation. For example, although self-efficacy predicts effective functioning, it is task-specific in its predictive utility and varies by task and person over time (Berry, 1999; Soederberg Miller & Lachman, 1999). Older adults tend to make less adaptive self-attributions, partly because of cultural values, which, in turn, can have negative effects on performance (Levy, 1996; Levy & Langer, 1994).

Finally, intellectual investment embodies cognitive skills, need for structure, tolerance for ambiguity, need for cognition, relativistic thinking, and attributional flexibility, among many other cognitive styles that have been well researched. For example, a high need for closure and low tolerance for ambiguity in situations lead older adults to produce greater social judgment biases (Blanchard-Fields & Hertzog, 2000; Blanchard-Fields & Norris, 1994).

This confluence of constructs becomes most noteworthy in the analyses of planful competence as a predictor of successful outcomes in later adulthood in the research presented in Chapter 5. Although planful competence measured in adolescence in the Terman studies predicts educational attainment in later adulthood, one still wonders what it is about planful competence that accounts for its predictive utility. The authors argue that the fact that the three measures of planful competence predicted educational attainment and occupational prestige across the two studies is evidence for its construct validity. Perhaps, but there are other rival hypotheses as to why these correlations would be found. For example, let us take perspective taking and self-efficacy. Either of these two variables may represent a third factor related to both planful competence and educational attainment that may account for the planful competence–education correlation. In other words, planful competence may simply represent an epiphenomenon. Similarly, analytic skills and perspective taking skills may account for adulthood educational attainment. Each of these constructs represents a rival predictor of educational attainment in its own right, as evidenced in the literature. Empirical examples abound, such as self-efficacy and well-being, self-efficacy and effective memory performance, and self-efficacy in everyday problem solving. Without a more precise operationalization of planful competence, none of these rival hypotheses can be ruled out.

Another concern raised by the conceptual overload of the construct planful competence is the issue domain specificity. Margie Lachman (e.g., Lachman & Weaver, 1998) and others have conducted numerous studies demonstrating the domain specificity of constructs such as controllability and self-efficacy. In other words, there are individual differences in self-efficacy (in the case of planful competence, self-confidence) when examined in domains of intelligence, health, and everyday problem solving. This is not accounted for by the data presented. In fact, if we go back to Clausen's original conceptualization, competence (in particular, self-confidence and dependability) is especially associated with a particular domain: social settings or interpersonal context. This seems to get lost in the analyses and interpretation. In fact, the majority of analyses focus on the "nonsocial" outcomes of educational attainment and occupational prestige.

The social and interpersonal component of the original conceptualization of planful competence also becomes particularly important when we examine gender differences. In general, planful competence was not a significant predictor of educational level or occupational prestige for women as it is for men. The authors make a reasonable argument that discrimination and stereotypes placed women in a disadvantaged context, whereas planfulness may favor individuals whose status is already advantaged. However, if we go back to the operationalization of planful competence, it seems to involve traits associated with masculinity in the gender role literature. For example, intellectual investment reflects assertiveness, decisiveness, achievement orientation, and perseverance. Dependability reflects such characteristics as the ability to get things done, controlling, ambitiousness, initiating, and levelheadedness. Self-confidence reflects self-satisfaction, being thick-skinned, proactive, and calm and cool. What is missing are constructs such as interpersonal sensitivity, affiliate concerns, interpersonal skills, and emotion. So, perhaps planful competence is a qualitatively different concept for women than it is for men.

This is illustrated in a study conducted in my lab. We examined the factorial invariance of the Bem Sex Role Inventory (BSRI) in women and men as well as across age groups (Blanchard-Fields, Suhrer Roussel, & Hertzog, 1994). When we correlated the gender identification item (masculinity and femininity) with scales such as interpersonal sensitivity, we found a striking difference for women and men. Women who rated themselves high on masculinity also rated themselves lower on interpersonal sensitivity, as one would expect. However, men who rated themselves high on masculinity rated themselves higher on interpersonal sensitivity. This interaction suggests that there is a qualitative difference in the way women and men construe the meaning of masculinity and femininity. For example, in other studies, when asked about social relationships, men saw themselves as "interpersonally sensitive" with important individuals in their life, such as getting along with an overbearing boss (Ashmore, 1990). In other words, more care needs to be taken to consider the individual's role in structuring the meaning of planful competence variables. Further research is needed to address such questions as how men versus women define planful competence.

Findings in the Shanahan et al. research also suggest that dependability predicts divorce rate in women. It would be interesting to find out whether women made better spousal choices in the spirit of good planful competence or simply persevered despite bad choices. In addition, divorce, as a status variable is a limited concept to indicate success in the family domain or social settings. Personality research on well-being focuses more on the quality of the marriage as the more important factor, given that divorce can occur for many reasons (Karney & Bradbury, 1995).

The authors also speculate that planfulness during adolescence or in early adulthood predicts well-being and adjustment in old age by way of life course achievements. For example, women with high planfulness in adolescence plotted higher levels of satisfaction across the life course. Several longitudinal studies of women's personality development have adopted a process approach in which they examine the interplay between social context and personality development. Helson and her colleagues (Helson & Moane, 1987; Helson, Stewart, & Ostrove, 1995) followed the lives of women who chose a typically feminine social clock (i.e., get married and have children) and how they adapted to the roles of wife and mother. This adaptation process was typically accompanied by a withdrawal from social life, the suppression of impulse and spontaneity, a negative self-image, and decreased feelings of competence. Twenty percent of the women who adhered to the social clock were divorced between the ages of 28 and 35. However, of these divorced women, those who also had careers by the age of 28 were less respectful of norms and more rebellious toward what they experienced. Note that these women were not lower on femininity or on well-being, they were simply more independent and self-assertive than those who followed the social clock. Follow-ups showed that these independent women remained so and showed greater confidence, initiative, and forcefulness than women who did not. Overall, Helson and her colleagues showed that women's personality change was systematic in early and middle adulthood, yet changes were evident in the context of specific changes in social roles and transitions in social contexts.

Finally, the authors considered a number of other interesting speculations about planful competence and the elderly. They suggest that planfulness may serve as a psychological resource throughout adulthood. Again, a further need for construct validity analyses is warranted. For example, the operational definition of planfulness typically used in this line of research may simply correspond well with the life stage of adolescents, who are at the peak of developing their logical skills and masculine identity (for boys). Thus, to clearly test the idea of heterotypic continuity, the construct again needs more clarification.

In conclusion, the construct validity issue is still of concern in this line of research, and the investigation of planful competence can be informed more by the psychological literature on related constructs such as personal control. At the same time, the psychological literature on constructs such as personal control can be well informed more by the approach these authors have taken; in other words, by placing psychological constructs into a historical/cohort framework. This could better address issues relevant to age differences in personal control. For example, it is argued that secondary control increases become more adaptive with age as a function of loss. Could it be that this is a cohort-specific phenomenon? Or is it a change in perspective given that goals and desires change as a function of life experience? In other words, it may not be a function of loss, but is less desire to pursue that particular goal given that the goal is no longer important.

REFERENCES

Ashmore, R. D. (1990). Sex, gender, and the individual. In L. A. Pervin (Ed.), *Handbook of personality: Theory and research* (pp. 486–526). New York: Guilford Press.

Berry, J. M. (1999). Memory self-efficacy in its social cognitive context. In T. M. Hess & F. Blanchard-Fields (Eds.), *Social cognition and aging* (pp. 69–96). San Diego: Academic Press.

Blanchard-Fields, F., & Hertzog, C. (2000). Age differences in social schematicity. In U. von Hecker, S. Dutke, & S. G. Sedek (Eds.), *Generative mental processes and cognitive resources: Integrative research on adaptation and control* (pp. 175–198). Dordrecht: Kluwer Academic.

Blanchard-Fields, F., & Norris, L. (1994). Causal attributions from adolescence through adulthood: Age differences, ego level, and generalized response style. *Aging and Cognition, 1,* 67–86.

Blanchard-Fields, F., Suhrer-Roussel, L., & Hertzog, C. (1994). A confirmatory factor analysis of the Bem Sex Role Inventory: Old questions, new answers. *Sex Roles, 30,* 423–457.

Brandtstädter, J. (1999). Sources of resilience in the aging self. In T. M. Hess & F. Blanchard-Fields (Eds.), *Social cognition and aging* (pp. 123–141). San Diego: Academic Press.

Clausen, J. S. (1991). Adolescent competence and the shaping of the life course. *American Journal of Sociology, 96,* 305–842.

Costa, P. T., Jr., & McCrae, R. R. (1992). Trait psychology comes of age. In T. Sonderegger (Ed.), *Nebraska symposium on motivation: Psychology and aging* (pp. 169–204). Lincoln, NE: University of Nebraska Press.

Costa, P. T., Jr., Zonderman, A. B., & McCrae, R. R. (1991). Personality, defense, coping, and adaptation in older adulthood. In E. M. Cummings, A. L. Greene, & K. H. Karraker (Eds.), *Life-span developmental psychology: Perspectives on stress and coping* (pp. 277–293). Hillsdale, NJ: Lawrence Erlbaum Associates.

Heckhausen, J., & Schulz, R. (1995). A life-span theory of control. *Psychological Review, 102,* 284–304.

Heckhausen, J., & Schulz, R. (1999). Selectivity in lifespan development: Biological and societal canalizations and individuals developmental goals. In J. Brandtstädter and R. M. Lerner (Eds.), *Action and self development: Theory and research through the lifespan* (pp. 67–130). Thousand Oaks, CA: Sage.

Helson, R., & Moane, G. (1987). Personality change in women from college to midlife. *Journal of Personality and Social Psychology, 53,* 176–186.

Helson, R., Stewart, A. J., & Ostrove, J. (1995). Identity in the cohorts of midlife women. *Journal of Personality and Social Psychology, 69,* 544–557.

Karney, B. R., & Bradbury, T. N. (1995). The longitudinal course of marital quality and stability: A review of theory, method, and research. *Psychological Bulletin, 118,* 3–34.

Lachman, M. E., & Weaver, S. L. (1998). Sociodemographic variations in the sense of control by domain: Findings from the MacArthur Studies of Midlife. *Psychology and Aging, 13,* 553–562.

Levy, B. (1996). Improving memory in old age through implicit self-stereotyping. *Journal of Personality and Social Psychology, 71,* 1092–1107.

Levy, B., & Langer, E. (1994). Aging free from negative stereotypes: Successful memory in China and among the American deaf. *Journal of Personality and Social Psychology, 66,* 989–997.

NEO, Professional Manual. (1992). Revised NEO Personality Inventory. Odessa, FL: Psychological Assessment Resources, Inc.

Soederberg Miller, L. M., & Lachman, M. E. (1999). The sense of control and cognitive aging: Toward a model of mediational processes. In T. M. Hess & F. Blanchard-Fields (Eds.), *Social cognition and aging* (pp. 17–41). San Diego: Academic Press.

Commentary

The Influence of Cohort on Personal Control Among Aging Persons

Margaret E. Ensminger

What has often been thought of as a personal characteristic may be influenced substantially by the social context. Although we tend to think of personal control as a good thing with beneficial outcomes, context may influence its impact. This has been illustrated in the chapter written by Shanahan and Hofer (this volume). In this brief discussion, I focus on the importance of cohort issues for examining personal control among the elderly. I also suggest that the same historical conditions may have a different impact and meaning for people who differ by social class, gender, and age. The two perspectives that focus on cohort and structural variations are both necessary in examining competence and personal control.

Shanahan and colleagues bring much needed focus on life course development and on how broad historical events can influence personal biographies and shape individual opportunities. Their analysis suggests that in some historically specific situations the attribute of perceived personal control may not be a particular advantage. For example, adolescent planfulness (personal control) among those who made the transition to adulthood at the time of the Great Depression of the 1930s did not predict education and occupational status. During the 1930s, the lack of jobs kept people in school longer than if work were readily available. Personal control was not particularly advantageous then, because there were limited options for exerting control. However, for later cohorts, planfulness during adolescence did contribute to the likelihood of continued schooling with the subsequent advantages that we associate with more schooling.

Furthermore, Shanahan and colleagues show that agency (personal control) in young adulthood was important for career success, but only for the older cohort, who had already started their careers before the onset of World War II. For men born fairly early in the twentieth century, the war disrupted their careers, and personal control was useful in getting their careers back on the right track. The younger cohort who started their careers right after the war found themselves in a very favorable career situation and were fairly successful, regardless of their personal control.

CONTEXT AND HISTORICAL EXPERIENCES

Such an analysis signifies some of the potential complications in thinking about personal control in the elderly without considering the context as uppermost. Other chapters in this volume attest that personal control no matter what stage in the life course is likely to be influenced by socioeconomic status, ethnicity, cultural values, and gender, as well as by age. We now need to add to this list cohort experiences. An article by Elder and Liker (1982) illustrates the complex interaction between early experiences with the Great Depression, social class, and reactions to financial stress among elderly women. Middle-class women whose families had experienced hardship during the 1930s and faced financial strain during old age were better able to emotionally handle the financial strain than those middle-class women who had not experienced family hardship. However, for lower class women whose families had experienced hardship, later financial difficulties were devastating to them emotionally. The trajectory differed not only by one's family experience but also by one's social class origins.

From this perspective, it seems that we cannot easily make conclusions about the elderly without reference to their historical cohort experiences. Those who are ages 65 to 70 today grew up as children and adolescents during World War II. Their childhood and young adult heroes were World War II–era icons such as John Wayne and Franklin D. Roosevelt. They have lived through great changes in civil rights. The view and place of women in society have greatly changed during their lifetime, with women assuming more control in both the workplace and the home. Divorce has become more commonplace. There has been relative economic prosperity during their lifetimes. How they will face aging and how the strengths and expectations that they will have for this stage of life is expected to differ from previous cohorts who were adults during World War II and who had more traditional conceptions of men's and women's roles. The role of personal control is likely to differ as well.

Kohli (1986) suggested that the increasing organization of the life course by age has made it easier to plan and predict life transitions. Social Security, rules about pension plans, employment opportunities that vary by age, and the funding of medical care for those over the age of 65 are examples of societal arrangements that greatly influence the transition to retirement. Because experiences based on these arrangements are relatively standard in American society, they may lead to certain similarities in retirement planning. In addition, the elderly may have more political power as a group because of their voting patterns and the effective organizing and lobbying of organizations that represent older Americans. These activities may provide a basis for affiliation related to age.

There are also forces that increase the diversity of the experiences of aging adults. The elderly now have more choices than did previous generations in terms of the kinds of living arrangements that are available: Assisted living and various types of retirement communities have increased the options that older adults have. Two other recent changes also influence how older adults make the transition to the next life stage. The increases in divorce and in the numbers of women in the workforce alter the resources of both men and women as they make the transition into the retirement phase of the life course. Within the framework of a predictable life course, based on many common experiences, but with important sources of diversity, there are more choices that older adults can make, increasing their opportunities for personal control (Kohli, 1986; Shanahan, 2000). It is difficult to discuss personal control of the elderly without reference to the particular historical cohort of which they are a part. This reminds us of Mills's (1959) central theme in sociology: how history shapes the individual's life course and how public issues are linked to personal troubles.

Similarly, it is hard to predict how future cohorts will be influenced by historical events. The communication revolution, the changing labor market structure, the dramatic changes that continue to occur in family life, and the globalization of most aspects of life cannot fail to have an impact on how people age and on their perceptions of personal control. The baby boom population (those born between 1946 and 1964) will soon reach the age of 65. How the high proportion of elderly in the population will affect issues of personal control can only be speculated. Throughout their life course, baby boomers have focused on the importance of making choices rather than accepting traditional ways. It is likely that this positive value placed on personal control and choice will continue. For those coming after the baby boomers, it is difficult to identify what patterns with regard to personal control will evolve.

For all cohorts currently in the workforce, employment patterns are changing so that individuals will be much more likely to change jobs frequently, to work for many companies with few expectations of mutual loyalty, to have the place of work be at home, and to have fairly diverse career trajectories. There may be several possible ramifications of this work history for the transition to retirement. First, the demarcation between being retired or still working may not be so obvious because there may be many spells of working and not working during their careers and home may be the site of many work activities. Second, the Social Security and pension systems and other means of saving for retirement may be much more varied than they are currently, suggesting more diverse paths to retirement. Finally, as Pescosolido and Rubin (2000) suggest, increasingly individuals are in short-term and serial relationships with limited commitment. Individuals have connections to many workplaces and to many families. Ties to other people and organizations may be so contingent that they are not integrative in the Durkheimian sense. In such a situation, personal control may be fairly prevalent, but it may have much less value in a context where individuals do not feel strongly connected to other people or organizations. Increasing structural social isolation may increase the value of communal decision making in which joint planning between spouses and among other family members or colleagues will have added importance.

Over the past 30 years, an important change that has occurred for the elderly has been the decreased likelihood that in general those who are over the age of 65 are poor. In the 1950s, older adults were overrepresented among those who were poor. Today, older adults are not more likely to be poor than are other age groups, and they are less likely to be poor than are younger age groups. However, this relative prosperity masks the reality that economic resources vary among the elderly. The increase in divorce has meant economic difficulties for those who are divorced, especially women. Widowed women traditionally have been at risk financially, but divorced women are even more so because they are not left with their husbands' resources. Divorce may influence personal control in several ways. To the extent that personal control is related to economic circumstances, the economic situations of those who are divorced will influence the extent of their personal control. On the other hand, to the extent that divorce changes the sense of power in relationships, divorce may enhance the feeling of personal control, especially for women.

An additional potential threat to older adults may come from the increasing inequality that is occurring within our society. That is, those who are in the top 5% of the population in terms of income and wealth are controlling more and more of the society's resources, whereas those on the bottom are controlling less and less. The potential ramifications of this for the elderly are not clear. This increasing inequality may undermine some of the power that comes to older adults because of their high political participation and organization. That is, if social class becomes more of an organizing force than age, then personal control may be more prevalent among those with more resources, regardless of age.

NEW DIRECTIONS FOR RESEARCH ON CONTROL

Another issue that Shanahan and Hofer brought us is that of measurement and conceptual refinement. Others in this volume have discussed the necessity for refining the conceptual and measurement issues surrounding personal control and mastery. Leonard Pearlin and Mark Pioli in Chapter 1 provide a rich history of the different definitions and dimensions of personal control. The concepts they discuss there pertaining to definitions and dimensions of control need to be better integrated with life course analyses. When using archival data, researchers are hampered by the available measures, and it is often necessary to use measures that are not very adequate. In the Shanahan et al. chapter, the measures for the concept of personal control were stretched. If the field had more conceptual clarity and defined measures, we could better gauge how far off these measures are or suggest better measures. Chapter 5 illustrates what we can learn from archival data, but we need to make sure that measures are as good as they can be. With the changes occurring in our society with regard to the workplace and family, we may need even better conceptualizations of the relevant social demarcations of age in the life course.

There are several suggestions for future research concerning life course and personal control. An important next step would be to explicitly consider the importance of both cohort and structural influences and to examine how they interact. Often in research when cohort influences are discussed, it is assumed that everyone in society is affected equally by the historical circumstances. However, some of the most exciting research on the life course has been concerned with the differential impact of societal changes on different groups within society. For example, the contrast in men's and women's trajectories from the same historical period may be informative. Because women in the Berkeley and Oakland longitudinal studies did not have career expectations, personal control may not have been as relevant for them as for the men. For women in cohorts where career achievement was not expected, what were the ramifications of high personal control? If we expect personal control to be influenced by how one is located in the social structure, we might expect that women will have higher levels of personal control as the autonomy of women in the labor force increases. Shanahan and Hofer cite findings that show that competence for women in the Berkeley studies did not predict education or career status. These data further support the importance of context in determining the impact of personal control. It is likely that those findings would not be found with current cohorts of women.

Similarly, those of different social backgrounds may have very different societal expectations and demands for personal competence in different time periods. Our understanding of these issues will further enhance how we think about personal control for the aging for a particular cohort in a specific social structural location.

The possibility that aging in future cohorts will be transformed because of the tenuous, serial, and weak affiliations that people have with their families, their workplace, and their communities suggests that social and behavioral scientists will have a full research agenda. Whether personal control is considered as a relevant issue in this context will be crucial to investigate. Shanahan and colleagues have provided a background to this question in the tradition of Mills and Elder in demonstrating how history can impinge on the relevance of personal control to the individual life course.

REFERENCES

Elder, G. H., & Liker, J. K. (1982). Hard times in women's lives: Historical influences across forty years. *American Journal of Sociology, 88,* 241–269.

Kohli, M. (1986). The world we forgot: A historical review of the life course. In V. W. Marshalll (Ed.), *Later life* (pp. 271–303). Beverly Hills, CA: Sage.

Mills, C. W. (1959). *The sociological imagination.* Oxford: Oxford University Press.

Pescosolido, B., & Rubin, B. A. (2000). The web of group affiliations revisited: Social life, postmodernism, and sociology. *American Sociological Review, 65,* 52–76.

Shanahan, M. J. (2000). Pathways to adulthood in changing societies: Variability and mechanisms in life course perspective. *Annual Review of Sociology, 26,* 667–692.

CHAPTER 6

The Life Span Theory of Control: Issues and Evidence

Richard Schulz, Carsten Wrosch, and Jutta Heckhausen

The primary goal of this chapter is to describe the life span theory of control and highlight key features of our theory that distinguish it from other conceptions of control. These include (1) its ability to address issues of development over the entire life course, with special emphasis on major life course transitions; (2) its universality with respect to culture and historical time; and (3) its link to the emotional system of humans. Although empirical tests of hypotheses derived from our theory are still limited, we report throughout this chapter findings from diverse literatures that lend support to our ideas. To set the stage for our life span theory of control, we begin by identifying four key parameters of life course development that frame our theory.

PARAMETERS OF LIFE COURSE DEVELOPMENT

The first requirement of any theory of the life course is that it acknowledge the broad biological and social forces that fundamentally shape the development of the organism (Elder, 2005; Heckhausen, 1999;

Heckhausen & Schulz, 1995). These forces typically are viewed as constraints and can be briefly summarized in four propositions (Schulz & Heckhausen, 1996). The first is that life is finite. Whatever is to be achieved or experienced in life has to be done in a finite period of time, typically less than 80 years. Second, biological development follows a sequential pattern. Although there is considerable interindividual variability in biological development, the overall biological resources across the life span resemble an inverted U function. Third, societies impose age-graded sociostructural constraints on development. Life span psychologists and life course sociologists emphasize that all societies can be characterized as having age-graded systems that constrain and provide a scaffold for life course patterns (Baltes, 1991; Hagestad, 1990; Hagestad & Neugarten, 1985; Heckhausen, 1990, 1995). These patterns provide predictability and structure at both individual and societal levels. Fourth, genetic potential is a limiting factor on functional development. Although the potential behavioral repertoire of humans is vast, the capacity to achieve extraordinary levels of functioning in a given domain may be constrained by the genetic makeup of an individual.

A second general requirement of a theory of life span development is that it must provide means for regulating development in ways that help maximize an individual's potential. This is achieved through four types of mechanisms (Heckhausen, 2001; Schulz & Heckhausen, 1996). First, there must be diversity in the opportunity to sample different performance domains. Second, there has to be selectivity in pursuing and allocating resources to developmental paths that are consistent with genetic and sociocultural opportunities. Third, the individual must compensate for and cope with failure encountered as different action-goals are pursued and with declines associated with late-life development. And fourth, the individual must manage trade-offs across domains and sequential life phases and recognize that the allocation of resources to one domain may compromise the opportunity to develop others.

LIFE SPAN THEORY OF CONTROL

The life span theory of control proposes the construct of control as the central theme for characterizing human development from infancy to old age (Heckhausen & Schulz, 1995; Schulz & Heckhausen, 1996). The underlying assumption of this position is that the ability to produce behavior–event contingencies and thus exert primary control over the environment is a fundamental building block of adaptive development in humans. We distinguish between primary control and secondary control. Primary control targets the external world and attempts to achieve effects in the immediate environment external to the individual, whereas secondary control targets the internal world of the individual (Rothbaum, Weisz, & Snyder, 1982) and is specifically aimed at optimizing the motivational and emotional resources required for primary control striving. Thus, practicing to improve tennis or basketball skills is an example of primary control, whereas convincing oneself that these skills are only minor indicators of one's physical capacities is an example of secondary control. As this example suggests, primary and secondary control strategies serve different functions, which are discussed later in this chapter.

We emphasize the functional primacy of primary over secondary control. Because primary control is directed outward, it enables individuals to explore and shape their environment to fit their particular needs and optimize their developmental potential. Without engaging the external world, the developmental potential of the organism cannot be realized. As a result, primary control is both preferred and has greater adaptive value to the individual. Striving for primary control is the engine that powers behavior.

Extensive empirical research suggests that striving for primary control is inherently part of the motivational systems of mammals. The developmental origin of activities directed at controlling external events and acquiring generalized expectations about control can be traced to the very beginning of life. Even neonates are able to detect behavior–event contingencies (Janos & Papousek, 1977), and most mammals prefer behavior–event contingencies to event–event contingencies even in the absence of consummatory behavior (Singh, 1970). The striving for primary control assures development within specific domains as well as the sampling of diverse domains over time (White, 1959). Primary control striving provides the foundation for diversity and selectivity throughout the life course.

Throughout the life course, primary and secondary controls work together to optimize development of the organism through selection processes and compensation of failure. We identify four types of control-related processes to achieve this goal (see Table 6.1). Selective primary control refers to the focused investment of resources such as effort, time, and abilities and skills required for pursuing a chosen goal. Selective

TABLE 6.1   Item Examples for Domain-General and Health-Specific Primary and Secondary Control Strategies

	Item Examples	
Type of Control Strategy	Domain-General Control Strategies	Health-Specific Control Strategies
Selective primary control	When something really matters to me, I invest as much time as I can on it.	I invest as much time and energy as possible to improve my health.
Selective secondary control	When I have decided on something, I know that I will achieve it.	When I decide to do something about a health problem, I am confident that I will do it.
Compensatory primary control	When I cannot solve a problem by myself, I ask others for help.	If I develop a new health problem, I immediately get help from a health professional (e.g., doctor or nurse).
Compensatory secondary control	When I do not reach a goal, I often tell myself that it wasn't my fault.	When I have a health problem, I remind myself that I am not to blame for it.

secondary control targets internal representations that are motivationally relevant to goal pursuit. Exemplary representations include the value ascribed to the chosen goal, the values associated with alternative goals, the perceived personal control of goal attainment, and the anticipated effects or consequences of a goal attainment. Thus, selective secondary control effectively enhances the value of a chosen goal while devaluing nonchosen alternatives. Compensatory primary control is required whenever the physical or cognitive capacities of the individual are insufficient to attain a chosen goal. This may happen not only in older adults, because of age-related declines, but also in infants, children, or inexperienced individuals, because of immaturity or insufficient skill development. Thus, compensatory primary control refers to the use of external resources such as assistance from others and technical aids such as wheelchairs and hearing aids. Compensatory secondary control serves to buffer the negative effects of failure or losses on the individual's motivation for primary control. Compensatory secondary control strategies include disengagement from prior goals, engagement with new alternative goals, self-protective causal attributions, strategic social comparison with others, and strategic intraindividual comparisons. Sample items used to measure primary and secondary controls are presented in Table 6.1 (Heckhausen, Schulz, & Wrosch, 1998; Heckhausen, Wrosch, & Fleeson, 2001; Wrosch & Heckhausen, 1999). To the extent that individuals are able to use these strategies in ways that maximize their long-term primary control potential, we would judge them to be optimizing development throughout the life course (see Figure 6.1).

Early development is characterized by an increased ability to exert primary control over the environment. The action–outcome experiences of the child provide the basis for the development of self-competence, including generalized and exaggerated expectancies of control and perceptions of self-efficacy. Children between the ages of 3 and 4 are able to experience appropriate emotional reactions to failure and therefore require compensating mechanisms to counteract this threat to their motivational resources (Geppert & Heckhausen, 1990; H. Heckhausen, 1984). During childhood and adolescence, a broad range of secondary control strategies develop, including changing aspiration levels, denial, egotistic attributions, and reinterpretation of action goals (see review in Heckhausen & Schulz, 1995).

Early adulthood is characterized by increasing levels of primary and secondary control as well as increased selectivity with respect to the domain specificity of control. Selectivity continues to increase throughout adulthood, whereas diversity gradually decreases. Because of the limited capacity of the individual and external constraints, the increased selectivity at older ages has to be compensated for with decreased diversity. This trade-off between diversity and selectivity is a hallmark of development in late middle and old age (Heckhausen, 2001; Heckhausen & Schulz, 1999a).

During late middle age and old age, increasing age-related biological and social challenges to selective primary control put a premium on secondary control strategies along with compensatory primary control as means for maintaining perceptions of primary control. As the ratio of gains to losses in primary control becomes less and less favorable, the individual increasingly resorts to compensatory control processes.

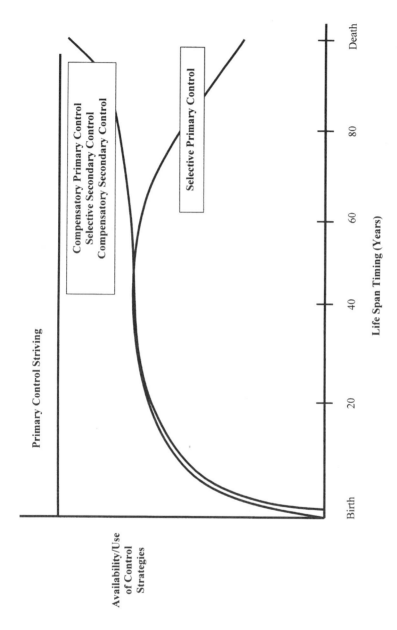

FIGURE 6.1 Availability and use of primary and secondary control strategies over the life course.

The sequential interplay of primary and secondary control strategies can be illustrated by focusing on a developmental goal such as having a child. Like other life goals, striving for a child is both socially and biologically constrained. It is characterized by a developmental window during which striving for the goal is optimal, as well as a deadline, after which striving for the goal becomes very difficult. Thus, we would expect different control processes to be optimal before and after the deadline. Before passing the deadline, adaptive control processes are those directed at goal attainment (i.e., selective primary and selective secondary controls). After passing a deadline without achieving the goal, the adaptive response is to deactivate goal pursuit strategies and activate goal disengagement strategies such as compensatory secondary control (e.g., devaluing the goal). Goal disengagement would serve the important function of helping the individual redirect his or her internal resources to other life domains with more favorable chances of success. Thus, existing levels of primary control and future primary control striving would remain intact. This line of reasoning could also be applied to individuals undergoing a life-threatening disease. In the early stages of a disease such as cancer, it should be adaptive to remain optimistic and aggressively fight the disease, but in later and irreversible stages of the disease, it may be more important to focus on substitute goals and find purpose in life elsewhere or restrict primary control striving to areas such as pain control in order to optimize functioning despite the illness.

Evidence: Importance of Control Strategies Across the Life Course

Although our theory emphasizes the stability of primary control striving throughout the life course, we also recognize the importance of adapting specific control strategies to take advantage of the opportunity structures available at different ages. Age-differential effects of control strategies are expected to be beneficial because older, as compared to younger, adults often face increasingly constrained opportunities for goal attainment. Control strategies aimed at goal attainment (primary control, selective secondary control) should be most beneficial in younger ages, when people face favorable opportunities for goal realization in a number of life domains (e.g., family and work). In old age, by contrast, self-protective control strategies (compensatory secondary control) may protect people's emotional and motivational resources and support disengagement from unattainable goals (Schulz & Heckhausen, 1996; Wrosch & Heckhausen, 1999).

A number of empirical studies have confirmed age-differential use of primary and secondary control strategies. With respect to compensatory secondary control, cross-sectional studies provide convergent evidence that older as compared to younger adults more frequently use strategies associated with compensatory secondary control (Heckhausen et al., 1998; Peng, 1993), as well as related constructs such as accommodation (Brandtstädter & Renner, 1990) and emotion-focused coping (Folkman, Lazarus, Pimley, & Novacek, 1987). In contrast, the empirical evidence with respect to age differences in primary control is inconsistent. Cross-sectional studies have shown an age-graded increase (Heckhausen et al., 1998), stability (Heckhausen, 1997; Peng, 1993), and decrease (Brandtstädter & Renner, 1990) in strategies associated with primary control (e.g., assimilation and problem-focused coping). Studies examining age-differential relations between control strategies and indicators of successful development are relatively rare at this point. To attain a more complete picture about control and successful development, however, life span research should study both age-related endorsement of control strategies and their relation to functional outcomes. We present in the following section results from three different studies that address the use of as well as the consequences of using different control strategies at different points in the life course.

Managing Partnership Separation in Young Adulthood and Late Midlife

The importance of primary and secondary control has been studied in the process of adaptation to partnership separation. Wrosch and Heckhausen (1999) examined the age-related use and predictive value of control strategies in young (age 23 to 39) and late midlife (age 49 to 59) adults who recently separated from their partners (see also Wrosch, 1999). People's age plays an important role in realizing intimate relationships: Young adults face favorable opportunities to attain a new partnership. Older adults, in contrast, confront a sharply reduced "marriage market" (Braun & Proebsting, 1986). The life span theory of control would predict that control strategies aimed at attaining partnership goals are particularly beneficial in younger separated individuals. In contrast, self-protective secondary control may preserve older separated people's motivational and emotional resources and facilitate disengagement from unattainable partnership goals.

The study measured partnership-specific versions of primary and secondary scales (Wrosch & Heckhausen, 1999). As illustrated in Figure

6.2, the results confirmed that younger, as compared to older, separated adults endorsed higher levels of selective primary and selective secondary control strategies. No significant age effect was obtained for compensatory primary control. In contrast, older separated persons reported higher levels of compensatory secondary control than younger separated adults did. A comparable pattern of result was shown for the nomination of personal goals and biases in information processing. On the one hand, older as compared to younger separated persons reported fewer partnership goals and enhanced recall of negative as compared to positive partnership aspect. On the other hand, older separated persons reported the highest number of social goals. Most importantly, the study showed that an age-adapted endorsement of compensatory secondary control predicted change in positive affect over time (Wrosch & Heckhausen, 1999). Older separated people reported improved positive affect if they mentioned high levels of compensatory secondary control. In contrast, younger separated adults suffered de-

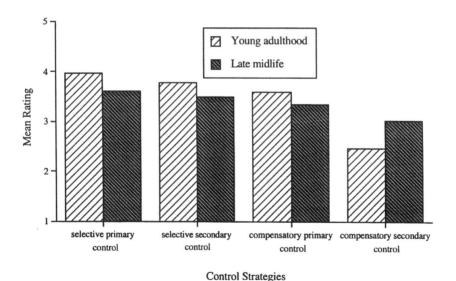

FIGURE 6.2 Mean levels of primary and secondary control strategies in young and late midlife adults who recently separated from an intimate partnership.
(Adapted from Wrosch & Heckhausen, 1999)

cline in positive affect if they used high levels of compensatory secondary control. The reported results suggest that people's control processes are well adapted to age-graded opportunities and constraints for development. In addition, an age-adapted investment of control may facilitate emotional well-being.

Managing Childbearing Goals Before and After Passing the Biological Clock

Another example of the importance of age-related investment of control strategies stems from a study on childbearing goals. Heckhausen and colleagues (2001) studied childless women who have and have not passed the biological clock for childbearing. Based on their chronological age, childless women were grouped as being "urgent" in regard to their childbearing goals (age 29 to 35), having "just passed" (age 39 to 46), and having "long passed" (age 49 to 56) the biological clock for childbearing. The main hypothesis of the study was that women in the urgency group would use control strategies aimed at having their own children. In contrast, women who have passed the biological clock were expected to invest in compensatory secondary control. We assessed whether age-adjusted endorsement of control strategies is related to women's subjective well-being.

The results of the study confirmed that women's use of control strategies is contingent on their age-related status according to having or not having passed the biological clock (Heckhausen et al., 2001). As depicted in Figure 6.3, women who were urgent in regard to their childbearing goals reported higher levels of selective primary, selective secondary, and compensatory primary controls than women who have already passed the biological clock for childbearing (just passed and long passed). In contrast, women who have passed the biological clock, as compared to urgent women, reported higher levels of compensatory secondary control. In addition, the study showed that among women whose biological clock had "run out," those who did not disengage from the goal of having children reported higher levels of depressive symptomatology (Heckhausen et al., 2001). Similar to the partnership study findings, this study shows that the appropriate investment in control strategies that are tailored to people's opportunities and constraints is critical for maintaining psychological well-being.

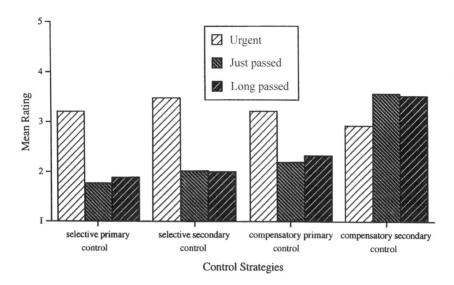

FIGURE 6.3 **Mean levels of primary and secondary control strategies in women who have passed (urgent) and have not passed (just passed and long passed) the biological clock for childbearing.**

(Adapted from Heckhausen, Wrosch, & Fleeson, 2001)

Managing Health and Financial Stress Across Adulthood

Age-related importance of control strategies has also been demonstrated in a study using a national probability sample ($N = 3,490$, age range: 25–76 years, see Wrosch, Heckhausen, & Lachman, 2000). The authors examined the use and predictive value of primary and secondary control strategies for managing health and financial stress. Among other constructs, the study assessed generic versions of two prototypical control strategies: persistence in goal striving and positive reappraisals. Persistence in goal striving can be seen as a core component of primary control striving, conceptually comparable to constructs such as selective primary control (Heckhausen & Schulz, 1993) or tenacious goal pursuit (Brandtstädter & Renner, 1990). Positive reappraisal, by contrast, is a compensatory secondary control strategy aimed at protecting individuals' motivational and emotional resources after experiencing failure and developmental losses.

Figure 6.4 illustrates the predictive associations between primary control and self-protective secondary control with subjective well-being (Wrosch et al., 2000). In young adulthood, primary control showed a significantly stronger effect on subjective well-being than in old age. In contrast, secondary control, as compared to primary control, showed a greater effect on subjective well-being in middle-aged and older adults. The study also examined whether the described age effects of control strategies were pronounced in people who faced health or financial stress. For both types of stress, it was found that age-related effects of control strategies on subjective well-being were more closely related among individuals confronting health or financial challenges. These results indicated that an age-adjusted use of control strategies facilitates

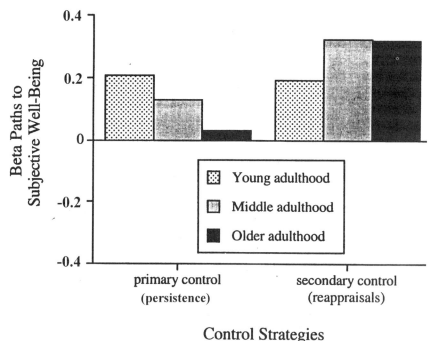

FIGURE 6.4   Predictive value of primary control (persistence) and secondary control (positive reappraisals) strategies on subjective well-being in young, middle-aged, and older adults.

(Adapted from Wrosch, Heckhausen, & Lachman, 2000)

successful development, particularly in people who confront problems that involve age-graded opportunities for goal attainment (e.g., chronic health stress in old age and financial problems after retirement).

EVOLUTIONARY AND CULTURAL PERSPECTIVES

We claim that striving for control is a human universal, invariant across historical time and diverse cultural settings. This is not to say that there are no cultural variations in the expression of control striving and in the extent to which different cultures afford opportunities for achieving control. Nevertheless, the preference for primary control is a fundamental human universal.

White (1959) was the first investigator to suggest that striving for control has an evolutionary basis when he concluded that effectance motivation—striving for competence or mastery—is intrinsic to both humans and animals. Striving for control is adaptive for all species that have the potential of influencing their environment. Controlling the environment is adaptive because it allows the organism to influence events relevant for survival, such as foraging, seeking and building shelter, searching for a mate, and caring for offspring. Human beings have been shaped by evolution to seek out, maintain, defend, and expand control by way of fundamental behavioral tendencies favoring active engagement with the environment. Such basic tendencies have been conceptualized as behavioral modules (Cosmides & Tooby, 1994; Fodor, 1983; Tooby & Cosmides, 1992), adaptive specializations (Rozin, 1976), or preadaptations (Mayr, 1960). Relevant modules for the promotion of control striving include (1) preferences for behavior–event contingencies over event–event contingencies in mammals (White, 1959), (2) an enhanced readiness to repeat responses when they lead to desirable consequences ("law of effect," Thorndike, 1898; "operant conditioning," Skinner, 1938), (3) curiosity and novelty-seeking behaviors among mammals (Schneider, 1996), and (4) an asymmetric affective system that favors responding to negative affect and the spontaneous dissipation of positive affect (Frijda, 1988; Heckhausen & Schulz, 1995; Schulz & Heckhausen, 1997).

Although control striving is clearly adaptive from an evolutionary perspective because it affords advantages for survival, procreation, and nurturing one's offspring, one might question its relevance to middle and old age. A number of researchers have emphasized that evolution poses little selective pressures for adaptive development during postre-productive ages (Baltes, Lindenberger, & Staudinger, 1998; Crews, 1993; Finch, 1990). Indeed, some researchers have argued that evolutionary selection in humans most likely has favored various maladaptive late-life onset by-products of early onset adaptive characteristics. For exam-ple, heart disease among individuals with a type A personality style may be a maladaptive midlife consequence of control-striving strategies developed during the reproductive phase of development.

Once evolutionary selection sets into motion a characteristic that is adaptive for procreation, there are no selection mechanisms available for altering the program during the postreproductive years. In other words, there are no built-in mechanisms for turning off a characteristic, such as control striving, simply because the primary goal (e.g., procre-ation) for that characteristic is no longer relevant. The motivation for primary control and the associated secondary control mechanisms that support this drive are perhaps unique in that they are functional adapta-tions at both young and old ages. Mechanisms that help the organism cope with failure and maintain primary control striving during early development turn out to be just as useful in middle and old age, during which humans must cope with a wide range of losses and declines.

Evidence: Universalism versus Cultural Relativism

Our universalistic position has been criticized by Gould (Gould, 1999; Heckhausen & Schulz, 1999b), who points out that some studies show that different cultural groups endorse higher ratings of or profit more from secondary control than primary control. Because virtually all of these studies were published prior to the publication of our theory and were therefore not intended to be critical tests of our ideas, their findings are open to multiple interpretations. Although we would argue that none of the findings contradict our views and at least some of them support our perspective, it is perhaps most fruitful to examine these studies in terms of the methodological issues they raise about testing the primacy hypothesis.

Different cultures provide different frameworks for expressing the universal behavioral tendency for maximizing primary control. A prime example of this is the relative emphasis on collectivistic or individualistic values (Triandis, 1989). Primary control striving can be applied to group goals as well as to individuals' goals. Thus, the fact that in some cultures (e.g., most of Asian cultures) collectivistic values, concerns, and goals are more salient than in other cultures (e.g., western industrial societies) (e.g., Seginer, Trommsdorff, & Essau, 1993) does not argue against the functional primacy of primary control. Similarly, studies comparing cultures with respect to the relative salience of interdependent versus independent selves (Markus & Kitayama, 1991) do not speak to culture-specific preferences for primary or secondary control, because an interdependent self can strive for primary control just as well as an independent self. Various studies cited as evidence for a primacy of secondary control in Asian cultures confound the measurement of primary control with individualistic and of secondary control with collectivistic goal orientations (e.g., sample item designed to indicate "secondary control" in a study by Seginer et al., 1993: "When I choose my future occupation, I will consider my parents' opinion because in important matters parents have the final say").

Another problem involves the conceptual and measurement confound of perceived control, actual control, and control striving. For example, Thompson, Collins, Newcomb, and Hunt (1996) compared White and African American HIV-positive inmates' beliefs about control (i.e., "How much control do you feel you have over _____?") and the extent to which they accept whatever happens (i.e., "How much do you feel OK about _____ because you just accept it and don't try to change it?"). Beliefs about control were interpreted as an indicator for primary control, and accepting outcomes was treated as a measure of secondary control. These operationalizations of primary and secondary control are problematic because beliefs about personal control do not necessarily correspond to attempts to realize primary control, nor does acceptance of negative outcomes correspond to secondary control. High control beliefs were found to be protective against distress in White Americans only, whereas passive acceptance, viewed by Thompson et al. (1996) as an indicator of secondary control, proved disadvantageous to both White and African Americans: The more acceptance, the more distress.

Research like the study by Thompson and colleagues (1996), which addresses control behavior in extremely uncontrollable settings, is very important because it provides critical tests about the potential of secondary control strategies for protecting primary control resources in areas of functioning where control is still possible. If primary control holds functional primacy, as we propose, one would expect that secondary control (e.g., blaming others, downward social comparisons, or disengaging from goal) would be used with regard to the uncontrollable aspects of a given situation, but primary control would be sought out in areas, however restricted, which still hold some control potential. Such investigations need to use appropriate measurement instruments that investigate self-report or, better still, behavioral indicators of primary control striving, as well as specific primary and secondary control strategies (Heckhausen et al., 1998).

Another problem of culture-comparative studies are cultural differences in the social norms about acceptable motives of behavior. Cultures differ in the extent to which they encourage or admonish the open expression of individual goals as motivators of behavior. Western industrial managers in their negotiations with their East Asian counterparts have long known that expressed flexibility, adaptability, and acquiescence do not usually mean their negotiating partners are actually willing to give in.

An approach to avoiding the problems of nonmatching semantic systems and variability in the social desirability of attitude expression in different cultures is to directly investigate primary control behavior. One such approach would be to directly study the basic mechanisms involved in primary control striving experimentally by investigating behavioral preferences for the fundamental modules of control striving (e.g., preference for behavior–event contingencies) described above. An interesting quasi-experimental method that tests both cultural and historical preferences for primary control would be to investigate the migration behavior of peoples around the world in terms of the relative control potential of emigrant compared to immigrant countries. From all we know as citizens in a globalized world, people try to escape low-control environments in favor of high-control environments. This is true for a great variety of determinants of control, be it economic, political, geographic (risk of earthquakes), climatic (floods, draught, storm, and famine), or in terms of social mobility. Systematic studies on control gradients between emigrant and immigrant countries would provide deeper insight into the dynamic of control striving as a human universal in different contexts of cultural origin.

Another source of evidence may be utility studies of invasive care procedures in medical treatments. These studies repeatedly demonstrate the astonishing preferences for survival at virtually any cost when compared to the alternative (Spilker, 1990). Studies of assisted suicide in Oregon consistently report that participation in the program among terminal patients is motivated by a desire for autonomy and control at the end of life (Sullivan, Hedberg, & Fleming, 2000). Culture-comparative work could reveal whether this finding is unique for western industrial societies or reflects a universal human condition.

Finally, to the extent that researchers continue to be interested in self-report measures of control, we think it important that we move away from measurement strategies that focus on the assessment of perceived control and pursue the development of measures that assess the use or endorsement of control-related strategies (Heckhausen et al., 1998). The latter approach is likely to be more informative about those characteristics of the motivational system that lie at the heart of our theory and is less vulnerable to social desirability effects.

EMOTION AND CONTROL

Throughout the life course, mastery of behavior–event contingencies or achievements is associated with positive affect such as happiness, pride, pleasure, and joy (Csikszentmihalyi, 1975; Oatley & Jenkins, 1992), and losses or failures tend to elicit negative affect such as sadness, shame, and anger (H. Heckhausen, 1984).

Positive affect resulting from contingency experiences serves as both a reinforcer for existing levels of primary control and a motivator for further primary control striving. Negative affect can serve the important role of increasing control striving when failure experiences are encountered. This would be the case, for example, when individuals fail to attain goals, then increase their efforts to gain the desired primary control (see Figure 6.5).

Negative affect can also have dysfunctional consequences when it undermines the motivation for primary control. Repeated failures at achieving important goals can undermine an individual's motivation to pursue them. In the long run, this would limit the primary control potential of the individual. To attenuate or buffer the impact of failure and loss experiences and the attendant negative affect, the individual has available a large repertoire of secondary control strategies. These strategies are invoked when opportunities for direct action are constrained, and they vary in direct proportion to the intensity of negative affect instigated by the loss experience. Poor performance on an important test may result in more practice or harder work to prepare for future similar challenges or it may result in making external attributions for poor performance (e.g., "I didn't get enough sleep the night before the test"). Together, these responses to failure help to protect existing levels of primary control and assure future primary control striving. In an analogous way, secondary control strategies can serve to enhance

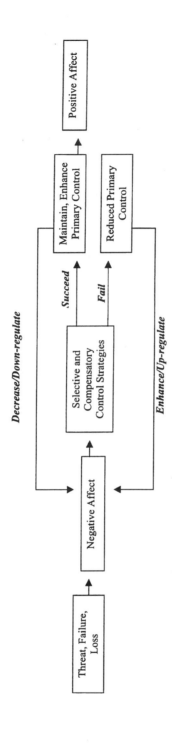

FIGURE 6.5 **A model for the relation between negative affect and control strategies.**

(Adapted from Schulz & Heckhausen, 1997)

the impact of positive affect and promote primary control striving. Thus, the pleasurable feelings resulting from achieving success on a particular task may result in heightened self-attributions about one's ability and encourage setting new goals that motivate primary control striving.

In some circumstances, losses or failures can be so overwhelming that neither primary nor secondary control mechanisms are able to overcome them. When this happens, the primary control potential of the individual is compromised, and we would expect negative affect to be both intense and long lasting. This may be the case, for example, when a permanent physical disability fundamentally undermines the primary control of an individual and all attempts to cognitively or physically compensate for this loss are unsuccessful. Situations such as these are frequently associated with the presence of clinical depression in late life (Alexopoulos et al., 1996; Schulz et al., 1994). This example is consistent with other findings showing that severe losses and threats, occurring in conjunction with vulnerability factors such as lack of social support, can cause psychiatric syndromes such as depression (Brown & Harris, 1989; Oatley & Bolton, 1985).

It is also possible to imagine positive affect so strong and persistent that motivation for further action is undermined, as may the case, for example, with addictions to mood-altering drugs such as heroin. However, like Frijda (1988), we believe that mechanisms have evolved to protect humans from the dangers of positive affect serving as the ultimate goal of human existence. Positive emotions spontaneously dissipate with time even in the presence of the eliciting event, whereas negative emotions persist as long as the instigating conditions are present: "One gets used to the events that, earlier, delighted and caused joy; one does not get used to continuous harassment or humiliation. Fear can go on forever; hopes have limited duration" (Frijda, 1988, pp. 353–354). The link between change and positive affect is consistent with our idea of the primacy of primary control. It assures that individuals continue striving beyond already attained levels of primary control, and the only way to achieve this is through action on the external environment. From an evolutionary perspective, an asymmetric affective system that requires continuous change for maintaining positive affect and heightened responsiveness to adverse conditions is likely to promote survival by way of maximizing primary control.

Emotional Intensity and Specificity of Response

Emotional experiences vary in intensity in direct proportion to the magnitude of threat to or loss of primary control (Frijda, 1988). Thus, threats to higher order domains of primary control such as survival or physical functioning elicit stronger emotional responses than threats to lower order domains such as specific cognitive or physical skills or abilities (Schulz & Heckhausen, 1997). The greater the loss or threatened loss, the greater the emotional response, and hence the greater the action readiness to respond. A rich repertoire of response options to loss are available to the individual, and they serve the dual purpose of maintaining or promoting the primary control of the individual and down-regulating the negative affect generated by the loss.

Both primary and secondary control strategies are available response options to threats, losses, and failures. Specific emotions may be associated with specific response tendencies. For example, an emotion like intense fear elicited by threat is more likely to result in a response involving selective action on the environment (i.e., selective primary control), whereas an emotion such as sadness elicited by loss or failure is likely to result in secondary control response targeting internal representations of the eliciting event and its likely consequences (i.e., compensatory secondary control) such as disengagement from prior goals, self-protective attributions, and strategic inter- and intraindividual social comparisons. Negative affect generated by a loss may also elicit compensatory primary control responses, such as seeking assistance from others and using technical aids such as wheelchairs and hearing aids.

Positive affect frequently leads to enhanced goal striving (selective primary control) but may also elicit selective secondary control such as targeting internal representations relevant to goal pursuit. This may involve enhancing the value ascribed to a chosen goal, the perceived personal control of goal attainment, or the anticipated positive effects of goal attainment.

In sum, both positive and negative affect can instigate specific control strategies that protect or enhance existing levels of primary control. Selective and compensatory control processes play the additional role of modulating the emotional experience itself, down-regulating negative affect, and maintaining positive affect for as long as possible.

Evidence: Emotions and Control

The evidence linking control strategies to emotions is fairly limited because few direct tests of these ideas have been carried out. Nevertheless, a large body of literature can be identified that is generally supportive of these views. For example, in the health literature, there are many studies showing that the threats or losses in primary control as a result of illness generate negative affect and increases in primary control because of improved functioning after treatment result in positive affect (Lenze et al., 2001; Nieboer, Schulz, Scheier, & Matthews, 1998). More direct evidence can be found in studies that link the use of selective and compensatory primary and secondary control strategies to affective outcomes. For example, Wrosch and colleagues (2000) found that older individuals confronting chronic health stress had higher levels of subjective well-being when they used a compensatory secondary control strategy (positive reappraisal) as opposed to primary control strategy (persistence) to deal with this stressor. Because complete recovery from chronic conditions such as arthritis and hypertension is not possible, a compensatory secondary control strategy such as reappraisal would be expected to be the more adaptive of the two strategies investigated. In contrast to these findings, Schulz, Wrosch, and Heckhausen (1998) found the use of goal pursuit control strategies when confronted with acute health stressors to be more adaptive. Older persons confronting acute health symptoms (i.e., indicators of potentially treatable acute conditions) who endorsed selective primary and secondary control strategies ("If I have a health problem that gets worse, I put in even more effort to get better"; "When I decide to do something about a health problem, I am confident that I will achieve it") and compensatory primary control ("When a treatment doesn't work for a health problem I have, I try hard to find out about other treatments") had lower levels of depressive symptomatology both cross-sectionally and longitudinally than individuals who did not endorse these strategies.

CONTROL STRATEGIES AND PERCEIVED CONTROL

The adaptive role of perceived control in human development is widely recognized and well documented. A large body of research has demonstrated that being optimistic and believing in one's own competencies relates to subjective well-being and good health (e.g., Bandura, 1997; Carver et al., 1993; Scheier et al., 1989; Seligman, 1991). One of the proposed mechanisms through which perceived control may operate has been described as an adaptive use of control strategies and active coping processes (Bandura, 1977; Carver & Scheier, 1981; Skinner, 1995). This would imply, in turn, that people's perceptions of control and their use of control strategies are different processes, although some of the literature has categorized primary and secondary control strategies under the label "perceived control" (e.g., Halliday & Graham,

2000; Thompson et al., 1996). As mentioned above, control strategies relate to individuals' active reactions and thus should be distinguished from perceived control. It remains an empirical question to examine the determinants and consequences of people's use of control strategies and perceptions of control (e.g., Skinner, 1996).

Although it would be reasonable to expect that individuals who endorse control-related strategies would also report higher levels of perceived control, this need not necessarily be the case. For example, positive control expectancies and the engagement in personal goals do not always work hand in hand in adaptive development (Schulz & Heckhausen, 1999). People may use control strategies to realize personal goals even if they have doubts about attaining their goals. Such situations may occur, for example, if a particular goal relates to a central feature of an individual's functioning or identity (e.g., hierarchy of goals, Carver & Scheier, 1981). Given that failure in the attainment of goals in central life domains may negatively affect people's primary control across a wide range of life domains, we would expect active goal pursuits to be adaptive, independent of people's levels of perceived control. In addition, perceived control may directly influence people's well-being, independent of the use of control strategies. For example, a person who has doubts about attaining a goal may directly experience distress, anxiety, and negative mood, whereas a person who believes that desirable outcomes are controllable should experience positive affect (e.g., Bandura, 1982; Kunzmann, 1999). Taken together, perceived control and control strategies may explain different portions of variance in individuals' well-being. In some cases, such as the management of highly central goals, people's active investments of control, as opposed to perceived control, may be even better precursors of successful development and subjective well-being.

Evidence: Control Strategies versus Perceived Control

We have studied the idea of independent effects of control strategies and perceived control in a longitudinal sample of older adults ($N =$ 154, age range: 68–92; see Wrosch et al., 2000). The study participants responded to a health-specific measure of goal engagement control strategies (composite of selective primary, selective secondary, and compensatory primary control), a scale of global perceived control (self-mastery; Pearlin & Schooler, 1978), and a self-report measure of depressive symptomatology (CES-D; Radloff, 1977). The basic assumption of the study was that an adaptive management of health-related threats would result in low levels of depression in the elderly. Both predictors—global perceived control and active pursuits of health-related goals—were expected to facilitate adaptive management of health problems in older adults. However, our main hypothesis was that high levels of active pursuits of health goals would predict low levels of depression, above and beyond individual differences in global perceived control.

The cross-sectional results showed that health-specific control strategies and global perceived control were only modestly correlated (Wrosch et al., 2000). In support of our hypotheses, we found independent main effects of health-specific control strategies and global perceived control on reduced levels of depression. In addition, active investments of control in health-related goals were particularly beneficial in older adults who confronted acute health problems. The longitudinal results confirmed a main effect of health-specific control strategies on change in depressive symptomatology. Older adults who reported high levels of health-specific control strategies showed reduced depression over time. This effect was independent of global perceived control, which did not explain change in depression over time.

The reported findings indicated beneficial effects of active investment of control, independent of individuals' levels of global perceived control. Thus, people who have doubts about attaining their goals may indeed profit from active primary control attempts. Moreover, only the investment of health-specific control strategies predicted reduction of depression over time; perceived control was unrelated to change in depression. These results suggest that it is particularly important for older adults to manage health-related problems by active attempts of goal attainment to compensate for threats in primary control potential. More generally, the findings provide evidence for the idea that control strategies can be empirically distinguished from levels of perceived control. However, the study of functional relations between control strategies, perceived control, and successful development needs more empirical research. In this regard, it would be useful to examine effects of domain-specific as well as global levels of perceived control and control strategies across the entire life course, in different life domains, and in different stages of adaptation processes.

CONCLUSION

The fundamental question emerging from our theoretical perspective is, how do individuals use primary and secondary control strategies to meet the dual challenges of selectivity and failure compensation throughout the life course? Our empirical research to date has focused on key life course transitions in which opportunities for exercising primary control in specific domains are either reduced or threatened. By focusing on these transitions, we have been able to show how the strategic use of different control strategies protects the emotional and motivational resources of the individual. A related question that has not been studied in detail concerns microanalysis of goal disengagement or goal deactivation processes. How do individuals give up major life goals, such as having a child or a particular career? What is the interplay between primary and secondary control processes that facilitate a successful transition from failed goal achievement to continued goal striving in other domains? In this context, perceived control may play a critical role in alternative goal selection.

In exploring the potential of the human control system, research on extreme circumstances that result in the breakdown of the control system should be particularly promising. For example, many older individuals progress through stages of pathology, impairment, and disability before they die. What role do compensation processes play in these transitions, and how effective are they in dealing with these threats? Under what circumstances do individuals give up primary control striving, and what are the health consequences of relinquishing primary control?

We feel that our theory also has the potential of informing intervention strategies to help individuals navigate challenging life course transitions and cope with losses. Several existing therapies, such as behavior therapy (Lewinsohn, 1974), cognitive-behavior therapy (Beck, Rush, Shaw, & Emery, 1979), and interpersonal therapy (Klerman, Weissman, Rounsaville, & Chevron, 1984), emphasize the importance of engaging the world and adjusting cognitions in the same way that we emphasize primary and secondary control. It would be useful to explore areas of convergence between our theoretical views and existing therapeutic interventions to identify ways in which treatment approaches may be amended based by our views of the life course and the role of control strategies.

Finally, because control-related processes are so central to the physical health and psychological well-being of human beings, it is useful to emphasize once again the importance of identifying behavioral and biological links between control and psychiatric and physical morbidity. This is particularly important for those of us interested in aging, because late life entails critical transitions in both control processes and health and well-being.

REFERENCES

Alexopoulos, G. S., Vrontou, C., Kakuma, T., Meyers, B. S., Young, R. C., Klausner, E., & Clarkin, J. (1996). Disability in geriatric depression. *American Journal of Psychiatry, 153,* 877–885.

Baltes, P. B. (1991). The many faces of human aging: Toward a psychological culture of old age. *Psychological Medicine, 21,* 837–854.

Baltes, P., Lindenberger, U., & Staudinger, U. (1998). Life-span theory in developmental psychology. In R. M. Lerner (Ed.), *Handbook of child psychology: 1. Theoretical models of human development* (5th ed., pp. 1029–1143). New York: Wiley.

Bandura, A. (1977). Self-efficacy: Toward a unifying theory of behavioral change. *Psychological Review, 84,* 191–215.

Bandura, A. (1982). Self-efficacy mechanisms in human agency. *American Psychologist, 37,* 122–147.

Bandura, A. (1997). *Self-efficacy: The exercise of control.* New York: Freeman.

Beck, A. T., Rush, A. J., Shaw, B. F., & Emery, G. (1979). *Cognitive therapy of depression.* New York: Guilford Press.

Brandtstädter, J., & Renner, G. (1990). Tenacious goal pursuit and flexible goal adjustment: Explication and age-related analysis of assimilative and accommodative strategies of coping. *Psychology and Aging, 5,* 58–67.

Braun, W., & Proebsting, H. (1986). Heiratstafeln verwitweter Deutscher 1979/82 und geschiedener Deutscher 1980/83 [Marriage tables of widowed, 1979/82, and divorced, 1980/83, Germans]. *Wirtschaft und Statistik, 86,* 107–112.

Brown, G. W., & Harris, T. (1989). *Life events and illness.* London: Unwin Hyman.

Carver, C. S., Pozo, C., Harris, S. D., Noriega, V., Scheier, M. F., Robinson, D. S., Ketchman, A. S., Moffat, F. L., & Clark, K. C. (1993). How coping mediates the effect of optimism on distress: A study of women with early stage breast cancer. *Journal of Personality and Social Psychology, 65,* 375–390.

Carver, C. S., & Scheier, M. F. (1981). *Attention and self-regulation: A control-theory approach to human behavior.* New York: Springer-Verlag.

Cosmides, L., & Tooby, J. (1994). Origins of domain-specificity: The evolution of functional organizations. In L. A. Hirschfeld & S. A. Gelman (Eds.), *Mapping the mind: Domain specificity in cognition and culture* (pp. 85–116). Cambridge: Cambridge University Press.

Crews, D. E. (1993). Biological anthropology and human aging: Some current directions in aging research. *American Review of Anthropology, 22,* 395–423.

Csikszentmihalyi, M. (1975). *Beyond boredom and anxiety.* San Francisco: Jossey-Bass.

Elder, G. H., Jr. (2002). The life course and human development. In R. M. Lerner (Ed.), *Handbook of child psychology* (Vol. 1, pp. 939–992). New York: Academic Press.

Finch, C. E. (1990). *Longevity, senescence, and the genome.* Chicago: University of Chicago Press.

Fodor, J. (1983). *The modularity of mind.* Cambridge, MA: MIT Press.

Folkman, S., Lazarus, R. S., Pimley, S., & Novacek, J. (1987). Age differences in stress and coping processes. *Psychology and Aging, 2,* 171–184.

Frijda, N. H. (1988). The laws of emotion. *American Psychologist, 43,* 349–358.

Geppert, U., & Heckhausen, H. (1990). Ontogenese der Emotion [Ontogenesis of emotion]. In K. R. Scherer (Ed.), *Enzyklopädie der Psychologie: Vol. C/IV/3. Psychologie der Emotionen* (pp. 115–213). Göttingen, Germany: Hogrefe.

Gould, S. J. (1999). A critique of Heckhausen and Schulz's (1995) life-span theory of control from a cross-cultural perspective. *Psychological Review, 106,* 597–604.

Hagestad, G. O. (1990). Social perspectives on the life course. In R. Binstrock & L. George (Eds.), *Handbook of aging and the social sciences* (3rd ed., pp. 151–168). New York: Academic Press.

Hagestad, G. O., & Neugarten, B. L. (1985). Age and the life course. In R. H. Binstock & E. Shanas (Eds.), *Handbook of aging and the social sciences* (2nd ed., pp. 35–61). New York: Van Nostrand Reinhold.

Halliday, C. A., & Graham, S. (2000). "If I get locked up, I get locked up": Secondary control and adjustment among juvenile offenders. *Personality and Social Psychology Bulletin, 26,* 548–559.

Heckhausen, H. (1984). Emergent achievement behavior: Some early developments. In J. Nicholls (Ed.), *The development of achievement motivation* (Vol. 3, pp. 1–32). Greenwich, CT: JAI Press.

Heckhausen, J. (1990). Erwerb und Funktion normativer Vorstellungen über den Lebenslauf: Ein entwicklungspsychologischer Beitrag zur sozio-psychischen Konstruction von Biographien [Acquisition and function of normative conceptions about the life course: A developmental psychology approach to the psychosocial construction of biographies]. *Kölner Zeitschrift für Soziologie und Sozialpsychologie, 31,* 351–373.

Heckhausen, J. (1995). *Developmental regulation in adulthood: Age-normative and sociostructural constraints as adaptive strategies.* Unpublished thesis, Free University of Berlin.

Heckhausen, J. (1997). Developmental regulation across adulthood: Primary and secondary control of age-related challenges. *Developmental Psychology, 33,* 176–187.

Heckhausen, J. (1999). *Developmental regulation in adulthood: Age-normative and sociostructural constraints as adaptive challenges.* Cambridge: Cambridge University Press.

Heckhausen, J. (2001). Adaptation and resilience in midlife. In M. E. Lachman (Ed.), *Handbook of midlife development* (pp. 345–391). New York: John Wiley.

Heckhausen, J., & Schulz, R. (1993). Optimization by selection and compensation: Balancing primary and secondary control in life-span development. *International Journal of Behavioral Development, 16,* 287–303.

Heckhausen, J., & Schulz, R. (1995). A life-span theory of control. *Psychological Review, 102,* 284–304.

Heckhausen, J., & Schulz, R. (1997, August). *Control striving across the life span: Developmental regulation via primary and secondary control.* Paper presented at the meeting of the American Psychological Association, Chicago.

Heckhausen, J., & Schulz, R. (1999a). Biological and societal canalizations and individuals' developmental goals. In J. Brandtstädter & R. Lerner (Eds.), *Action and self development: Theory and research through the life span* (pp. 67–103). London: Sage.

Heckhausen, J., & Schulz, R. (1999b). The primacy of primary control is a human universal: A reply to Gould's critique of the life-span theory of control. *Psychological Review, 106*(3), 605–609.

Heckhausen, J., Schulz, R., & Wrosch, C. (1998). *Developmental regulation in adulthood: Optimization in primary and secondary control—a multiscale questionnaire.* Berlin: Max Planck Institute for Human Development.

Heckhausen, J., Wrosch, C., & Fleeson, W. (2001). Developmental regulation before and after a developmental deadline: The sample case of "biological clock" for child-bearing. *Psychology and Aging, 16,* 400–413.

Janos, O., & Papousek, H. (1977). Acquisition of appetitional and palpebral conditioned reflexes by the same infants. *Early Human Development, 1,* 91–97.

Klerman, G. L., Weissman, M. M., Rounsaville, B. J., & Chevron, E. S. (1984). *Interpersonal psychotherapy of depression.* New York: Basic Books.

Kunzmann, U. (1999). *Being and feeling in control: Two sources of older people's emotional well-being.* Berlin: Sigma.

Lenze, E., Rogers, J. C., Martire, L. M., Mulsant, B. H., Rollman, B. L., Dew, M. A., Schulz, R., & Reynolds, C. F., III. (2001). The association of late-life depression and anxiety with physical disability: A review of the literature and prospectus for future research. *American Journal of Geriatric Psychiatry, 9,* 113–135.

Lewinsohn, P. M. (1974). Clinical and theoretical aspects of depression. In K. S. Calhoun, H. E. Adams, & K. M. Mitchell (Eds.), *Innovative treatment methods in psychopathology* (pp. 63–120). New York: Wiley.

Markus, H. R., & Kitayama, S. (1991). Culture and the self: Implications for cognition, emotion, and motivation. *Psychological Review, 98,* 224–253.

Mayr, E. (1960). The emergence of evolutionary novelties. In S. Tax (Ed.), *Evolution after Darwin: The evolution of life* (Vol. 1). Chicago: University of Chicago Press.

Nieboer, A., Schulz, R., Scheier, M., & Matthews, K. (1998). Spousal caregivers' activity restriction and depression: A model for changes over time. *Social Science and Medicine, 47,* 1361–1371.

Oatley, K., & Bolton, W. (1985). A social cognitive theory of depression in reaction to life events. *Psychological Review, 92,* 372–378.

Oatley, K., & Jenkins, J. M. (1992). Human emotions: Function and dysfunction. In M. R. Rosenzweig & L. W. Porter (Eds.), *Annual review of psychology* (Vol. 43, pp. 55–85). Palo Alto, CA: Annual Reviews.

Pearlin, L. I., & Schooler, C. (1978). The structure of coping. *Journal of Health and Social Behavior, 19,* 2–21.

Peng, Y. (1993). *Primary and secondary control in American and Chinese-American adults: Cross-cultural and life-span developmental perspectives.* Unpublished doctoral dissertation, Brandeis University. Waltham, MA.

Radloff, L. (1977). The CES-D scale: A self-report depression scale for research in the general population. *Applied Psychological Measurement, 1,* 385–401.

Rothbaum, F., Weisz, J. R., & Snyder, S. S. (1982). Changing the world and changing the self: A two-process model of perceived control. *Journal of Personality and Social Psychology, 42,* 5–37.

Rozin, P. (1976). The evolution of intelligence and access to the cognitive unconscious. In J. A. Sprague & A. N. Epstein (Eds.), *Progress in psychobiology and physiological psychology* (Vol. 6, pp. 245–280). New York: Academic Press.

Scheier, M. F., Matthews, K. A., Owens, J. F., Magovern, G. J., Lefebvre, R. C., Abbott, R. A., & Carver, C. S. (1989). Dispositional optimism and recovery from coronary artery bypass surgery: The beneficial effects on physical and psychological well-being. *Journal of Personality and Social Psychology, 57,* 1024–1040.

Schneider, K. (1996). Intrinsisch (autotelisch) motiviertes Verhalten—dargestellt an den Beispielen des Neugierverhaltens sowie verwandter Verhaltenssysteme (Spielen und leistungsmotiviertes Handeln) [Intrinsically motivated behavior—as demonstrated in examples of curiosity and related behavioral systems (play and achievement-oriented behavior)]. In J. Kuhl & H. Heckhausen (Eds.), *Enzyklopädie der Psychologie: Motivation, Volition und Handlung* (pp. 119–152). Göttingen: Hogrefe.

Schulz, R., & Heckhausen, J. (1996). A life-span model of successful aging. *American Psychologist, 51,* 702–714.

Schulz, R., & Heckhausen, J. (1997). Emotions and control: A life-span perspective. In M. P. Lawton & K. W. Schaie (Eds.), *Annual review of gerontology and geriatrics* (Vol. 17, pp. 185–205). New York: Springer.

Schulz, R., & Heckhausen, J. (1999). Aging, culture, and control: Setting a new research agenda. *Journal of Gerontology: Psychological Sciences, 54B,* P139–P145.

Schulz, R., Mittelmark, M., Kronmal, R., Polak, J. F., Hirsch, C. H., German, P., & Bookwala, J. (1994). Predictors of perceived health status in elderly men and women. *Journal of Aging and Health, 6,* 419–447.

Schulz, R., Wrosch, C., & Heckhausen, J. (1998). *Health engagement control strategies and depression in the elderly.* Paper presented at the biannual meeting of the International Society for the Study of Behavioral Development, Bern, Switzerland.

Seginer, R., Trommsdorff, G., & Essau, C. (1993). Adolescent control beliefs: Cross-cultural variations of primary and secondary orientations. *International Journal of Behavioral Development, 16,* 243–260.

Seligman, M. E. P. (1991). *Learned optimism.* New York: Knopf.

Singh, D. (1970). Preference for bar-pressing to obtain reward over freeloading in rats and children. *Journal of Comparative and Physiological Psychology, 73,* 320–327.

Skinner, B. F. (1938). *The behaviors of organisms.* New York: Appleton-Century-Crofts.

Skinner, E. A. (1995). *Perceived control, motivation, and coping.* Thousand Oaks, CA: Sage.

Skinner, E. A. (1996). A guide to constructs of control. *Journal of Personality and Social Psychology, 71,* 549–570.

Spilker, B. (Ed.). (1990). *Quality of life assessment in clinical trials.* New York: Raven Press.

Sullivan, A. D., Hedberg, K., & Fleming, D. W. (2000). Legalized physician-assisted suicide in Oregon—the second year. *New England Journal of Medicine, 342,* 598–604.

Thompson, S. C., Collins, M. A., Newcomb, M. D., & Hunt, W. (1996). On fighting versus accepting stressful circumstances: Primary and secondary control among HIV-positive men in prison. *Journal of Personality and Social Psychology, 70,* 1307–1317.

Thorndike, E. L. (1898). Animal intelligence: An experimental study of the associative processes in animals. *Psychological Monographs, 2*(8).

Tooby, J., & Cosmides, L. (1992). The psychological foundations of culture. In J. H. Barkow, L. Cosmides, & J. Tooby (Eds.), *The adapted mind: Evolutionary psychology and the generation of culture* (pp. 19–136). New York: Oxford University Press.

Triandis, H. C. (1989). The self and social behavior in differing cultural contexts. *Psychological Review, 96,* 506–520.

White, R. W. (1959). Motivation reconsidered: The concept of competence. *Psychological Review, 66,* 297–333.

Wrosch, C. (1999). *Entwicklungsfristen im Partnerschaftsbereich: Bezugsrahmen für Prozesse der Aktivierung und Deaktivierung von Entwicklungszielen* [Developmental deadlines in the partnership domain: Reference frame for activation and deactivation of developmental goals]. Berlin: Waxmann.

Wrosch, C., & Heckhausen, J. (1999). Control processes before and after passing a developmental deadline: Activation and deactivation of intimate relationship goals. *Journal of Personality and Social Psychology, 77,* 415–427.

Wrosch, C., Heckhausen, J., & Lachman, M. E. (2000). Primary and secondary control strategies for managing health and financial stress across adulthood. *Psychology and Aging, 15*(3), 387–399.

Commentary

Is the Life Span Theory of Control a Theory of Development or a Theory of Coping?

Corinna E. Löckenhoff and Laura L. Carstensen

In this commentary, we discuss the conceptual contributions that the life span theory of control makes to the understanding of development across the *life span*. We point out that the theory is one of very few truly life *span* theories of development and, as such, contributes rare conceptual coherence to developmental processes that unfold throughout life. We also argue that the theory can offer important insights into adaptive coping over the life course. Moreover, it provides the context within which to understand the temporal processes involved in choosing and rejecting specific goals. At the same time, we question whether the theory provides an adequate basis for understanding life course development more generally. In particular, we critically examine the contention that primary control is always preferred over secondary control as well as the tendency to characterize later life as a process of continuous decline. We suggest that these theoretical presumptions— rooted in evolutionary models of human aging—constrain, as opposed to increase, the utility of the theory. Although evolutionary approaches hold value in understanding human aging, we argue that uniquely human characteristics, involving consciousness—particularly the subjective appreciation for temporal qualities of life—limit the degree to which biological decrements principally drive aging outcomes. Finally, we argue that life span theories of human development must be able to account for observed gains in later life without invariably presuming that they reflect efforts to cope with decline and loss. We draw on theoretical considerations and empirical findings from our own work as well as others to support our arguments and illustrate our central points.

The life span theory of control, presented originally by Heckhausen and Schulz in 1995 and elaborated in subsequent years (Heckhausen & Schulz, 1998; Schulz & Heckhausen, 1998, 1999; Schulz, Wrosch, & Heckhausen, this volume) explains development over the life span and major life course transitions by means of two control-related processes. Primary control, defined as the active pursuit of a chosen goal, refers to efforts to modify the environment or change one's circumstances. Secondary control is directed toward motivationally relevant internal representations, such as the relative value ascribed to particular goals. Both control strategies are thought to be in a constant interplay with each other. They allow for diversity of experience, selection of developmental paths, compensation for failures, and management of the inevitable trade-offs among pursuits in different domains at different phases in life.

The life span theory of control postulates that primary and secondary control processes follow different trajectories over the life course. The ability to exert primary control is hypothesized to increase rapidly in early childhood, peak in midlife, and decline as people get older. Secondary control strategies are developed in childhood and continue to grow throughout life. They are seen as compensatory mechanisms that become important when primary control over the environment is not possible.

A central tenet of the theory concerns the functional primacy of primary control over secondary control. Schulz, Wrosch, and Heckhausen (this volume) argue that only primary control allows for active exploration and modification of the environment and that survival and procreation are impossible without the ability to induce environmental change. From an evolutionary perspective, this is thought to translate into higher adaptive potential of primary control processes. In turn, secondary control efforts, namely, those that influence internal states, are thought to hold less adaptive value. Claims for the primacy of primary control are based on the assumption that striving for primary control is a central part of the mammalian motivational system. Schulz and colleagues support this postulate with empirical evidence gathered from human and animal studies. The evidence they present concerns the universality of instrumental learning mechanisms, preference for behavior–event contingencies over event–event contingencies, and preference for novel stimuli. Furthermore, Schulz and colleagues suggest that primary control strivings generate positive emotional experience. Specifically, mastery experiences are thought to lead to positive emotions, whereas loss of primary control results in negative affect.

CONCEPTUAL STRENGTHS

A central feature of the life span theory of control is its coherent view of the life course. In contrast to stage theories (e.g. Erikson, 1994), the life span theory of control does not assume that the life course is split into qualitatively different phases. Instead, the same mechanisms are thought to influence development from childhood to old age. Based on hypotheses about life span changes in primary and secondary control, concrete predictions for individual developmental trajectories can be derived.

Because of the fundamental limitations of the human condition (finiteness of life, age-related biological changes, age-graded societal norms, and limited genetic potential), development can occur only when selection processes are activated. According to the theory, the preference for primary control ensures that individuals explore their environment and identify multiple domains in which the external world can be changed. However, limited resources make it impossible to exert control across all domains. Primary control leads to selective engagement in domains that can be influenced by the individual and that increase access to resources. Secondary control strategies are thought to increase engagement with chosen goals and decrease the value ascribed to alternative goals that are not selected for further pursuit. Secondary control also can lead to disengagement from areas in which primary control is not possible.

Thus, the theory is not limited to the explanation of normative life changes that affect most individuals within a society (e.g., retirement). It also can account for more unusual, nonnormative life events (e.g., paralysis after an accident) that alter individual development. At first, decreased primary control in a certain domain should lead to increased efforts to regain active control. If individuals do not have sufficient resources themselves, external resources (such as technical aids and assistance from others) can be used to exert compensatory primary control. For example, a person with quadriplegia can use an electric wheelchair to regain mobility. He or she may also delegate housekeeping tasks and everyday errands to family members or paid helpers while retaining control about what is being done. Theoretically, irreparable loss of primary control will lead to increases in secondary control strategies. A person may develop new goals targeting areas of life in which primary control is still possible. For example, a paralyzed person may give up unattainable goals for athletic achievement and focus on educational goals instead. Thus, the theory offers a way to integrate adaptive coping efforts into a life span developmental framework using the same principles to explain coping with normative and nonnormative life events.

Schulz and colleagues (this volume) suggest that "[d]uring late middle age and old age, increasing age-related biological and social challenges to selective primary control put a premium on secondary control strategies" (Schulz et al., this volume, p. 237). They argue that older adults have greater difficulties coping actively with losses because reserve capacities concomitantly decline with age. However, there is considerable evidence that older adults cope just as—if not more—effectively than their younger counterparts. We concur that older adults may be likely to employ disengagement strategies and focus on emotion regulation instead of the attainment of other types of goals. However, alternative explanations for such tendencies are viable. For example, it is important to keep in mind that this can be explained by age-related differences in sources of stress. Lazarus and colleagues (Folkman, Lazarus, Pimley, & Novacek, 1987; Lazarus, 1996) found that age differences in emphasis on emotion- versus problem-focused strategies could be fully explained by differences in the types of stressors encountered by younger and older adults. Older adults were more concerned with health issues, whereas younger adults were facing problems with work and child rearing. There is no evidence that older adults are more likely to use secondary control strategies regardless of the problem type. In fact, it seems that older people are better at tailoring their problem-solving approaches to the specific characteristics of a problem (Blanchard-Fields, 1996), a point to which we return below.

Overall, by describing the lifelong interplay between primary and secondary control, the life span theory of control offers a useful framework to understand adaptive coping strategies as they are employed by different age groups. In the arena of coping, the theory is extremely valuable. However, it becomes problematic if it is offered as a life span theory of human development because it does not offer a parsimonious explanation for developmental gains observed in adult development. In the absence of empirical evidence that gains reflect coping with loss, they cannot be simply presumed to reflect psychological reactions to biological loss.

IMPLICATIONS FOR AGING

Like a number of life span developmental theories (e.g., Brandstädter & Greve, 1994), the life span theory of control presumes that age-related psychological changes reflect adaptation to a steady downhill course with regard to resources and abilities. There is no doubt that loss is a central part of aging. Albeit variable, all people experience loss and decline at some point in old age, and, granted, there are people whose experience of old age is one of a series of ultimately lethal blows. On the other hand, many people—according to some studies, most people (Field, 1997)—experience old age as a very positive time in life. Consequently, theories of aging grounded on the premise that aging is synonymous with losing at best lack parsimony and at worst provide tautological models that cannot be empirically validated.

Viewing old age as a time of gradual and pervasive decline in biological and psychological functioning is conceptually problematic. Even the presumption that physical aging follows a steady downhill slope is inconsistent with empirical data across different domains of functioning. Physical health does not decline gradually as people age. Fries (1990) argued that advanced medical technology may lead to a compression of morbidity into a shorter period of time before death. Manton and his colleagues (Manton, 1997; Manton, Stallard, & Corder, 1998) investigated broad trends as well as individual trajectories in the National Long-Term Care Survey (1982–1994). Individual trajectories showed both declines and improvements in old age functioning and disability status over time, indicating that disability often reverses even very late in life.

Similarly, cognitive change does not occur at a steady rate. Kaufman and Horn (1996) compared age changes in experience-based (crystallized) and information-processing (fluid) abilities. Age-related declines occurred primarily in the latter domain. Although the majority of older people show decline in some primary mental abilities, very few people show significant decline in most of their abilities (Schaie, 1996). Riegel and Riegel's (1972) terminal drop hypothesis postulates a sudden decline in cognitive performance within 5 years before death instead of a steady decrease throughout old age. This hypothesis has been supported by a number of studies (e.g., Bosworth, 1997; White & Cunningham, 1988).

These findings illustrate that it is crucial to differentiate between illness and death, on the one hand, and normal age-related changes, on the other. If one considers only the age-related changes that are normative and unrelated to specific disease processes, it is clear that they are insufficient to cause developmental disengagement. In addition, assuming a steady decline of abilities in old age clouds detection of positive changes and growth in late life. Although the majority of biological changes in old age are indeed negative, age-related psychological changes clearly include both developmental gains and losses. Breadth of knowledge and experience (as measured by the concept of crystallized intelligence) continue to grow in late life (Horn & Hofer, 1992). In emotional and social domains, improvement is a more common finding than loss.

Carstensen and her colleagues (Carstensen, Pasupathi, Mayr, & Nesselroade, 2000), for example, investigated everyday emotional experience across the life span. During a 1-week period, participants reported their current levels of 19 different emotions at 35 randomly selected times. Frequency, intensity, complexity, and regulation of emotional experience were examined. There were no age differences in the intensity of positive or negative emotions or in the frequency of positive emotions. However, the frequency of negative emotions decreased until the age of 60. After this age, the decrease ceased. In addition, older adults reported a more complex emotional experience (as measured by the number of factors yielded in principal component analyses within each individual). Complexity of emotional experience was negatively correlated with the intensity of negative affect and neuroticism. Furthermore, older people were more effective in regulating their emotional experience. Highly positive experiences were more stable among older participants, whereas periods of highly negative experiences were less likely to last. These findings suggest that emotional experience improves over the life span. Interestingly, gradual improvement in emotion regulation seems to start in young adulthood—long before the onset of age-related losses.

Older adults are also more flexible in their approaches to everyday problem solving. Blanchard-Fields (1996) emphasized that everyday problems are rarely well structured and can only be solved by considering multiple criteria for solutions and the interpersonal context of the situation. According to Blanchard-Fields, more mature problem-solving strategies are characterized by increased complexity of problem interpretation and flexibility in responding. Thus, effective solutions for everyday problems may require changes in the self as well as changes in the material and social environment. As people grow older, they seem to become more effective in integrating both strategies. They also show greater flexibility when approaching different kinds of problems. Blanchard-Fields and Irion (1988b) investigated the relationship between coping strategies and locus of control with regard to stressors. Internality among younger adults was associated with negative outcomes such as self-blame, hostility, and avoidance. In contrast, internality among older adults was related to positive outcomes such as conscious self-reflection. In another study, the same authors asked older adults and adolescents to complete measures of emotion-focused and problem-focused coping strategies (Blanchard-Fields & Irion, 1988a). Older adults preferred problem-focused coping strategies in situations that were perceived as controllable and emotion-focused strategies in uncontrollable situations. In contrast, adolescents reported the use of emotion-focused and defensive coping styles regardless of the situation. Thus, older adults were in fact less likely to use secondary control strategies than adolescents. Also, they were more flexible in their approach to different types of problems. Blanchard-Fields, Chen, and Norris (1997) asked people of different ages how they would deal with problems in the following three domains: consumer problems, managing a home, and conflict with friends. With regard to the instrumental domains, older adults were more problem focused than younger people, who reacted in a more passive-dependent manner. With regard to conflict with friends, older adults were more likely to endorse avoidant strategies, whereas younger adults were more emotionally reactive. Again, older adults seemed to be more flexible in managing different types of problems.

These findings suggest age-related improvements in psychological factors such as emotional experience, emotion regulation, and problem-solving skills. There is no reason to presume that such improvements are driven by loss. These processes show linear improvements from early to late life, beginning too early to result from age-related decline.

THE INTERPLAY BETWEEN PRIMARY AND SECONDARY CONTROL

The life span theory of control presumes age-related loss of primary control as a central cause of age-related changes in secondary control. Thus, it can address age-related gains in emotion regulation and problem solving only in terms of coping with loss of primary control. In consequence, developmental growth is interpreted as a self-protective reaction to frustrated goal pursuits. This is by no means a parsimonious explanation for improvements in old age. Other factors such as experience and changes in goal structure (see below) are neglected by this perspective.

The tendency to interpret age-related gains as coping efforts arises from the theoretical presumption that primary control processes have primacy over secondary control processes. This assertion has been criticized by Gould (1999), who suggests that the primacy of primary control is limited to western contexts and is less salient in Asian cultures, where secondary control processes are more prominent. In response, Heckhausen and Schulz (1999) argue, and we concur, that there may be different behavioral expressions of primary control striving in different cultures. For example, western cultures may focus on primary control over individual goals, whereas Asian cultures may put more emphasis on collectivistic primary control. Furthermore, we agree with Heckhausen and Schulz (1999) that the measurement of control tendencies through self-reports may be problematic because there are cultural differences in social norms regarding the expression of individual goals. Additional research would be needed to disentangle control strategies and goal orientations and to supplement self-reports with behavioral measures

However, presuming a primacy of primary control is problematic for other reasons. First, the authors have no true empirical support for their claim. Instead, they use evolutionary argumentation and draw parallels between human and mammalian aging. Second, in addition to the lack of empirical support, there is no conceptual reason to claim primacy of primary over secondary control. It is a theoretical point that adds no predictive value to the theory and cannot be proven or disproven because, as Schulz and colleagues (this volume) acknowledge, primary and secondary control strategies are inseparable elements of successful problem solving throughout the life span. Even among children and adolescents it may be hard to disentangle emotion-focused from problem-focused coping and difficult to differentiate between environment-directed and self-directed strategies. Compas and his colleagues (Compas, Connor, Saltzman, Thomsen, & Wadsworth, 2000; Connor, Compas, Wadsworth, Thomsen, & Saltzman, 2001), for example, developed the Responses to Stress Questionnaire (RSQ) based on a multidimensional model of stress that views response effectiveness as a function of both coping response and the specific nature of the stressor. When determining the factorial structure of the RSQ in a sample of children and adolescents, several dimensions were found. Within the dimension of voluntary engagement responses, analyses revealed two distinct factors that Compas and colleagues identified as "primary" and "secondary control." Interestingly, the "primary control" factor encompassed problem solving as well as emotional expression and emotion regulation, whereas the "secondary control" factor was composed of cognitive restructuring, positive thinking, acceptance, and distraction. No evidence was found for a factorial differentiation between coping strategies targeting the environment and coping strategies targeting the self. The findings suggest that primary and secondary control strategies are inseparable parts of successful coping starting very early in the life span.

As the authors acknowledge, human development is characterized by a constant interplay between primary and secondary control processes. No doubt, successful development involves the ability to actively influence the environment. However, regardless of age, humans cannot survive without secondary control mechanisms. Indeed, effective execution of any act of primary control requires secondary control processes to guide and orchestrate the activity. Successful functioning is possible only if active attempts to change the environment are moderated and directed by estimations about the relative value of certain goals, comparisons with societal and individual standards, and anticipation of the consequences of goal attainment. Also, the resources to achieve one's goals are limited at all stages of the life span. Thus, people of all ages need to employ secondary control strategies to make optimal use of their resources. Subsequently, the real value of the life span theory of control will be demonstrated by generating knowledge about the temporal interplay of these processes.

The life span theory of control assumes that human control striving originates in effectance motivation (White, 1959), which is common to all mammals. Because primary control striving targets the outside world, it is considered highly adaptive. Life span changes in primary control among humans are assumed to resemble age-related changes among other animal species. Schulz and colleagues use an evolutionary argument to support these claims. Within this framework, they argue that selective pressures in both animals and humans are not effective in postreproductive years. Thus, characteristics that are useful early in life (e.g., control striving) continue into old age, although the "primary goal" of procreation is no longer achievable.

The attempt to explain both human and mammalian aging within the same theoretical framework is intriguing because it acknowledges the common biological factors that influence the aging process of all living organisms. However, extrapolating from animal aging to human aging poses the danger of neglecting important differences between human development and the development of other species.

First, selective pressures among humans are by no means limited to the reproductive years. According to current research, the decisive steps of human evolution took place in small social groups (Gaulin & McBurney, 2001). Even in postreproductive years, individuals contributed to the replication of their genes through altruistic behavior toward relatives and the preservation and communication of knowledge. In what is termed the "grandmother hypothesis," Hawkes, O'Connell, and Blurton Jones (1997) propose that after a certain age it is better for female reproductive fitness to care for existing kin instead of having more own children. This has been posited to account for the abrupt loss of fertility during menopause. Hawkes and her colleagues (Hawkes, O'Connell, Blurton-Jones, Alvarez, & Charnov, 1998) studied a group of hunter-gatherers in Tanzania. They found that women with young babies had little time available to forage food for themselves. The children who had grandmothers who helped with the gathering of food developed better than children whose mother did not receive help. This suggests that selective pressures among humans can be effective beyond the reproductive years.

Animal models also neglect the influence of higher cognitive functions that are unique to human beings. Consciousness allows humans, unlike other mammals, to anticipate future events, including their own death (Carstensen, Isaacowitz, & Charles, 1999). They also can compare their own performance to the performance of others and to their own personal standards (Bandura, 1989). Expected future events and individual standards of performance are important motivators of human behavior (see below).

Overall, evolutionary argumentation adds an essential perspective to the understanding of life span development. However, it is just as important to acknowledge evolutionary developments that distin-guished humans from other species along with those that made us similar. All species lose some of their physical capabilities as they age. This biological decline and associated losses in reserve capacity and primary control may be the cardinal feature of mammalian aging. But humans differ from other mammals in higher order cognitive abilities that allow us to appreciate temporal dimensions, hold implicit beliefs about developmental trajectories, and regulate our emotional experi-ence. According to the life span theory of control, all of these uniquely human characteristics are regarded as strategies that are "second best," useful only when primary control is not possible. We argue the opposite. Understanding life and death and taking systematic steps to reduce mortality is what led to a near doubling of life expectancy in one century. We offer two theoretical frameworks that conceptualize the influence of higher cognitive abilities on human development. The first of these models, socioemotional selectivity theory, links life span changes in social goals to changes in time perspective. The second conceptual framework is rooted in implicit theories of aging and their influence on individual developmental trajectories.

According to the life span theory of control, individual goal selection is influenced by sequential patterns of biological development and age-graded sociostructural constraints. In this theoretical framework, goal disengagement is seen as a result of secondary control processes after frustrated goal pursuit. However, age-related goal change can and does occur for reasons other than loss or lack of resources.

Socioemotional selectivity theory emphasizes the proactive, agentic character of human motivation and the uniquely human ability to moni-tor one's position in the life span (Carstensen et al., 1999). It is postu-lated that perceptions of time play a fundamental role in the selection and pursuit of social goals. People can planfully adjust their goals ac-cording to their individual time perspective. Socioemotional selectivity theory claims that knowledge-related goals (e.g., education) are prior-itized when time is perceived as open-ended. However, if time is perceived as limited, emotion-related goals (e.g., positive social interac-tions) become more important. Although time perspective is associated with chronological age, these factors are not rigidly tied to each other. A number of studies illustrated the malleability of time perspective and the flexibility of associated social goals. Fredrickson and Carstensen (1990) assessed preferences for novel versus familiar social partners as an indicator of knowledge versus emotion-related social goals. Under open-ended conditions, older people preferred the familiar social partner (i.e., emotionally meaningful social goals), whereas younger participants did not show such a preference. However, if participants were asked to imagine that time was limited (due to a geographic move), younger and older adults' social preferences did not differ from each other. In another study (Fung, Carstensen, & Lutz, 1999), future time perspective was expanded by asking participants to imagine a medical treatment that would add 20 years to their life. Under this condition, older adults' preferences were indistinguishable from younger adults' social partner choices. Further evidence was gathered in a Hong Kong sample (Fung, Carstensen, & Lutz, 1999). Under open-ended conditions, older adults were more likely than younger adults to prefer familiar social partners. However, if time was imagined as limited (due to hypothetical emigration plans), both younger and older adults preferred familiar social partners. This suggests that the influence of perceived time perspective on social goals is consistent across different cultural contexts and can be disentangled from chronological age.

Time perspective is not only subject to micro-level changes within an experimental context. It is also influenced by larger societal factors and macro-level political developments (Fung et al., 1999). Before Hong Kong was returned to the People's Republic of China in 1997, mass media reports described the approaching handover as the end of the current way of life. The limited societal time perspective had an impact on individual social goals. One year before the handover, older adults were more likely to prefer familiar social partners than younger adults. However, when the handover was only 4 months away, all age groups preferred familiar social partners. One year after the handover, when the political situation had stabilized, social partner preferences among the different age groups resembled the data collected 1 year before the handover (Fung et al., 1999). These findings suggest that age-related changes in social goals are not caused by chronological age per se, but by changes in time perspective that are associated with the aging process. Time perspective is malleable and can be changed by individual as well as societal factors.

Within the framework of socioemotional selectivity theory, increased emotional complexity among older adults can be explained by their preferences for emotion-related goals. Pursuing such goals may lead to mixed experiences, especially when the time left in life is perceived as limited. Similarly, age-related improvements in emotion regulation can be attributed to the increased salience of emotionally meaningful goals.

Thus, socioemotional selectivity theory offers a plausible explanation for age-related gains in emotional functioning.

IMPLICIT THEORIES OF AGING

Implicit theories regarding life span changes in abilities and personality characteristics can influence the retrospective recall of the past as well as expectations for the future. Interpretations and expectations regarding the aging process in general and one's own aging in particular can influence current well-being and personal goals. Thus, implicit theories of aging can modify the influence of age-related biological changes on developmental trajectories.

Ross (1989) hypothesized that some characteristics and attributes are expected to be stable across the life span, whereas others are expected to change with age. As predicted, college students' descriptions of life span changes in personality traits, abilities, and opinions followed four dominant prototypical trajectories. Two of these prototypes emphasized change, the other two indicated stability over the life span.

Heckhausen, Dixon, and Baltes (1989) examined people's beliefs about developmental changes in adulthood. Participants of different age groups were given a list of person-descriptive adjectives and asked to indicate developmental increase, desirability, and onset/closing age of changes for each adjective. People of different ages were relatively similar in their views on human development. However, older adults had more complex perspectives than younger people. Developmental expectations were multidirectional, encompassing gains and losses and stability as well as change. However, participants expected fewer developmental gains and more developmental losses with increasing chronological age. Overall, these findings suggest that adults of all ages have specific expectations regarding developmental trajectories.

Such implicit theories of developmental change seem to influence the recall of past personality characteristics. Woodruff and Birren (1972) examined longitudinal changes in personality and social adjustment over 25 years (age 20 vs. age 45). Self-reports changed little over time. However, when participants were asked to describe their personality as it had been at the age of 20, the retrospective self-reports were significantly more negative. This could have been caused by implicit theories of improvement over time (Woodruff, 1983).

Fleeson and Baltes (1998) asked their adult participants to complete a set of personality questionnaires under three conditions: with regard to the present, retrospectively (how they were at age 20 to 25), and anticipative (how they would be at age 65 to 70). Interestingly, positive retrospective descriptions of one's personality were negatively correlated with current well-being. In contrast, positive current and anticipative personality descriptions were positively correlated to current well-being. Across the different studies, there is clear evidence that people have implicit theories about changes in personality characteristics and abilities across the life span.

Ross (1989) suggested that implicit theories originate in sociocultural conceptions of the aging process. These societal notions often emphasize differences among age groups. However, age-related changes are very subtle and occur over long periods of time. As a result, individuals may perceive themselves as relatively consistent across the life span (Epstein, 1973). This may create a discrepancy between societal expectations for change and individual perceptions of continuity. Societal notions may lead people to expect age-related changes, although they would not perceive any such changes in themselves without expecting them. For example, when misplacing the car keys, an older person may become concerned and interpret the event as the first sign of dementia. In contrast, a younger person may blame the same slip of memory on being tired or any other harmless cause. The findings by Fleeson and Baltes (1998) suggest that expectations about developmental trajectories are related to current well-being. Implicit theories may also influence developmental goals for the future. For example, older people with positive expectations for cognitive development in old age should be more likely to set challenging educational goals for themselves. Implicit theories of aging may also influence people's reactions to age-related biological decline. Depending on their implicit expectations, some people may treat physical difficulties as an inevitable consequence of old age, whereas others may be more likely to react with increased efforts and attempts to regain independence. Future research needs to investigate the links between implicit theories of aging and motivation.

CONCLUSION

Overall, the life span theory of control makes important conceptual contributions to the understanding of age-related changes over the life course. Throughout life, people pursue varying goals, and every selection in favor of one goal is also a decision to give up alternative goals.

These processes have important implications for mental health. Schulz and colleagues (this volume) offer a theoretical framework to understand how goal selectivity and compensatory efforts to attain them influence life span development. They propose an interesting way to conceptualize adaptive coping processes in response to normative and nonnormative life events. Limitations arise if the theory is offered as a general life span theory of human development. Although physical changes in old age are predominantly negative, there are both gains and losses in psychological domains as people get older. Knowledge, emotional experience, emotion regulation, and problem-solving skills continue to improve with age. Unfortunately, the life span theory of control can account for gains only in terms of creative coping with loss. We presented evidence for alternative explanations and pointed out that many changes begin too early in life for biological decline to account for them.

In contemporary developmental theory, there is a pervasive tendency to define old age in terms of its relative deficits compared to youth without consideration of its relative strengths. This approach places an emphasis on negative changes and loss of abilities that were present earlier in life. But, although loss occurs, new skills and abilities emerge concomitantly. It is true that old age as a life phase inevitably ends in death. However, it is inappropriate to interpret a very long (indeed, roughly a 30-year period) by its final years before death. For the first time in human history, the majority of people in the western world can expect to live into their 70s and 80s in relatively good health. So far, there are no clear role models and societal blueprints for this new phase of life. As more and more people enter old age, extrapolations from earlier life phases (e.g., viewing old age as an extension of midlife) become increasingly inadequate. Now is the time to define old age as a normative life phase in its own right that is more than just lost youth. The roles and guidelines for late life must be disentangled from the dying process. Theoretical frameworks need to acknowledge the diversity among older adults and the problems as well as the opportunities and skills that are unique to old age.

REFERENCES

Bandura, A. (1989). Self-regulation of motivation and action through internal standards and goal systems. In L. A. Pervin (Ed.), *Goal concepts in personality and social psychology* (pp. 19–85). Hillsdale, NJ: Erlbaum.

Blanchard-Fields, F. (1996). Emotion and everyday problem solving in adult development. In C. Magai & S. H. McFadden (Eds.), *Handbook of emotion, adult development, and aging* (pp. 149–165). San Diego: Academic Press.

Blanchard-Fields, F., Chen, Y., & Norris, L. (1997). Everyday problem solving across the adult life span: Influence of domain specificity and cognitive appraisal. *Psychology and Aging, 12,* 684–693.

Blanchard-Fields, F., & Irion, J. C. (1988a). Coping strategies from the perspective of two developmental markers: Age and social reasoning. *Journal of Genetic Psychology, 1*(49), 141–151.

Blanchard-Fields, F., & Irion, J. C. (1988b). The relation between locus of control and coping in two contexts: Age as a moderator variable. *Psychology and Aging, 3,* 197–203.

Bosworth, H. B. (1997). Terminal change: A longitudinal and cross-sectional examination of confounding factors in the Seattle longitudinal study. *Dissertation Abstracts International: Section B: The Sciences and Engineering, 57*(12-B), 7436.

Brandstädter, J., & Greve, W. (1994). The aging self: Stabilizing and protective processes. *Developmental Review, 14,* 52–80.

Carstensen, L. L., Isaacowitz, D. M., & Charles, S. T. (1999). Taking time seriously: A theory of socioemotional selectivity. *American Psychologist, 54,* 165–181.

Carstensen, L. L., Pasupathi, M., Mayr, U., & Nesselroade, J. R. (2000). Emotional experience in everyday life across the adult life span. *Journal of Personality and Social Psychology, 79,* 644–655.

Compas, B. E., Connor, J. K., Saltzman, H., Thomsen, A. H., & Wadsworth, M. E. (2001). Coping with stress during childhood and adolescence: Problems, progress and potential in theory and research. *Psychological Bulletin, 127,* 87–127.

Connor, J. K., Compas, B. E., Wadsworth, M. E., Thomsen, A. H., & Saltzman, H. (2000). Responses to stress in adolescence: Measurement of coping and involuntary stress response. *Journal of Consulting and Clinical Psychology, 68,* 976–992.

Epstein, S. (1973). The self-concept revisited: Or a theory of a theory. *American Psychologist, 28,* 404–416.

Erikson, E. H. (1994). *Identity and the life cycle.* New York: Norton.

Field, D. (1997). Looking back, what period of your life brought you the most satisfaction. *International Journal of Aging and Human Development, 45,* 169–194.

Fleeson, W., & Baltes, P. B. (1998). Beyond present-day personality assessment: An encouraging exploration of the measurement properties and predictive power of subjective lifetime personality. *Journal of Research in Personality, 32,* 411–430.

Folkman, S., Lazarus, R. S., Pimley, S., & Novacek, J. (1987). Age differences in stress and coping processes. *Psychology and Aging, 2,* 171–184.

Fredrickson, B. L., & Carstensen, L. L. (1990). Choosing social partners: How old age and anticipated endings make people more selective. *Psychology and Aging, 5,* 335–347.

Fries, J. F. (1990). Medical perspectives upon successful aging. In P. B. Baltes & M. M. Baltes (Eds.), *Successful aging: Perspectives from the behavioral sciences* (pp. 35–49). Cambridge: Cambridge University Press.

Fung, H. H., Carstensen, L. L., & Lutz, A. M. (1999). Influence of time on social preferences: Implications for life-span development. *Psychology and Aging, 14,* 595–604.

Gaulin, S. J. C., & McBurney, D. H. (2001). *Psychology: An evolutionary approach.* Upper Saddle River, NJ: Prentice Hall.

Gould, S. J. (1999). A critique of Heckhausen and Schulz's (1995) life-span theory of control from a cross-cultural perspective. *Psychological Review, 106,* 597–604.

Hawkes, K., O'Connell, J. F., & Blurton Jones, N. G. (1997). Hadza women's time allocation, offspring provisioning, and the evolution of post-menopausal lifespans. *Current Anthropology, 38,* 551–578.

Hawkes, K., O'Connell, J. F., Blurton-Jones, N. G., Alvarez, H., & Charnov, E. L. (1998). Grandmothering, menopause, and the evolution of human life histories. *Proceedings of the National Academy of Sciences of the United State of America, 95,* 1336–1339.

Heckhausen, J., Dixon, R. A., & Baltes, P. B. (1989). Gains and losses in development throughout adulthood as perceived by different adult age groups. *Developmental Psychology, 25,* 109–121.

Heckhausen, J., & Schulz, R. (1995). A life-span theory of control. *Psychological Review, 102,* 284–304.

Heckhausen, J., & Schulz, R. (1998). Developmental regulation in adulthood: Selection and compensation via primary and secondary control. In J. Heckhausen & C. S. Dweck (Eds.), *Motivation and self-regulation across the life span* (pp. 50–77). New York: Cambridge University Press.

Heckhausen, J., & Schulz, R. (1999). The primacy of primary control is a human universal: A reply to Gould's (1999) critique of the life-span theory of control. *Psychological Review, 106,* 605–609.

Horn, J. L., & Hofer, S. M. (1992). Major abilities and development in the adult period. In R. J. Sternberg & C. A. Berg (Eds.), *Intellectual development* (pp. 44–99). New York: Cambridge University Press.

Kaufman, A. S., & Horn, J. L. (1996). Age changes on tests of fluid and crystallized ability for women and men on the Kaufman Adolescent and Adult Intelligence Test (KAIT) at ages 17–94 years. *Archives of Clinical Neuropsychology, 11,* 97–121.

Lazarus, R. S. (1996). The role of coping in the emotions and how coping changes over the life course. In C. Magai & S. H. McFadden (Eds.), *Handbook of emotion, adult development, and aging* (pp. 289–306). San Diego: Academic Press.

Manton, K. G. (1997). Chronic morbidity and disability in the U.S. elderly populations: Recent trends and population implications. In D. I. Mostofsky & J. Lomranz (Eds.), *The Plenum series in adult development and aging* (pp. 37–67). New York: Plenum Press.

Manton, K. G., Stallard, E., & Corder, L. S. (1998). The dynamics of dimensions of age-related disability 1982 to 1994 in the U.S. elderly population. *Journals of Gerontology: Series A: Biological Sciences and Medical Sciences, 53*, B59–B70.

Riegel, K. F., & Riegel, R. M. (1972). Development, drop, and death. *Developmental Psychology, 6*, 306–319.

Ross, M. (1989). Relation of implicit theories to the construction of personal histories. *Psychological Review, 96*, 341–357.

Schaie, K. W (1996). Intellectual development in adulthood. In J. E. Birren & K. W. Schaie (Eds.), *The handbooks of aging* (pp. 266–286). San Diego: Academic Press.

Schulz, R., & Heckhausen, J. (1998). Emotion and control: A life-span perspective. In K. W. Schaie & M. P. Lawton (Eds.), *Annual review of gerontology and geriatrics* (pp. 185–205). New York: Springer.

Schulz, R., & Heckhausen, J. (1999). Aging, culture and control: Setting a new research agenda. *Journals of Gerontology: Series B: Psychological Sciences and Social Sciences, 54*, P139–P145.

White, N., & Cunningham, W. R. (1988). Is terminal drop pervasive or specific? *Journals of Gerontology, 43*, 141–144.

White, R. W. (1959). Motivation reconsidered: The concept of competence. *Psychological Review, 66*, 297–333.

Woodruff, D. S. (1983). The role of memory in personality continuity: A 25-year follow-up. *Experimental Aging Research, 9*, 31–34.

Woodruff, D. S., & Birren, J. E. (1972). Age changes and cohort difference in personality. *Developmental Psychology, 6*, 252–259.

Afterword

Applications of Personal Control

Steven H. Zarit and Sara A. Leitsch

The exploration of personal control by the authors of this volume has yielded a basic and obvious point: Control matters. The demonstration that personal control and its related constructs have far-reaching implications for the health and well-being of people in adulthood and later life and for blunting the effects of adverse events has been a well-established finding. Although it is useful to be reminded of the pivotal role that personal control plays over the life span, we also embarked with a wish list of goals for these chapters that would expand and clarify key issues in the study of mastery and control (see Chapter 1). In this chapter, we examine where we stand in relation to three of these goals: (1) identifying the social influences that shape and modify personal control, (2) understanding how these social influences interact with other factors over the adult years, and (3) clarifying the concept of personal control and its measurement. We also take a logical step by extending our examination of personal control for the design and development of interventions to enhance functioning.

SOCIAL ORIGINS OF PERSONAL CONTROL

Personal control has long been regarded as a relatively stable personal characteristic to be studied at the individual level. This volume clearly demonstrates that resources available to people based on their position in society, as well as the contingencies in the immediate and broader social context, shape the development of personal control over the life span and influence the extent to which exercise of personal control is likely to be effective and adaptive. The argument regarding social influences can be grouped into three levels: (1) the immediate social context, such as the effect of family and friends; (2) social stratification; and (3) cultural influences on the expression of personal control.

Perhaps the most obvious yet overlooked influence on personal control is the immediate social context. Krause (this volume) demonstrates how the exercise of personal control is embedded in social processes. The type of social support one receives, whether anticipated, enacted, or collaborative, affects the dimensions of personal control. Anticipated support is consistent with primary control and may in fact enhance it. Enacted support, in turn, facilitates secondary control processes, and the mutual exchange of enacted support addresses feelings of collaborative control. Thus, dimensions of control beliefs depend, in part, on the type of social support experienced within the immediate social context.

Krause stresses the importance of examining these relationships of support and control in terms of specific roles and functions. Consistent with the process of selective optimization with compensation, turning control of one role or function over to another person may enhance continued control in other, more valued domains. Of particular importance is Krause's delineation of the consequences of collaborative control. On the one hand, it may enhance the quality of social support during stressful events because of strong feelings of reciprocity between the individual and his or her social network. Conversely, collaborative control may be subject to a variety of conflicts and tensions. Just as giving control to another person can be experienced in positive and negative ways, the same may be the case for collaborative control (McLeod, this volume).

Krause also suggests that the effects of an adverse event usually reverberate through the person's social network. Financial losses, for example, will influence not only an individual but also that person's spouse and children. The individual's response is affected in part by how the other involved people respond.

There is an obvious link from an analysis of support and control to macro-level variables such as socioeconomic status (SES). As emphasized by several of the authors in this volume (e.g., Avison & Cairney, Krause, McLeod), people who are higher in SES will have more opportunities to exercise personal control. William Avison and John Cairney, in Chapter 4, for example, argue that the sense of personal control is entangled with "the experience of power and opportunity." People with higher SES have more financial resources and a variety of other life experiences that reinforce mastery and control (e.g., through work experiences and opportunities for higher education). Likewise, people with higher SES will generally (though not always) be able to draw upon more support resources to help maintain control. Furthermore, as McLeod notes, people from lower SES groups will turn to family and friends for support who generally also have low resource levels. Thus, for people with lower SES, there is less potential and actual support available, although there may be more opportunities for collaborative support.

Cultural factors add another layer of complexity. Culture affects the meaning and contingencies for personal control. The acceptability of exercising personal control in various roles can differ from one cultural group to another. Particularly among some nonwestern cultures, control may be expressed in indirect or collaborative ways, and its saliency for well-being is reconceptualized. For ethnic minority groups within the United States, we need to consider both the meaning of control within each group and SES and other potentially constraining factors. The history of discrimination against African Americans in combination with low SES may lead to lower expectations about being able to exercise control in a variety of roles (Skaff, this volume). There may, of course, be experiences that blunt these effects, such as the support provided by extended kin networks and by the church. Overall, opportunities and resources for control have emerged from the interaction of historical and cultural experiences and the availability of resources in one's own family and community.

Clearly, investigation of the social dimensions of personal control is a potentially fruitful, important, and complex endeavor. Further clarification is needed in how social stratification, in combination with ethnicity or race, leads to differential control beliefs and consequences in a variety of roles. We also need to move beyond a focus on individual differences in control to consider how exchanges within one's immediate social network affects the exercise and experience of control.

CHANGES IN PERSONAL CONTROL OVER THE LIFE SPAN

A widely held expectation is that personal control decreases over the life span, but the evidence remains limited. There are two compelling reasons for this expectation: that older people experience losses of status and resources and that illness and disability may reduce the ability to exercise control in many domains of life. Despite this strong rationale, global ratings of mastery and control remain high, even in the oldest old (Femia, Zarit, & Johansson, 1997; Johnson & Barer, 1997). Findings of a decrease of mastery or internality may be strongest when focusing on a specific role or life domain. As an example, the chronic stress of caregiving can lead to an erosion of role-specific mastery (Aneshensel, Pearlin, Mullan, Zarit, & Whitlatch, 1995).

Schulz, Wrosch, and Heckhausen (this volume) and Löckenhoff and Carstensen (this volume) propose that the discrepancy in findings about control and age may reflect a process of selective optimization, whereby people maintain primary control for valued roles and functions but can give up control in other areas. Krause (this volume) adds that although age-related events (including mental and physical changes) can lead to an erosion of control, one's social network can help a person maintain control or prevent its erosion through provision of anticipated and actual support. Older people who are wealthy may be able to maintain high levels of personal control in most circumstances by purchasing needed assistance, whereas people with fewer resources may be more vulnerable to adverse effects.

The observations made by Johnson and Barer (1997) in their study of the oldest-old support these speculations. They describe people in their late 80s who score high in mastery and employ a great deal of control in their daily lives over a limited range of activities and roles. Many people in their sample were homebound but maintained a routine that allowed them to keep control over their household. They conserved energy by rarely venturing out and maintaining a strict basic routine that allowed them to do the things necessary to support their independence. These observations of the oldest-old also illustrate Krause's link between support and control, because some degree of external help is critical for maintaining their fragile independence.

Although these examples can be described as the outcome of selective optimization, little is known about how the process of selection takes place, or its timing, as well as how personal and social factors influence selection. It is also likely that not all selection leads to optimal management of resources, nor that the loss of control associated with some types of selection is acceptable to everyone. We also know little about the relation of global expectations of mastery or control to the selection process. It is possible that the oldest-old described by Johnson and Barer

(1997) were a select sample of survivors whose high expectations of control led them to take steps necessary to maintain control in their lives despite declining abilities. People for whom control was not important may already have given up their homes and moved into a setting where assistance was readily available.

Finally, the study of personal control in adulthood and aging is subject to the same complexities as investigations of other constructs. There may be cohort differences both in global and role-specific control, as well as in what roles people value and how they allocate resources to maintain control. Historical events as well can have an impact on valued roles. It could be argued that expectations of control have become more likely for today's older population due to the creation of Medicare and to changes in Social Security (e.g., the automatic adjustment of payments to the cost of living index). These benefits may have the same effect as Krause suggests in Chapter 2 for anticipated support. That is, they allow people to take risks and maintain control when they otherwise might be unable due to a less secure financial situation. Of course, if there were serious deterioration of benefits in these programs at some time in the future, that could have the opposite effect on perceived control.

CONCEPTS AND MEASURES OF PERSONAL CONTROL

Personal control incorporates several related constructs that address different aspects of the phenomenon. At times, the plethora of terms and measures creates confusion and leads to a lack of comparability across studies exploring similar issues. But, as Pearlin and Pioli (this volume) state in Chapter 1, the diversity of terminology and measures is also a strength, reflecting the vitality of research on personal control. There should be a balance between development of more precise definitions and measures, on the one hand, and finding creative ways of exploring new aspects of personal control, on the other. Premature designation of a "gold standard" for measuring personal control could have the unintended consequence of precluding new directions in research. Although there is a need for better measures that meet appropriate psychometric standards, it is also the case that some existing measures with good psychometric properties have turned out to be weaker measures of the control construct. That disparity between precision and content is not an inherent problem in measurement, but underscores the need for an iterative process in conceptualization and development of measures for a complex construct such as personal control.

The field has matured to the point that it is possible to adopt some consistency in terminology. Multidimensional models of personal control, such as those proposed by Skinner (1995) and Abeles (1990; this volume) provide a useful framework for representing the process by which control beliefs, expectancies, and actions affect one another. Abeles (this volume) points out the importance of differentiating among types of control beliefs, such as self-beliefs, task beliefs, and self-efficacy expectations. Skaff and Gardiner (this volume) suggest a way of viewing personal control as embedded in social processes by considering where control is located (in the individual, group, or a powerful other), how control is exercised (behavior or cognitive), and what the target of control is (self, one's own responses, or the environment).

Within this type of general framework, several useful distinctions can be made. The first is between global and specific measures of personal control beliefs. Generally, there has been a movement toward domain-specific measures. As studies adopt more specific measures, however, it is important not to lose sight of the value of global assessments of mastery or personal control. These global expectancies undoubtedly influence beliefs about control and effectiveness for specific roles and activities. There is also a trade-off in generalizability; that is, measures such as those used in self-efficacy studies are so specific to a particular situation that it is often difficult to compare findings across settings and groups.

A second distinction suggested by Pearlin and Pioli (this volume) is that there can be different types of specific measures. They identify role-specific measures, for example, caregiving mastery and function specific, as in the case of many self-efficacy measures.

A third distinction is between control beliefs and actions. It remains controversial if it would be more parsimonious to classify the types of control discussed by Schulz, Wrosch, and Heckhausen (this volume) as coping, as Skinner argues (1995), or if they are more properly considered as an extension of control beliefs.

There is, then, no simple answer to the question of what measure to use. Good research will proceed from conceptual clarity about the control processes that are of interest and the selection of measure that best address those particular aspects of the control process. As Pearlin and Pioli (this volume) state at the outset, the best approach to measurement of personal control may be "flexible multidimensionality." In other words, we need to use good measurement principles that reflect a complex, multidimensional process, but which remain somewhat elastic as we continue to explore and modify the concepts and relationships in personal control.

PERSONAL CONTROL AND TREATMENT: PROSPECTS AND RISKS

The focus on control, particularly in the gerontological literature, has largely been descriptive, that is, examining its role in contributing to valued outcomes such as good health, or as a resource that lessens the impact of adverse events in a person's life. A logical extension is to consider how our understanding of the role of personal control in adaptation can be used to design effective interventions and treatments that help people maintain or regain well-being in challenging circumstances. The influence of personal control on many different types of outcomes—work stress and unemployment, family stress, and health problems, to name some of the notable ones discussed in this volume—underscores the importance of exploring how we might apply these in the design and evaluation of interventions. These interventions could be at the personal level, but as the focus on the social structural influences of control suggests, there also needs to be consideration of how immediate environmental influences as well as broader community and societal processes affect control beliefs.

There are several directions that applications of personal control might take. As it has been argued that personal control is a pivotal resource in adapting to stressful life situations (Krause, this volume), a focus on control beliefs may help us understand why a particular treatment or intervention is successful. It may be that treatments are effective by mobilizing appropriate control beliefs and strategies (Bandura, 1977, 1997; McAuley & Katula, 1998; Seligman, 1998; Williams, Turner, & Peer, 1985). Various models of personal control as a mediator or moderator of stress may help clarify the process of how treatment leads to desired outcomes. For a treatment to be effective, it may be important that the method of control addressed in the treatment is consistent with an individual's control beliefs. Alternatively, there may be situations in which people's control beliefs interfere with their using adaptive strategies. In those instances, it may be possible to focus on modifying control beliefs to achieve more positive outcomes. Changing personal control could be affected at an individual level through the implementation of treatment strategies, or it could be addressed by influencing the opportunities and constraints in the person's social environment. Treatment models could incorporate a focus on control beliefs and strategies as a way of addressing specific problems, or as part of a preventive approach to enhance resources for managing anticipated problems. We will consider these approaches below.

Control as a Mediator or Moderator

The most common application of personal control is as a mediator or moderator of treatment effects. Through the influential work of Bandura (1977, 1997), self-efficacy has come to be widely regarded as a mediator of treatment for a variety of outcomes, including reducing phobic behavior (Hoffart, 1995; Williams, 1992; Williams et al., 1985), smoking cessation (Coelho, 1984; Scholte, Breteler, & Marinus, 1997), recovery from alcoholism and other substance abuse (Cisler & Nawrocki, 1998; Coon, Pena, & Illich, 1998; Maisto, Connors, & Zywiak, 2000), use of HIV-prevention strategies (Sanderson & Jemmott, 1996), improved health (O'Leary, 1992), and the effects of job training (Gist & Mitchell, 1992; Gist, Stevens, & Bavetta, 1991; Saks, 1995). According to Bandura, treatment is successful when it creates expectations that a person's actions in a particular setting can be effective. Only a limited amount of this research has focused on older adults (e.g., Dittmann-Kohli, Lachman, Kliegl, & Baltes, 1991; McAuley & Katula, 1998).

Bandura's work has led to the development of treatments that specifically address personal control. As an example, Williams and colleagues (Williams, 1992; Williams et al., 1985; see also Hoffart, 1995) have used a variation on desensitization in the treatment of phobias. Classic behavior theory suggests that exposure to feared stimuli while a person is in a relaxed state prevents avoidance and leads to extinction of the fear response. Williams and colleagues, however, argue that self-efficacy is the mediating mechanism by which people exposed to fear-arousing stimuli overcome their phobias. Their treatment, guided mastery, combines exposure to the fear-arousing stimuli with specific mastery experiences, such as breaking a task into small, manageable steps and working up toward difficult outcomes. In a comparison of guided mastery with classic desensitization and a no treatment control, Williams and colleagues found that guided mastery had a greater effect in reducing fear of heights. Self-efficacy related to heights also improved most in that treatment and correlated positively with approach behavior (to heights) and inversely with anxiety. Williams, Kinney, and Falbo (1989) reported that self-efficacy predicted generalization of training to untreated fears, although the effects were lower than for the target of treatment.

The role of self-efficacy as a mediator is usually demonstrated, as in the studies by Williams and colleagues (1985, 1989), by showing that it increases during treatment and correlates with the desired outcomes. Saks (1995) conducted a more rigorous statistical analysis of mediational and moderational effects of self-efficacy on the relation of job training to work adjustment during the first year of training. Using the Baron and Kenny (1986) criteria for evaluating mediation, Saks found that training was related to work adjustment (ability to cope, job performance, and intention to quit the profession) at 1 year, that training and work adjustment were related to self-efficacy, and that self-efficacy reduced the relation between training and work adjustment. In other words, Saks was able to show that the effects of training were achieved partly (i.e., mediated) through increases in self-efficacy. Saks also found evidence of a moderating effect of initial levels of self-efficacy. Trainees who were low in self-efficacy had disproportionately higher gains than trainees who were high in self-efficacy.

This brief review suggests several critical issues in this research. First, in most studies, with Saks (1995) as a notable exception, the specific mediating mechanisms are inferred from associations between self-efficacy and treatment outcomes. Second, although the presumed mechanism of treatment is increased self-efficacy, it is only occasionally addressed specifically in the treatment protocol (e.g., Williams et al., 1985). Third, there has only been limited attention to the role of initial levels of self-efficacy in influencing response to treatment, and even less attention to related personal control constructs. Fourth, following Bandura's (1977) original conception, self-efficacy is assessed in a highly particularistic way as one's expectations for performance in a given situation. There has not been much consideration of the relation of self-efficacy to other personal control constructs, or if training that affects self-efficacy for one situation generalizes to other situations or to more global beliefs about personal control

An examination of the process of how personal control affects outcomes can help us understand better how treatments succeed and how to design more effective intervention strategies. Avison and Cairney (this volume) suggest a possible direction for interventions with their systematic examination of the mechanisms by which mastery may influence outcomes. Rather than testing a single model, Avison and Cairney put forward several possible pathways by which mastery may lead to better outcomes. Although they did not specifically address interventions, their models suggest how intervention effects may be conceptualized as well as the analytic approaches that can be taken to examine these effects. Building on the work of Wheaton (1985), Avison and Cairney articulate five processes by which mastery may affect outcomes:

1. The classic interactive buffering effect (also known as a moderating effect), in which high levels of mastery lessen the distress experienced during times of stress;
2. The additive model, in which exposure to stresses mobilizes personal control, which in turn lessens distress;
3. The mediator model, in which stress erodes one's sense of personal control, which leads to increasing distress;
4. The stress deterrence model, in which mastery reduces exposure to stress, thereby indirectly reducing distress; and
5. The distress deterrence model, in which stressors and personal control operate independently on distress.

It is possible to extend these models from their focus on stress to look at how personal control might mediate or moderate the effects of treatment on outcomes. Indeed, we could substitute other resources for mastery, for example, social support, or a very traditional psychotherapy resource, personal insight, and the framework would be equally useful. In other words, rather than conceptualizing treatment effects as a black box in which something magical happens, we can look at the process by which the proposed mechanisms of treatment (e.g., increased personal control) affect outcomes.

The most fundamental point emerging from these analyses is that there are many different processes by which treatment may have a positive outcome. Another implication is that the benefits of treatment will not necessarily be divided equally across all individuals. Rather, mastery or personal control may act as a resource that enhances or limits an individual's response to treatment.

Using this framework, we can conceptualize different scenarios for treatment as we would expect different outcomes from mediator and moderator models. As discussed, treatment studies have presumed mediation; that is, the interventions increase personal control, which leads to a more positive outcome. There may, however, be other ways that treatment and control lead to different outcomes. As suggested by moderator models, some combinations of control and stress may respond more optimally to intervention than other combinations. It is also possible that stress can activate mastery and coping approaches, suggesting that treatment may be more effective when some threshold of activation has been passed. Conversely, people exposed to high levels of chronic stress may experience an erosion of mastery (Aneshensel et al., 1995), which limits their response to treatment. There is an indication that family caregivers respond to respite services in this fashion. Many caregivers do not choose to use respite services until they are highly stressed, but their stress levels may concomitantly limit their ability to benefit from treatment (Zarit, Stephens, Townsend, Greene, & Leitsch, 1999). Additionally, interventions can erode resources such as personal control. Caregivers often complain that in-home respite services take away control over such crucial matters as which respite worker the family will use, when the worker will come, and an overall lack of predictability in receiving help (MaloneBeach, Zarit, & Spore, 1992). Already faced with uncontrollable stress, these caregivers may experience a further decrease in their personal resources when they cannot exercise some control over the help they are receiving.

Another important distinction raised by Avison and Cairney (this volume) is the notion of stress deterrence. The role of treatment may not be to reduce stress or increase personal control, but to reduce exposure to stressors. As an example, respite services such as adult day care could be conceptualized as stress deterrence interventions, because they reduce exposure of family caregivers to primary stressors (Zarit, Stephens, Townsend, & Greene, 1998). Personal control may also play a role in this type of deterrence model by leading to greater or lesser acceptance of the intervention. In any case, we can understand the effects of the intervention better by conceptualizing its effects as deterring exposure to stress, which might have different consequences than another treatment that improves management of stress.

An interesting variation of a stress deterrence model is suggested by Price (this volume; see also Vinokur & Schul, 1997). The effects of a job-training program appeared to inoculate participants against a second job loss; that is, they were less likely to experience discouragement and depressive symptoms because they had a sense of mastery over the process of finding new employment. In this situation, cognitive skills (job search strategies combined with optimistic expectations) may have led to a different appraisal of the threat involved in job loss and, consequently, to fewer adverse consequences. These cognitive skills, of course, also contribute to more rapid reemployment.

Beyond specific models of treatment effectiveness, there generally needs to be greater attention to the role of personal control in the response of older adults to interventions. As the evidence suggests, it is logical to include a focus on control in the development and evaluation of prevention and treatment programs for older adults.

A consideration of control may lead to more elaborated treatment models. In a longitudinal study of the oldest-old, for example, it was found that higher initial levels of mastery were related to continued independence over time (Femia et al., 1997). One application of those findings would be to attempt to find ways of increasing levels of mastery as a way of preventing disability. Mastery, however, may be a few steps removed from the processes that have a direct effect on disability. It may be, for example, that people with higher levels of mastery engage in more optimal health behaviors (e.g., exercise and diet), which lead to better outcomes. In that case, interventions may more appropriately focus on health behaviors and efficacy expectations related to them. It is likely that application of findings on the relation of personal control to positive outcomes in later life would need that type of elaboration of more proximal effects.

Individual differences in control may also affect one's response to treatment. Particularly when people are in situations that directly threaten their ability to maintain control in valued domains of their lives (e.g., with caregivers or people with chronic disabilities), the effectiveness of interventions may depend on initial levels of personal control or a combination of initial level and some other factor, such as social support. It may well be that how treatment is organized and delivered should be modified in accordance with personal control levels.

Finally, there should be consideration of how directly an intervention should focus on control beliefs, as opposed to performance. As stressed by Pearlin and Pioli and by others in this volume, personal control is learned, so it should be possible to introduce new learning. Given all the positive things with which personal control is correlated, should we embark on programs that help increase control among older people? Several issues should be considered when planning how much of a focus treatment should have on control. First, there needs to be clarification of the target of the intervention, whether to change beliefs, behavior, or mood. In many cases, beliefs are a step in the process toward some other goal, which should properly be the focus of treatment. On the other hand, it may be necessary to include some attention to changing beliefs to affect behavior change. There has been a long debate in psychotherapy over whether meaningful changes in behavior can occur without changing beliefs. Contemporary psychotherapies, such as cognitive behavioral therapy (Beck, Rush, Shaw, & Emery, 1979) and interpersonal psychotherapy (Klerman, Weisman, Rounsaville, & Chevron, 1984), have found that doing some of both is the most effective strategy. These approaches combine tasks that are graded for difficulty, which lead to increased feelings of mastery, with a focus on beliefs about the efficacy of actions in valued life domains.

Second, the beliefs that change with treatment and mediate its effects are very specific in nature, such as the self-efficacy required to carry out a particular behavior. Whether general control beliefs, or even something relatively focused, such as health locus of control, are amenable to intervention remains to be seen.

Third, if control training were part of a preventive strategy to inoculate older people against the adverse effects of stressors that might occur in the future, then a critical issue would be the maintenance of training effects. Part of maintenance, of course, would be the support for enhanced control beliefs and related behaviors in the person's social settings.

A FINAL CAVEAT: ARE INTERVENTIONS FOR PERSONAL CONTROL ALWAYS A GOOD THING?

The popularity of personal control as an explanatory concept and its congruence with cultural precepts about independence and personal autonomy raise the risk that it will become another gerontological fad that is more rhetoric than substance. We want to emphasize the importance of proceeding with interventions in a cautious and skeptical way. It could be that personal control is not readily amenable to intervention, that control beliefs are stable and difficult to change, or that the very act of intervening has the paradoxical effect of undermining those aspects of the person's beliefs that are adaptive. Although all the hazards of focusing on personal control in treatment are not known, we raise three caveats: (1) Control may not always be associated with positive outcomes, (2) control may not be necessary for well-being, and (3) people may not always want more control.

Personal control may not always lead to positive outcomes. The efficacy of control beliefs and behaviors depends, to a considerable extent, on the context. A noteworthy example is people's experiences with institutional settings such as nursing homes. It has long been recognized that settings such as nursing homes discourage independent and reward dependent behaviors, or what Margaret Baltes evocatively called "dependency scripts" (Baltes, Burgess, & Stewart, 1980). In that type of setting, control beliefs may not have the same association with positive outcomes as in noninstitutional contexts.

The possibility that personal control leads to different outcomes in community and institutional settings was tested using a longitudinal sample of family caregivers (Aneshensel et al., 1995). Predictors of well-being were examined at two points, when caregivers were actively assisting their relative at home and again after they placed their relative in a nursing home. During home care, mastery was associated with better outcomes; that is, caregivers with higher mastery were more likely to have lower feelings of depression and anxiety. When caring for someone at home, caregivers higher in mastery are more likely to seek active solutions to problems, which may, in turn, lower the stress they are experiencing. After placement, however, mastery was related to poorer outcomes. Caregivers with higher mastery were more likely to report symptoms of depression and anxiety. Once they have turned the care of their relative over to someone else, high mastery may cause them to feel ineffective and frustrated, because they are no longer in control of many aspects of care.

One intervention strategy in this context would be to target secondary control. Family members whose relative is institutionalized may have unrealistic expectations for care and the ability to control how the care is given. A program in which they have the opportunity to examine and change those expectations may have beneficial effects by decreasing their feelings of distress and guilt and by helping them interact with staff in more positive ways (Zarit & Zarit, 1998). It would be requisite, of course, not to train caregivers to accept poor care, but to understand that there are times when they cannot determine when and how care is given, and that their relatives' needs cannot always be met promptly or in an individualized way.

It may also be possible to increase caregivers' use of primary control strategies in ways that are effective within the care setting. They could, for example, learn which staff person to talk with about which complaints. They could also learn ways of phrasing their concerns. Caregivers who only complain to staff are likely to be ignored. Combining requests for changes along with positive statements is more likely to be effective (Zarit & Zarit, 1998). In effect, a training program could teach them the rules of the game, how nursing homes operate, and where it is possible to have an effect. In doing so, caregivers could come to exercise some limited degree of control in the setting, and at the same time ensure that their relative is receiving good care.

Interventions may need to focus on the environmental system to change the usual reward and punishment contingencies that perpetuate a loss of control. Changes might involve new administrative regulations that allow staff and residents more latitude in the decisions they make. A controversial change would be to tolerate certain risks, such as allowing a patient at a moderate risk of falling to ambulate without assistance, and in that way maintain personal control. Structural and administrative changes could also fundamentally alter the amount of control residents have over their daily lives. In Swedish group homes for dementia, for example, residents have their own apartment, which they lease and furnish, and, as any other apartment dweller, they can shut and lock the door if they prefer. These arrangements may support personal control and reduce the behavior problems typically associated with institutional care of people with dementia (Malmberg & Zarit, 1993).

The history of interventions in nursing home settings, however, is replete with failures. Even the most sophisticated and straightforward interventions, such as retraining incontinence, usually are abandoned once the research team leaves the facility. It is important, then, not to approach change in a naive or overly optimistic way. Processes such as excess disabilities and dependency scripts can be described, but not necessarily changed. Issues of control may be pivotal to understanding why these systems are so resistant to change and where the points of leverage may be.

Besides consideration of the setting for personal control, the broader cultural context affects how control beliefs may play out in a given situation. Skaff and Gardiner (this volume) discuss how personal control expectations vary in different cultures. Another example is the research conducted Berit Ingersoll-Dayton and her colleagues (Ingersoll-Dayton, Saengtienchei, Kespichayawattana, & Aungsuroch, 2001) on well-being in Thai elders. They drew on the model of well-being developed by Ryff (1989) that has six components: autonomy, environmental mastery, positive relations with others, purpose in life, personal growth, and self-acceptance. This model was based on the works of western personality theorists (e.g., Maslow, Jung, and Erikson) and reflects many assumptions common in western culture. Ingersoll-Dayton and colleagues conducted open-ended interviews with Thai elders to ascertain if similar dimensions of well-being would emerge. In contrast to Ryff's dimensions that emphasized personal control and fulfillment, the salient features of well-being identified during the interviews with Thai elders focused on traditional eastern ideals: harmony, interdependence, acceptance, respect, and enjoyment. The lack of domains reflecting personal control and mastery suggests that it may not be a necessary component or correlate of well-being in some cultures. Of course, control still may play an important role in these cultures, but where it is expressed in ritualized and indirect ways.

Finally, we should consider if people always want more control. There may be instances where all of us would be happier turning control over to someone else. Krause (this volume) illustrates this point with the example of a mother who turns management of her finances over to her son. Another example is in health care. Trends in health care have placed more control in the hands of patients, who must learn to advocate for their own care in a managed care environment. Many people would undoubtedly prefer going back to the days of TV's Marcus Welby, M.D., when they could depend on their doctor to make informed judgments about their treatment.

The misfit between desired and perceived control has been shown to affect well-being. Guided by person–environment–fit theory, Wallace and Bergeman (1997) examined the mismatch between reported perceived control of older adults and their desired control on matched items. The misfit between perceived and desired control accounted for depression levels above and beyond perceived control alone. Although most participants reported having less control than desired, a sizable portion reported a mismatch in the other direction; they desired less control than they were currently exercising. These results highlight the importance of individual differences in the desire for control and raise a cautionary flag about sweeping generalizations that more control is good for everyone.

CONCLUSION

Personal control and its related constructs can be expected to remain a vital area of inquiry in the coming years. The chapters in this volume suggest several possible directions for this work. At the most basic level, there needs to be continued development of measures, particularly domain-specific, and studies that focus at least in part on the relation of general and domain-specific measures. Research needs increasingly to go beyond examination of individual differences, whether studying adaptation to stressful events or age effects, and instead consider both the individual and social context. The roles of family and community, as well as the effects of social stratification, are all integral to control beliefs. Extending this point, we need to consider how culture affects control beliefs and how the expression of control varies from one group to another. Finally, a focus on personal control may enhance interventions designed to support the functional abilities and well-being of older people. There is considerable evidence that control beliefs mediate a variety of treatments. Changes in these beliefs may even be necessary for a positive outcome. The variety of constructs and studies of personal control underscores the theoretical and practical significance of this area. Continue exploration of dimensions of personal control will enrich our understanding of processes of adaptation in adulthood and aging.

REFERENCES

Abeles, R. P. (1990). Schemas, sense of control, and aging. In J. Rodin, C. Schooler, & K. W. Schaie (Eds.), *Self-directedness: Cause and effects throughout the life course* (pp. 85–94). Hillsdale, NJ: Erlbaum.

Aneshensel, C. S., Pearlin, L. I., Mullan, J. T., Zarit, S. H., & Whitlatch, C. J. (1995). *Profiles in caregiving: The unexpected career.* New York: Academic Press.

Baltes, M. M., Burgess, R. L., & Stewart, R. (1980). Independence and dependence in self-care behaviors in nursing home residents: An operant-observational study. *International Journal of Behavioral Development, 3*, 489–500.

Bandura, A. (1977). Self-efficacy: Toward a unifying theory of behavioral change. *Psychological Review, 84*, 191–215.

Bandura, A. (1997). *Self-efficacy: The exercise of control.* New York: Freeman.

Baron, R. M., & Kenny, D. A. (1986). The moderator–mediator variable distinction in social psychological research: Conceptual, strategic, and statistical considerations. *Journal of Personal and Social Psychology, 51*, 1173–1182.

Beck, A. T., Rush, A. J., Shaw, B. F., & Emery, G. (1979). *Cognitive therapy of depression.* New York: Guilford.

Cisler, R. A., & Nawrocki, J. W. (1998). Coping and short-term outcomes among dependent drinkers: Preliminary evidence for enhancing traditional treatment with relapse prevention raining. *Alcoholism Treatment Quarterly, 16,* 5–20.

Coelho, R. J. (1984). Self-efficacy and cessation of smoking. *Psychological Reports, 54,* 309–310.

Coon, G. M., Pena, D., & Illich, P. A. (1998). Self-efficacy and substance abuse: Assessment using a brief phone interview. *Journal of Substance Abuse Treatment, 15,* 385–391.

Dittmann-Kohli, F., Lachman, M. E., Kliegl, R., & Baltes, P. B. (1991). Effects of cognitive training and testing on intellectual efficacy beliefs in elderly adults. *Journal of Gerontology, 46,* 162–164.

Femia, E. E., Zarit, S. H., & Johansson, B. (1997). Predicting change in activities of daily living: A longitudinal study of the oldest old in Sweden. *Journals of Gerontology Psychological Sciences, 52B,* P294–P302.

Gist, M. E., & Mitchell, T. R. (1992). Self-efficacy: A theoretical analysis of its determinants and malleability. *Academic of Management Review, 17,* 183–211.

Gist, M. E., Stevens, C. K., & Bavetta, A. G. (1991). Effects of self-efficacy and post-training intervention on the acquisition and maintenance of complex interpersonal skills. *Personnel Psychology, 44,* 837–861.

Hoffart, A. (1995). A comparison of cognitive and guided mastery therapy of agoraphobia. *Behaviour Research and Therapy, 33,* 423–434.

Ingersoll-Dayton, B., Saengtienchei, C., Kespichayawattana, J., & Aungsuroch, Y. (2001). Psychological well-being Asian style: The perspective of Thai elders. *Journal of Cross-Cultural Gerontology, 16,* 283–302.

Johnson, C. L., & Barer, B. M. (1997). *Life beyond 85 years: The aura of survivorship.* New York: Springer.

Klerman, G. L., Weissman, M. M., Rounsaville, B. J., & Chevron, E. (1984). *Interpersonal psychotherapy of depression.* New York: Basic Books.

Maisto, S. A., Connors, G. J., & Zywiak, W. H. (2000). Alcohol treatment, changes in coping skills, self-efficacy, and levels of alcohol use and related problems 1 year following treatment initiation. *Psychology of Addictive Behaviors, 14,* 257–266.

Malmberg, B., & Zarit, S. H. (1993). Group homes for dementia patients: An innovative model in Sweden. *Gerontologist, 31,* 682–686.

MaloneBeach, E. E., Zarit, S. H., & Spore, D. (1992). Caregivers' perceptions of case management and community-based services: Barriers to service use. *Journal of Applied Gerontology, 11,* 146–159.

McAuley, E., & Katula, J. (1998). Physical activity interventions in the elderly: Influence on physical health and psychological function. *Annual Review of Gerontology and Geriatrics, 18,* 115–154.

O'Leary, A. (1992). Self-efficacy and health: Behavioral and stress-physiological mediation. *Cognitive Therapy and Research, 16,* 229–245.

Ryff, C. D. (1989). In the eye of the beholder: Views of psychological well-being among middle-aged and older adults. *Psychology and Aging, 4,* 195–201.

Saks, A. M. (1995). Longitudinal field investigation of the moderating and mediating effects of self-efficacy on the relationship between training and newcomer adjustment. *Journal of Applied Psychology, 80,* 211–225.

Sanderson, C. A., & Jemmott, J. B., III. (1996). Moderation and mediation of HIV-prevention interventions: Relationship status, intentions, and condom use among college students. *Journal of Applied Social Psychology, 26,* 2076–2099.

Scholte, R. H., & Breteler, M. H. M. (1997). Withdrawal symptoms and previous attempts to quit smoking: Associations with self-efficacy. *Substance Use and Misuse, 32*(2), 133–148.

Seligman, M. E. P. (1998). *Learned optimism: How to change your mind and your life.* New York: Pocket Books.

Skinner, E. A. (1995). *Perceived control, motivation, and coping.* Thousand Oaks, CA: Sage.

Vinokur, A. D., & Schul, Y. (1997). Mastery and inoculation against setbacks as active ingredients in the JOBS intervention for the unemployed. *Journal of Consulting and Clinical Psychology, 65,* 867–877.

Wallace, K. A., & Bergeman, C. S. (1997). Control and the elderly: "Goodness-of-fit." *International Journal of Aging and Human Development, 45,* 323–339.

Wheaton, B. (1985). Models for the stress-buffering functions of coping resources. *Journal of Health and Social Behavior, 26,* 352–364.

Williams, S. L. (1992). Perceived self-efficacy and phobic disability. In R. Schwarzer et al. (Ed.), *Self-efficacy: Thought control of action* (pp. 149–176). Washington, DC: Hemisphere Publishing.

Williams, S. L., Kinney, P. J., & Falbo, J. (1989). Generalization of therapeutic changes in agoraphobia: The role of perceived self-efficacy. *Journal of Consulting and Clinical Psychology, 57,* 436–442.

Williams, S. L., Turner, S. M., & Peer, D. F. (1985). Guided mastery and performance desensitization treatments for severe acrophobia. *Journal of Consulting and Clinical Psychology, 53,* 237–247.

Zarit, S. H., Stephens, M. A. P., Townsend, A., & Greene, R. (1998). Stress reduction for family caregivers: Effects of adult day care use. *Journals of Gerontology Series B—Psychological Sciences and Social Sciences, 53B*(5), S267–S277.

Zarit, S. H., Stephens, M. A. P., Townsend, A., Greene, R., & Leitsch, S. A. (1999). Patterns of adult day service use by family caregivers: A comparison of brief versus sustained use. *Family Relations, 48,* 355–361.

Zarit, S. H., & Zarit, J. M. (1998). *Mental disorders in older adults: Fundamentals of assessment and treatment.* New York: Guilford.

Author Index

Subject Index